GUIDE TO FOOD STORAGE

Follow this guide for food storage, and you can be sure that what's in your freezer, refrigerator, and pantry is fresh-tasting and ready to use in recipes.

In the Freezer (at -10° to 0° F)

Dairy and Eggs

Cheese, hard	6 months
Cheese, soft	6 months
Egg substitute, unopened	1 year
Egg whites	1 year
Egg yolks	1 year
Ice cream, sherbet	1 month

Fruits and Vegetables

Commercially frozen fruits	1 year
Commercially frozen vegetables	8 to 12 months

Meats, Poultry, and Seafood
Beef, Lamb, Pork, and Veal

Chops, uncooked	4 to 6 months
Ground and stew meat, uncooked	3 to 4 months
Ham, fully cooked, half	1 to 2 months
Roasts, uncooked	4 to 12 months
Steaks, uncooked	6 to 12 months

Poultry

All cuts, cooked	4 months
Boneless or bone-in pieces, uncooked	9 months

Seafood

Fish, fatty, uncooked	2 to 3 months
Fish, lean, uncooked	6 months

In the Refrigerator (at 34° to 40° F)

Dairy and Eggs

Butter	1 to 3 months
Buttermilk	1 to 2 weeks
Cheese, hard, wedge, opened	6 months
Cheese, semihard, block, opened	3 to 4 weeks
Cream cheese, fat-free, light, and ⅓-less-fat	2 weeks
Egg substitute, opened	3 days
Fresh eggs in shell	3 to 5 weeks

Meats, Poultry, and Seafood
Beef, Lamb, Pork, and Veal

Ground and stew meat, uncooked	1 to 2 days
Roasts, uncooked	3 to 5 days
Steaks and chops, uncooked	3 to 5 days

Chicken, Turkey, and Seafood

All cuts, uncooked	1 to 2 days

Fruits and Vegetables

Apples, beets, cabbage, carrots, celery, citrus fruits, eggplant, and parsnips	2 to 3 weeks
Apricots, asparagus, berries, cauliflower, cucumbers, mushrooms, okra, peaches, pears, peas, peppers, plums, salad greens, and summer squash	2 to 4 days
Corn, husked	1 day

In the Pantry (keep these at room temperature for 6 to 12 months)

Baking and Cooking Staples

Baking powder
Biscuit and baking mixes
Broth, canned
Cooking spray
Honey
Mayonnaise, fat-free, low-fat, and light (unopened)
Milk, canned evaporated fat-free
Milk, nonfat dry powder
Mustard, prepared (unopened)
Oils, olive and vegetable
Pasta, dried
Peanut butter
Rice, instant and regular
Salad dressings, bottled (unopened)
Seasoning sauces, bottled
Tuna, canned

Fruits, Legumes, and Vegetables

Fruits, canned
Legumes (beans, lentils, peas), dried or canned
Tomato products, canned
Vegetables, canned

WeightWatchers®

ANNUAL RECIPES *for* SUCCESS
2009

Oxmoor
House®

©2008 by Oxmoor House, Inc.
Book Division of Southern Progress Corporation
P. O. Box 2262, Birmingham, Alabama 35201-2262

ISBN-13: 978-0-8487-3234-9
ISBN-10: 0-8487-3234-0
ISSN: 1526-1565
Printed in the United States of America
First Printing 2008

Be sure to check with your health-care provider before making any changes in your diet.
Weight Watchers, **POINTS**, and the Core Plan are registered trademarks of Weight Watchers International, Inc., and are used under license by Oxmoor House, Inc.

OXMOOR HOUSE, INC.
Editor in Chief: Nancy Fitzpatrick Wyatt
Executive Editor: Katherine M. Eakin
Art Director: Keith McPherson
Managing Editor: Allison Long Lowery

WEIGHT WATCHERS® ANNUAL RECIPES *for* SUCCESS 2009
Editor: Rachel Quinlivan, R.D.
Project Editor: Diane Rose
Senior Designer: Emily Albright Parrish
Copy Chief: L. Amanda Owens
Director, Test Kitchens: Elizabeth Tyler Austin
Assistant Director, Test Kitchens: Julie Christopher
Test Kitchens Professionals: Jane Chambliss; Patricia Michaud; Kathleen Royal Phillips;
    Catherine Crowell Steele; Ashley T. Strickland; Kate Wheeler, R.D.
Photography Director: Jim Bathie
Senior Photo Stylist: Kay E. Clarke
Associate Photo Stylist: Katherine Eckert Coyne
Director of Production: Laura Lockhart
Production Manager: Theresa Beste-Farley

CONTRIBUTORS
Compositor: Carol O. Loria
Copy Editor: Dolores Hydock
Proofreader: Leah Marlett
Indexer: Mary Ann Laurens
Interns: Anne-Harris Jones, Erin Loudy, Lauren Wiygul
Menu Planner Editor: Carolyn Land Williams, M.Ed., R.D.
Recipe Development: Gretchen Feldtman Brown, R.D.; Jennifer Cofield; Georgia Downard;
    Caroline Grant, M.S., R.D.; Nancy Hughes; Ana Price Kelly; Jackie Mills, R.D.; Karen Wilcher
Food Stylist: Margaret Dickey
Photographer: Lee Harrelson

COVER: White Chocolate–Raspberry Cheesecake, page 39

contents

Cranapple Cobbler, *page 46*

Catfish Sandwiches with Tartar Sauce, *page 122*

Greek Egg and Lemon Soup, *page 158*

Weight Watchers® Annual Recipes for Success 2009

This new cookbook empowers you to make the right food choices every day. There's never been a better time to make a positive change for your health, and you can do it while still enjoying the foods you love. Here's how:

- An introduction to the Weight Watchers Experience
- Nine truly inspiring weight-loss Success Stories from people just like you
- Over 300 great-tasting recipes that bring pleasure back to mealtime
- A **POINTS**® value for every recipe
- Core Plan® recipes marked with ✓
- Complete nutritional analysis with every recipe (see "About Our Recipes" on page 189)
- More than 40 color photographs of delicious recipes
- Step-by-step recipe instructions, how-to photography, prep and cook times, and secrets from our Test Kitchens
- Five Seasonal Menus, each with a Game Plan for preparing the meal to help you enjoy the fruits of the season
- Four weeks of 7-Day Menu Planners that incorporate many recipes from the cookbook plus some new ones, too

Our Favorite Recipes

All of our recipes are rigorously tested to ensure ease of preparation, excellent taste, and good nutrition. But some are a cut above the rest. These recipes are so outstanding that they've each earned a place as one of our favorites. We hope you'll enjoy them just as much.

Mojito'd Melon Mix-Up, **POINTS** value: 2 *(page 42)*. Using a calorie-free sweetener helps keep the **POINTS** value low for this refreshing dessert inspired by the classic Cuban cocktail.

Lemon Drop Tartlets, **POINTS** value: 1 *(page 46)*. Lemon curd is the secret ingredient in these intensely flavorful tartlets.

Strawberry-Rhubarb Turnovers, **POINTS** value: 2 *(page 47)*. The sweet-tart filling provides a pleasing contrast to the flaky phyllo.

Seared Scallops with Lemon-Butter Sauce, *POINTS* value: 5 *(page 73).* A citrusy Lemon-Butter Sauce coats the seared scallops with rich flavor.

Moroccan Lamb with Tomato Chutney, *POINTS* value: 5 *(page 92).* The chutney is the star of this dish. Its beautiful color and fantastic flavor helped this recipe earn our Test Kitchens' highest rating.

Rosemary-Garlic Pork Tenderloin, ✓ *POINTS* value: 3 *(page 95).* A fragrant herb paste is used both on the exterior and to stuff the tenderloin, making for a pretty presentation.

Fast Asian Slaw, *POINTS* value: 0 *(page 114).* This quick salad can easily become a main dish with the addition of shrimp, chicken, or tofu.

Fresh Orange and Spring Greens Salad, *POINTS* value: 1 *(page 112).* Orange sections add brightness to this simple green salad.

Grilled Chicken with Avocado Salsa, ✓ *POINTS* value: 6 *(page 103).* Fresh avocado-based salsa gives a boost to the simply seasoned chicken.

Mushroom and Swiss Panini, *POINTS* value: 6 *(page 128).* Melted cheese and meaty baby portobellos make this hot vegetarian sandwich a tasty meal.

Braised Brussels Sprouts with Cranberries and Bacon, *POINTS* value: 4 *(page 148).* The sweet cranberries and salty bacon used to flavor these sprouts create an extraordinary side dish.

Greek Egg and Lemon Soup, *POINTS* value: 4 *(page 158).* Orzo's texture complements this creamy lemony soup.

The Weight Watchers® Experience

Weight Watchers has been a recognized leader in weight management for over 40 years, with a history of helping people successfully lose weight.

At Weight Watchers, weight management is a partnership that combines our knowledge with your efforts. We help you on your journey to make the positive changes required to lose weight. We guide you to make positive behavioral changes in your life, inspiring you with our belief in your power to succeed and motivating you every step of the way.

THE MEETINGS ARE THE MAGIC

Weight Watchers provides information, knowledge, tools, and motivation to help you make the decisions about nutrition and exercise that are right for you. We help you make healthy eating decisions, and we encourage you to enjoy yourself by becoming more active. To provide motivation, mutual support, encouragement, and instruction from our Leaders, Weight Watchers organizes group meetings around the world. Meeting Leaders, who were all once meeting members, share their inspiring stories of personal success with others.

The weekly meeting has continued to be at the core of the Weight Watchers program throughout its 40-year history. In fact, research shows that people who attend Weight Watchers meetings lose three times more weight than those who go it alone.[1] The meetings promote weight loss through education and group support in conjunction with a flexible, healthy diet that does not require the purchase of specific foods.

[1] Heshka S et al. Weight loss with self-help compared with a structured commercial program: a randomized trial. JAMA 289 (14):1792; 2003.

Each week, approximately 1.5 million members attend approximately 50,000 Weight Watchers meetings around the world, which are run by more than 15,000 leaders.

THE WEIGHT WATCHERS PHILOSOPHY

Weight Watchers stands behind healthy weight loss. Weight loss of up to two pounds per week is encouraged by decreasing caloric intake and through physical activities that burn calories. Food choices meet scientific recommendations for satisfying nutrition needs and for lessening the risk of developing long-term diseases. Activities include a broad range of options that boost both weight loss and overall health. Weight Watchers recognizes that these same strategies are vital for keeping weight off.

Weight Watchers is realistic, practical, livable, and flexible. Weight Watchers encourages members to set realistic weight-loss goals. An initial loss of 10% of body weight—for example, a 200-pound person losing 20 pounds—is a smart milestone that has important health benefits. A practical, livable, and flexible approach is easier to follow because it can fit easily into different lifestyles.

Our Leaders help set a member's weight goal within a healthy range, based on body mass index. When members reach their weight goal and maintain it for six weeks, they achieve Lifetime Member status. This gives them the privilege to attend our meetings free of charge as long as they maintain their weight within a certain range.

Weight Watchers believes in imparting knowledge in a way that enables members to learn the what, how, and why of weight loss. Smart choices are easier to make when a person understands the principles of weight loss.

FLEXIBLE FOOD PLANS

The Weight Watchers approach recognizes that each person has unique preferences for particular foods that are satisfying to eat and that fit into their own weight-management routine and busy lifestyle. Some people prefer tracking and controlling what they eat. Others prefer focusing on a group of wholesome foods without counting or tracking. **Weight Watchers Turnaround**® offers both types of food plans and allows you to switch back and forth between plans for maximum flexibility and lasting weight loss.

The Flex Plan is based on the Weight Watchers *POINTS*® Weight-Loss System.

- **Every food has a *POINTS* value that is based on calories, fat grams, fiber grams, and portion size.**

- **Members who use the Flex Plan keep track of *POINTS* values and maintain their daily *POINTS* values within a set range called the *POINTS* Target.**

- **You can enjoy a full range of food options at home, on the go, or when dining out.**

The Core Plan® offers foods from a list of wholesome, nutritious foods from all food groups—fruits and vegetables; grains and starches; lean meats, fish, and poultry; eggs; and dairy products.

- **No measuring or counting is required, as Core Foods provide eating satisfaction without empty calories and allow you to use your hunger cues as a guide.**

- **For the occasional treat, you can also eat foods outside of this list in a controlled amount.**

The Weight Watchers food plans empower you to make food choices in a way that suits your preferences and lifestyle.

The Weight Watchers Commitment to Science

Weight Watchers backs up its weight-management plans with a strong commitment to the science of weight loss. The research and conclusions of experts and health organizations worldwide, including the World Health Organization and the National Institutes of Health, are incorporated into the Weight Watchers offerings. Weight Watchers also conducts its own research on weight-loss methods. As scientific findings change, the Weight Watchers plans evolve.

TESTIMONY TO SUCCESS

At Weight Watchers, we celebrate the success and triumphs of all of our members in their weight-loss journeys because they are a testament to the effectiveness of our weight-loss plans. When our customers successfully lose weight, people notice. Family members, friends, colleagues, and acquaintances inquire about how they achieved such amazing results. The pages that follow will take you through a sample of those success stories.

For more information about the Weight Watchers program and a meeting nearest you, call 1-800-651-6000 or visit online at **www.weightwatchers.com**

"With some guidance from my Leader,
I found my way to the Core Plan."

In the fall of 2003, my family dropped me off at college, and I felt freedom for the first time. No curfew, no chores, no parents, and none of the same old foods for dinner. It was time to let loose and have fun. I quickly learned that most of my socializing revolved around food, and food was never that hard to find! With more than five dining halls, I always had an all-you-can-eat buffet at my fingertips.

DENYING THE TRUTH At the end of freshman year, I noticed that my high school friends looked a little heavier, having put on the infamous "15." But I was in denial—I thought I may have put my jeans in the dryer one too many times; so I resorted to hanging my clothes on the line.

In the spring of junior year, I could deny it no longer; I had gained "the freshman 15," and then some. I knew I had to turn my life around, but admitting that I needed help was no easy task. My cousin Morgan suggested Weight Watchers, and I decided to give it a go.

That summer of 2006, I walked into my first Weight Watchers meeting, and knew I had found the right path. I started losing weight on the **POINTS**® Weight-Loss System and began seeing both physical and mental changes in myself.

THE SWITCH I made steady progress until I hit a plateau. With some guidance from my Leader, I found my way to the Core Plan. I struggled with it for two weeks with no success, but by the third week, I found my rhythm. Suddenly I was losing again and realizing that I would achieve my desired weight goal.

Last February, I became a Lifetime Member of Weight Watchers. Although I had reached my goal, I felt as though my journey was not yet complete. Being a strong Christian, I believed that I needed to extend my hands, heart, and time to others in need. I knew then that I wanted to be on the Weight Watchers staff so that I could do that.

Cybrina

AGE **22** HEIGHT **5'3"**

WAS **167.6 lbs** LOST **30.6 lbs***

WEIGHT **137 lbs**

AS OF **4/1/2008**

*Results Not Typical

Cybrina tackled weight loss at a time when many others gain weight: her college years. Today, she is a Leader who shares her love of the Core Plan® with her members.

CYBRINA'S TIPS:

- Keep already-calculated snacks in your car to avoid going through the drive-thru.
- Make time for yourself. The Weight Watchers plan isn't just about your relationship with food; it also helps you learn how to make yourself a priority.
- Always celebrate. Your weight-loss journey is a *fun* experience, so why not acknowledge it that way?

*"It took me nearly two and
a half years to lose the weight,
but each day was a discovery."*

At more than 100 pounds overweight, I truly felt as if I wasn't participating in my own life. I didn't really know myself and felt both embarrassed and shy around others. I found that I was simply invisible. It was amazing how people could look through the largest person in the room.

DIABETES SCARE   I began to notice that I was sick all the time. I started talking to some of my close friends about the endless illnesses and how thirsty I was all the time. They informed me that excessive thirst could be a symptom of diabetes. This freaked me out, as I was definitely a prime candidate for the disease, even though I was only 26 years old.

I went to get tested and was expecting the worst. I found myself wondering why I was making life so hard on myself. The test came back negative, and I knew that day would change my life forever. I called my best friend, and she accompanied me as I joined Weight Watchers meetings and started following the *POINTS*® Weight-Loss System. I never looked back!

SLOW AND STEADY   I jumped into the process with both feet. It took me nearly two and a half years to lose the weight, but each day was a discovery. During that time, I discovered that some things should just not be optional. I get myself to work every day without considering it an option, so why would it be optional to do the other things that come along with taking good care of myself?

I knew I had to start slowly. I decided a 15-minute daily walk would suffice at the beginning. I built up from there. The best thing about the plan was that I never looked at it as a diet, but as a way of life. Now I have all the tools necessary to continue my lifelong journey.

Christina

AGE **31**   HEIGHT **5′6″**

WAS **285.4 lbs**   LOST **133.6 lbs***

WEIGHT **151.8 lbs**

AS OF **2/1/2008**

*Results Not Typical

There are many difficulties that come from carrying over 100 pounds of extra weight as a young person. Christina decided that she couldn't pay that price any longer.

CHRISTINA'S TIPS:

- Use zip-top bags! I used them to portion out food, writing *POINTS* values on the front to remind myself just what I was eating.
- I keep a bottle of vitamins on my desk and another bottle in my purse. If you keep them in sight, it's easier to remember to take them.
- Order first when dining out—there will be less temptation from hearing what others order.

"I still go to brunch on Sunday and have my pancakes—I just won't have five!"

When I looked at pictures of myself, I saw how heavy I was, double chin and all. I said, "No more. I can't have this." Also, my mother is a nurse. She was concerned for me from a medical standpoint because high blood pressure and diabetes run in my family.

TAKING THE FIRST STEP It was tough for me to walk into a meeting room dominated by women. But I got over that when I realized that we all had a common goal. We all wanted to change our lives and feel better. I found the more I went, the more I got out of it. I started to enjoy the camaraderie and group support. It helps to learn what other people are going through.

FACING CHALLENGES One large obstacle I faced was changing my relationship with food. I was an emotional eater. If I was angry, depressed, overwhelmed, or stressed, I'd find myself overeating Chinese food or chips.

I followed the Core Plan® in the beginning because, as a bulk eater, I didn't want to be overwhelmed with a drastic change in my eating habits. I needed some freedom in regard to portion sizes. I knew that any weight-loss plan I was on was not going to work if I felt deprived.

GETTING FIT, LITTLE BY LITTLE Building up my fitness level was difficult. I started by walking on the treadmill, and I gotta tell you, I felt really heavy. It's demotivating when the guy next to you is running effortlessly, and you're panting and sweating.

Now, I run three miles a day and do 25 minutes of abdominal exercise. I am looking into running a marathon next year.

JOE'S EATING HABITS: While I ate everything [I liked] while I was on plan, there were little changes:
- I went from eating regular enriched pasta to whole-grain pasta.

Joe

AGE **29**   HEIGHT **5'4"**

WAS **193.8 lbs**   LOST **36.8 lbs***

WEIGHT **157 lbs**

AS OF **5/3/2008**

*Results Not Typical

Having previously dropped pounds with Weight Watchers meetings, Joe returned with the mission of losing those last 30 pounds and reaching his goal.

- I went from regular to skim milk.
- I eat a lot of lean meat, and I have fish twice a week.
- I started eating more fruits and vegetables.

"When I first signed up, my goal was to push my weight down below 200 pounds. Remarkably, that happened after about 10 weeks, and I found it very easy."

Long, frequent flights and late work nights: That's what Marc had to contend with in his efforts to get healthy. Juggling his demanding profession and travel-heavy calendar, this California lawyer dropped 37 pounds and managed to keep his passion for fine wine and cheese intact.

A lot of San Franciscans refer to themselves as foodies, and that's a category I definitely fall into. We spend a lot of time eating, talking about food, and drinking wine. Before I started tracking my **POINTS**® values, I would frequently eat foods like duck confit or really heavy cheeses.

About a year ago when I was on my way to lunch, I felt my sides jiggle as I was walking. The idea that there was enough of me to move involuntarily made me very uncomfortable. I weighed 218 pounds; that was the heaviest I'd ever been in my life. That's when I decided to sign up for Weight Watchers Online.

MAN ON THE RUN My job has me on the move constantly. I'm a lawyer for a multinational healthcare company with offices all over the world, and when my clients need help navigating through murky legal waters, I meet with them face-to-face wherever they're located. I have day trips about 12 times a year, three-day trips six times a year, and week-long trips two or three times a year.

I chose to start following the plan at a time when I knew I didn't have any business trips coming up for about a month. Every day at work, I'd enter my breakfast in the **POINTS** Tracker as soon as I sat down at my desk. I'd leave WeightWatchers.com open in a browser window all day, so whenever I ate anything, I could track it right away. If I grabbed a chocolate candy off my secretary's desk, I would track that, too.

Marc

AGE **43** HEIGHT **6'0"**

WAS **218 lbs** LOST **37 lbs***

WEIGHT **181 lbs**

AS OF **3/17/2008**

*Results Not Typical

Breakfast à la Marc
POINTS value: 3

1. Combine three egg whites and some fresh spinach in a microwave-safe container and cook for about a minute.

2. Place the egg whites and spinach on an English muffin with ¼ cup salsa. YIELD: 1 SERVING.

I tracked my food and activity every day of that first week, and I lost 2 pounds. Right away, I knew the plan was working. Slowly but surely, I was able to move one more notch over on my belt and fit into a pair of pants I hadn't worn in years!

"In the beginning, I decided I would simply sit on the sidelines, watch, and soak up information."

At 24, I weighed over 275 pounds. In fact, most of my adult life had been spent in a body that made the simple act of climbing a flight of stairs difficult. Diabetes, high blood pressure, and heart disease run rampant in my family. Subscribing to Weight Watchers Online and following the **POINTS**® Weight-Loss System was a decision I made for my health. I wanted the chance to live an active life, not watch as life passed me by.

GATHERING INFORMATION In the beginning, I decided I would simply sit on the sidelines, watch, and soak up information from the site. I wouldn't try to count **POINTS** values or lose weight, but would browse the message boards, read articles, and investigate the tools available. I allowed myself the freedom to jump in when I felt ready. After about a month of listening to members talk about favorite recipes and meal plans, I felt I had enough information to get started.

Once I gained momentum and confidence, I stepped out of the shadows completely. I started posting to the message boards, asking questions, and sharing my own experiences. I allowed others to inspire and teach me, and eventually I started inspiring others. I made sure to welcome new members, giving them any information I could. That's how I met Kevin. One lonely Friday night, I saw a "newbie" asking for a little boost as he got started.

UNDENIABLE CONNECTION The connection was nearly immediate. We started chatting online, and just four days later I told a friend I was falling in love with someone I had never met. Just weeks later we were flying across the country to meet one another. We were married in June. Together we have lost over 180 pounds.

I have read tons of success stories, and in a lot of them, the person says, "The plan truly changed my life." I think I would have to say that's true for me, too. Not only did I find the love of my life, I found myself!

Julie

AGE **27**   HEIGHT **5'5"**

WAS **307 lbs**   LOST **127 lbs***

WEIGHT **180 lbs**

AS OF **3/8/2008**

*Results Not Typical

Julie subscribed to Weight Watchers Online and not only lost over 100 pounds, but also found the love of her life via the message boards.

JULIE'S TIPS:

- When you tally losses, also tally gains. It puts everything in perspective. Over the course of three years, I have lost over 100 pounds and gained so much along the way.

- Look at your first weight gain like you do the first dent in a new car. It's hard to deal with, but after a while it isn't as big of a deal. There will be gains and losses, but overall, you're making your life healthier.

"The secret this time around was tracking POINTS® values online."

I went on my first diet when I was in 8th grade, and that started my 25-year history as a yo-yo dieter. I actually followed Weight Watchers before, but after I reached my goal weight, I resumed old eating habits and regained the weight.

A MILESTONE BIRTHDAY I turned 40 in March of 2004. I felt old, out of shape, and unattractive. I was 30 pounds heavier than when I got married in 1989. I decided to take a big step: I signed up for a triathlon that October (my first). At the same time, I knew I needed help and structure. That's when I subscribed to Weight Watchers Online and started following the **POINTS®** Weight-Loss System.

ONLINE TRACKING WORKS For me, the secret this time around was tracking **POINTS** values online. The online **POINTS** tracker is genius. Every food item you can think of is in the database, and it adjusts for portion size. Plus, I could log on from anywhere.

SLOW BUT STEADY I lost 8 pounds in my first 8 weeks on the plan, and I felt very encouraged. I dropped a pants size, and my physical training got easier as I got slimmer.

THE FINISH LINE After five months following the plan, I hit my 10 percent goal—and crossed the finish line of my first-ever triathlon. Talk about empowering! Will, my trainer, even came and took photos. He's helped me train for two more triathlons since then. I know that without the change in my diet, I couldn't have accomplished such a huge physical feat. I let Will be my fitness coach, and Weight Watchers Online provided expert nutrition advice.

Rina

AGE **44**   HEIGHT **5'0"**

WAS **147 lbs**   LOST **28 lbs***

WEIGHT **119 lbs**

AS OF **2/20/2008**

*Results Not Typical

Rina entered her 40s feeling "dowdy." But when she let herself be coached in eating right and exercising, she found her inner athlete—and dropped to a weight she hadn't seen since high school.

RINA'S TIPS:

- I travel a lot, and when I'm in an unfamiliar restaurant, I stick with lots of fruit, green salads, and nonfried lean chicken or seafood. Sometimes I take a tiny bite if there's something amazing that I have to try.

- Don't use middle age as an excuse. Before I subscribed to Weight Watchers online, I figured my metabolism had slowed down and I could never be slim again. Baloney! It took a year and a lot of persistence, but now I weigh what I did in high school.

13

> *"I know Weight Watchers is an excellent vehicle to touch and teach my community to conquer their weight issues."*

At just 23 years old, I found myself in the unenviable position of making a choice between major surgery and weight loss. I was extremely overweight and sidelined with serious health issues, including hyperthyroidism and congestive heart failure. I couldn't even wrap my brain around the fact that at such a young age, I was gravely ill and the underlying cause was the excess weight I was carrying.

FEELING LOW My heaviest point came after the birth of my first daughter. Feeling unattractive, worthless, and desperate—and against my mother's wishes—I turned to weight-loss supplements. I lost a dramatic amount of weight very quickly, but I began coughing incessantly, my heart rate increased, and I experienced shortness of breath.

Eventually, after gaining much of the weight back, I ended up in the emergency room and was told I needed a heart transplant or weight loss. In my mind, weight loss was the only answer. I followed my sister to a Weight Watchers meeting and started following the **POINTS**® Weight-Loss System.

TURNING THE PAGE With strength of purpose, I attended my meetings and lost the weight, and my health began to improve. My heart became strong again, and I looked healthy. All of the things that the doctors told me I wouldn't be able to do, I did and am doing, including running!

Today, I am both proud and honored to be a Weight Watchers Leader who gets the chance to empower others. I look around my community—the African-American community—and I see the pain and affliction that comes with being overweight. I know Weight Watchers is an excellent vehicle to touch and teach my community to conquer their weight issues. Being African-American myself, I have the greatest opportunity to provide the hope and inspiration to overcome the many illnesses associated with excess weight.

Sharifa

AGE **30** HEIGHT **5'4"**

WAS **168 lbs** LOST **35.4 lbs***

WEIGHT **132.6 lbs**

AS OF **2/28/2008**

*Results Not Typical

Plagued by health issues, Sharifa was given the choice of having open-heart surgery or losing weight. She took the weight off and decided to help others do the same by becoming a Leader.

SHARIFA'S TIPS:

- Never go it alone. Being around people who could identify with my struggles made everything seem simpler.
- Walking is the best way to start any exercise routine. I started moving one foot at a time, literally. When I was strong enough to move my body, that is what I did.

> ## *"I am a testament to the value of consistently attending weekly meetings."*

The hardest thing I've ever done, other than losing weight, was walking into a Weight Watchers meeting. You see, I am a registered dietitian. I spend my days telling people how to eat right to achieve optimal health. Going to a meeting and having to admit that I had a problem was embarrassing to me. At the end of my rope and feeling like a failure both personally and professionally, I went to visit my doctor. When I asked her to sign a consent form for a different weight-loss program, she refused.

HOPE FADING Having been overweight my whole adult life and feeling that my last hope was slipping away, I started to cry. She looked at me and said, "Teresa, you are a smart woman who knows how to eat right, and I have faith that you will figure out a solution to this problem."

When I showed up at home with eyes blackened by mascara from crying, my husband looked at me and said, "Why don't you go to Weight Watchers?" He pointed out that losing weight had never been my problem, but keeping it off was.

CONSISTENCY IS THE KEY The next week, I walked into my first Weight Watchers meeting and started following the *POINTS*® Weight-Loss System. I am a testament to the value of consistently attending weekly meetings. I was at my meeting on the day after Thanksgiving, two days before Christmas, two days before my birthday, and every week in between.

FABULOUS AT 50 I love the fact that I turned 50 this year and wore a bikini to the beach. I have not worn one since I was 18 years old! Even better is knowing that I am an inspiration to my entire family, my profession, and my clients.

Teresa

AGE **50**   HEIGHT **5'2"**

WAS **223.2 lbs**   LOST **88.2 lbs***

WEIGHT **135 lbs**

AS OF **1/18/2008**

*Results Not Typical

As a registered dietitian, Teresa had all the facts about how to eat right. It wasn't until she walked into a Weight Watchers meeting that she realized knowing the facts doesn't mean you have all the tools to lose weight on your own.

TERESA'S TIPS:

- Don't wait for life to give you the right conditions to lose weight. It will never happen. Start now, work through the challenges, and stay committed to your goals.
- Make use of the meetings and the friends from those meetings because they will pick you up and dust you off when you fall.
- Create a strong catalog of meals you love to eat. Eat only what you truly love, and the plan will be a joy.

"Everything I needed in order to lose my excess weight was inside of me already. I knew what I had to do; I just needed to learn the guidelines."

I got married in October of 2004. About three months after our wedding, we received our photo proofs; my beautiful wife was standing next to a not-so-good-looking guy. I didn't recognize the person in those pictures. That was the moment that I realized how overweight I was.

SEEING THE SIGNS   Overeating at Thanksgiving wasn't what made me overweight. The problem was inside me. I didn't eat because I was hungry; I ate because I was trying to forget about my problems.

I had horrible back pain and was making countless visits to the chiropractor. What I really needed was someone to tell me, "You're too heavy. If you lose weight, it will reduce stress on your back." I also had sleep apnea. My snoring would keep my poor wife, Danielle, awake the whole night, and I would wake up not feeling refreshed.

FIRST STEPS   My wife suggested that I go with her to her Weight Watchers meetings, but I told her that she should go and I would just try to make healthy changes with her. I was scared. I didn't want to get weighed. She eventually convinced me to go to one meeting, but it wasn't until the second try that I found the perfect meeting for me and the perfect Leader who motivated me.

When I walked into Weight Watchers, they told me my ideal weight was 175, and I immediately said, "That's unobtainable. Let me just see if I can reach 250." Once I reached that goal, I knew I could do it. I just needed to set small goals for myself.

I come from a big Italian family, and I'm the odd one out now. They think I'm too thin! They're not used to seeing me like this, but I'm happy with myself.

Vincent

AGE **29**   HEIGHT **5'10"**

WAS **278.6 lbs**   LOST **117.6 lbs***

WEIGHT **161 lbs**

AS OF **4/23/2008**

*Results Not Typical

At over 300 pounds, back pain and sleep apnea were just a couple of reasons why newlywed Vincent knew it was time to get serious about his health.

VINCENT'S ADVICE:

- You should eat breakfast every morning.
- Exercise to relieve stress.
- You can't think of Weight Watchers as a diet. It's a way of life. If you fall off the wagon, you have to get back on with the next bite, the next meal. The next chance you get, get back on the plan.

appetizers & beverages

Ambrosia Smoothie, *page 25*

ROASTED RED PEPPER AND CHIPOTLE HUMMUS ☑.

POINTS value: 1

PREP: 7 minutes

The chipotle chile lends a subtle smokiness to this flavorful version of hummus. Serve with raw vegetables or baked pita chips for dipping, or spread on a sandwich for a tasty departure from mayonnaise.

- 1 (16-ounce) can chickpeas (garbanzo beans), rinsed and drained
- ½ cup bottled roasted red bell peppers
- ¼ cup fat-free sour cream
- 1 tablespoon fresh lime juice
- 1 garlic clove
- 1 chipotle chile
- ¼ teaspoon salt
- 1 tablespoon extravirgin olive oil

1. Combine first 7 ingredients in a food processor; process until smooth. With processor on, slowly pour oil through food chute; process until well blended. YIELD: 7 SERVINGS (SERVING SIZE: ¼ CUP).

PER SERVING: CAL 82 (27% from fat); FAT 2.5g (sat 0.3g); PRO 2.8g; CARB 12.2g; FIB 2g; CHOL 1mg; IRON 0.6mg; SOD 214mg; CALC 32mg

KALAMATA AND TOMATO-BASIL SPREAD

POINTS value: 1

PREP: 13 minutes

You can prepare the bean mixture and the olive mixture ahead of time and then complete the spread when you're ready to serve it. Serve with water crackers, toasted pita wedges, or crostini. To make this a Core Plan ☑. recipe, substitute fat-free feta in place of the regular feta cheese.

- 2 cups finely chopped plum tomato (about 4), divided
- 1 (16-ounce) can navy beans, rinsed and drained
- ½ cup fresh basil
- 2 garlic cloves
- ¼ teaspoon salt
- ½ cup finely chopped pitted kalamata olives (about 24)
- 2 tablespoons chopped fresh basil
- 2 teaspoons extravirgin olive oil
- 2 teaspoons red wine vinegar
- 3 tablespoons crumbled feta cheese (about 1 ounce)

1. Combine 1½ cups tomato and next 4 ingredients in a blender; process until smooth. Set aside.
2. Combine remaining ½ cup tomato, olives, and next 3 ingredients in a small bowl.
3. Spoon bean mixture into a shallow bowl; top with cheese. Spoon olive mixture over cheese. YIELD: 16 SERVINGS (SERVING SIZE: ¼ CUP).

PER SERVING: CAL 52 (45% from fat); FAT 2.6g (sat 0.6g); PRO 2g; CARB 5.6g; FIB 1.4g; CHOL 2mg; IRON 0.5mg; SOD 199mg; CALC 25mg

TUSCAN SPREAD

POINTS value: 2

PREP: 6 minutes

This tasty spread comes together in minutes. Try it with fresh vegetables, toasted pita wedges, or thin breadsticks. To make this a Core Plan ☑. recipe, simply omit the nuts.

- 1 (19-ounce) can cannellini beans, rinsed and drained
- 3 tablespoons toasted pine nuts
- ½ teaspoon grated fresh lemon rind
- 2 tablespoons fresh lemon juice
- 2 tablespoons water
- 1 tablespoon extravirgin olive oil
- 1 tablespoon fresh oregano
- ½ teaspoon freshly grated black pepper
- ½ teaspoon salt

1. Combine all ingredients in a food processor; process until smooth. YIELD: 6 SERVINGS (SERVING SIZE: ¼ CUP).

PER SERVING: CAL 90 (55% from fat); FAT 5.5g (sat 0.5g); PRO 2.6g; CARB 8.3g; FIB 2.2g; CHOL 0mg; IRON 1mg; SOD 258mg; CALC 21mg

PINE NUTS

Pine nuts—also known as *pignoli*, *pignolia*, and *piñon*—are not actually nuts. They're actually the seeds of several species of pine trees. To harvest the seeds, the pinecones generally must be heated and the seeds removed by hand. This labor-intensive process is what makes pine nuts so expensive. Because of their high fat content (the "good" mono- and polyunsaturated fats), pine nuts can turn rancid quickly, so store them in a sealed container in the refrigerator for up to 3 months or freeze them for up to 9 months.

FRESH CRAB DIP

POINTS value: 1

PREP: 15 minutes

Serve this dip with cracked pepper–flavored water crackers or toasted baguette slices.

  1 tablespoon prepared horseradish, divided
½ cup (4 ounces) tub-style light cream cheese, softened
⅓ cup fat-free sour cream
¼ teaspoon salt
¼ cup chili sauce
¾ teaspoon fresh lemon juice
¼ teaspoon Worcestershire sauce
  4 ounces lump crabmeat, shell pieces removed
  2 tablespoons finely chopped green onions

1. Combine 1½ teaspoons horseradish and next 3 ingredients in a medium bowl; stir until smooth. Spread mixture evenly in a shallow bowl.
2. Combine remaining 1½ teaspoons horseradish, chili sauce, lemon juice, and Worcestershire sauce in a small bowl, stirring well. Spoon a thin layer evenly over cream cheese mixture. Mound crabmeat in center, and sprinkle evenly with green onions. **YIELD: 12 SERVINGS (SERVING SIZE: ABOUT 2 TABLESPOONS).**

PER SERVING: CAL 46 (35% from fat); FAT 1.8g (sat 1.2g); PRO 3.2g; CARB 3.7g; FIB 0.1g; CHOL 13mg; IRON 0.1mg; SOD 297mg; CALC 37mg

CREAMY COCKTAIL SAUCE

POINTS value: 1

PREP: 6 minutes

This creamy sauce is great with seafood or fresh raw vegetables.

¼ cup light mayonnaise
  3 tablespoons fat-free sour cream
⅓ cup ketchup
1½ tablespoons prepared horseradish
  1 tablespoon fresh lemon juice

1. Combine mayonnaise and sour cream in a small bowl, stirring with a whisk until smooth. Add ketchup, horseradish, and juice; stir to combine. **YIELD: 8 SERVINGS (SERVING SIZE: 2 TABLESPOONS).**

PER SERVING: CAL 42 (56% from fat); FAT 2.6g (sat 0.5g); PRO 0.6g; CARB 4.4g; FIB 0.1g; CHOL 3mg; IRON 0.1mg; SOD 185mg; CALC 15mg

CREAMY PEANUT-BUTTERY JAVA DIP

POINTS value: 1

PREP: 7 minutes ■ **COOK:** 30 seconds

Be sure that the whipped topping is completely thawed before folding it into the warm peanut butter. Otherwise, the peanut butter will firm up, making it more difficult to blend evenly with the topping. Serve with sliced apples, pears, or bananas.

  1 teaspoon instant coffee granules
  2 teaspoons water
  1 tablespoon creamy peanut butter
  2 cups frozen fat-free whipped topping, thawed
  1 tablespoon dark brown sugar
½ teaspoon ground cinnamon

1. Combine coffee granules and water in a small bowl, stirring until granules dissolve.
2. Place peanut butter in a medium microwave-safe bowl; microwave at HIGH 30 seconds or until peanut butter begins to melt. Fold in whipped topping. Add coffee mixture, brown sugar, and cinnamon, and stir gently to combine. Refrigerate, covered, until ready to serve. **YIELD: 6 SERVINGS (SERVING SIZE: ¼ CUP).**

PER SERVING: CAL 39 (30% from fat); FAT 1.3g (sat 0.3g); PRO 0.7g; CARB 5.7g; FIB 0.3g; CHOL 0mg; IRON 0.2mg; SOD 14mg; CALC 5mg

STRAWBERRY-MANGO SALSA

POINTS value: 0

pictured on page 51

PREP: 12 minutes ■ **OTHER:** 10 minutes

This colorful salsa scoops up nicely with baked cinnamon-sugar pita chips, but it can also freshen up grilled fish or chicken. A ¾-cup serving has a **POINTS** value of 1.

  1 cup chopped strawberries
  1 diced peeled ripe mango
¾ cup finely chopped orange bell pepper
  2 tablespoons chopped fresh mint
  1 teaspoon grated fresh orange rind
  2 tablespoons fresh orange juice
1½ teaspoons sugar
⅛ teaspoon crushed red pepper

1. Combine all ingredients in a medium bowl. Let stand at least 10 minutes before serving, or cover and chill until ready to serve. **YIELD: 9 SERVINGS (SERVING SIZE: ¼ CUP).**

PER SERVING: CAL 27 (7% from fat); FAT 0.2g (sat 0g); PRO 0.4g; CARB 6.9g; FIB 1g; CHOL 0mg; IRON 0.2mg; SOD 1mg; CALC 7mg

MEDITERRANEAN VEGETABLE PLATTER

POINTS value: 1

PREP: 11 minutes

Perk up your next party with this quick antipasto platter. Serve it immediately or make it ahead and refrigerate it overnight. The flavor will only get better.

   1 tablespoon extravirgin olive oil
   1 tablespoon red wine vinegar
   1 large garlic clove, minced
   1 teaspoon dried oregano, crushed
   ¼ teaspoon salt
  16 grape tomatoes
  16 small pitted ripe olives
   6 ounces small mushrooms, quartered
   2 (1-ounce) reduced-fat mozzarella string cheese sticks, each cut crosswise into 5 pieces
   1 (14-ounce) can quartered artichoke hearts, drained
   5 pickled okra pods, drained and cut in half lengthwise

1. Combine first 5 ingredients in a large bowl. Add tomatoes and next 3 ingredients; toss well to coat. Add artichoke hearts and okra; toss gently. Spoon onto a platter or into a shallow bowl; serve immediately or cover and chill. YIELD: 10 SERVINGS (SERVING SIZE: ½ CUP).

PER SERVING: CAL 57 (46% from fat); FAT 2.9g (sat 0.8g); PRO 3.4g; CARB 5.3g; FIB 1.7g; CHOL 3mg; IRON 0.5mg; SOD 292mg; CALC 95mg

CREAMY ARTICHOKE AND ROASTED PEPPER–STUFFED ENDIVE

POINTS value: 1

PREP: 20 minutes

You can use romaine lettuce hearts instead of the endive, if you'd like. If using romaine, trim the tops of 16 inner leaves (about 4 inches long), and fill the leaves as directed in the recipe. Use the remaining romaine to make Steak Salad with Beets and Blue Cheese on page 118.

   ½ cup (4 ounces) tub-style light cream cheese, softened
   2 teaspoons fresh lemon juice
   1 small garlic clove, minced
   ⅛ teaspoon salt
  Dash of ground red pepper (optional)
   ¾ cup drained canned quartered artichoke hearts
   ⅓ cup bottled roasted red bell peppers
   2 heads Belgian endive (about 10 ounces), separated into leaves

1. Combine first 4 ingredients and, if desired, ground red pepper in a small bowl; stir until blended.
2. Arrange artichokes and bell peppers in a single layer between several sheets of paper towels; pat gently to remove excess moisture. Chop artichokes and bell peppers, and stir into cream cheese mixture. Spoon about 1 tablespoon cream cheese mixture onto end of each endive leaf. YIELD: 8 SERVINGS (SERVING SIZE: 2 STUFFED ENDIVE LEAVES).

PER SERVING: CAL 48 (43% from fat); FAT 2.3g (sat 1.6g); PRO 2.3g; CARB 4.5g; FIB 1.7g; CHOL 7mg; IRON 0.1mg; SOD 223mg; CALC 25mg

ROASTED RED PEPPER PESTO DIP WITH TORTELLINI SKEWERS

POINTS value: 2

PREP: 10 minutes ■ **COOK:** 12 minutes

Use this quick, versatile dip as a spread for sandwiches or as a sauce to toss with pasta. Store it in the refrigerator, covered, for up to 1 week.

   1 (9-ounce) package fresh cheese tortellini
   5 tablespoons extravirgin olive oil, divided
   1 (12-ounce) bottle roasted red bell peppers, drained
   2 cups fresh basil
   ⅓ cup grated fresh Parmesan cheese
   ¼ cup pine nuts or chopped walnuts, toasted
   2 garlic cloves
   2 teaspoons fresh lemon juice
   ¼ teaspoon salt
   ¼ teaspoon freshly ground black pepper
  21 (6-inch) wooden skewers

1. Cook pasta according to package directions, omitting salt and fat. Toss with 1 tablespoon oil.
2. Combine red bell peppers and next 7 ingredients in a food processor; process until minced. With processor on, slowly pour remaining ¼ cup oil through food chute; process until well blended.
3. Arrange 3 tortellini on each wooden skewer and serve with dip. YIELD: 21 SERVINGS (SERVING SIZE: 1 SKEWER AND ABOUT 1 TABLESPOON DIP).

PER SERVING: CAL 90 (57% from fat); FAT 5.7g (sat 1.1g); PRO 2.6g; CARB 7.2g; FIB 0.5g; CHOL 5mg; IRON 0.2mg; SOD 152mg; CALC 33mg

DEVILISH EGGS

POINTS value: 1

PREP: 18 minutes

You can prepare these eggs up to a day in advance. Just store them covered in the refrigerator until you're ready to serve them.

    6 hard-cooked large eggs
    ½ cup prepared hummus
    2 tablespoons fat-free sour cream
    1½ teaspoons prepared mustard
    ¼ teaspoon black pepper
    1 tablespoon sweet or dill pickle relish

1. Cut eggs in half lengthwise; remove yolks. Place 3 yolks in a small bowl; reserve remaining yolks for another use. Add hummus and next 3 ingredients to yolks; mash with a fork until smooth. Stir in pickle relish. Spoon egg mixture evenly into egg white halves. **YIELD: 12 SERVINGS (SERVING SIZE: 1 STUFFED EGG HALF).**

PER SERVING: CAL 42 (45% from fat); FAT 2 1g (sat 0.5g); PRO 3.4g; CARB 2.5g; FIB 0.6g; CHOL 52mg; IRON 0.4mg; SOD 85mg; CALC 16mg

SMOKED SALMON BRUSCHETTA WITH SUN-DRIED TOMATO RELISH

POINTS value: 3

pictured on page 49

PREP: 14 minutes ■ **COOK:** 10 minutes

    16 (½-inch-thick) slices French bread
    Olive oil–flavored cooking spray
    ½   cup chive-and-onion light cream cheese
    1½ tablespoons chopped fresh dill
    1   (3-ounce) package julienne-cut sun-dried tomatoes, chopped
    1   tablespoon minced shallots
    1   tablespoon chopped fresh flat-leaf parsley
    1   tablespoon white balsamic vinegar
    1   tablespoon extravirgin olive oil
    1   (4-ounce) package sliced smoked salmon, cut into 16 pieces
    ⅛   teaspoon freshly ground black pepper
    Fresh dill sprigs (optional)

1. Preheat oven to 400°.
2. Place bread slices on a baking sheet coated with cooking spray; coat bread slices with cooking spray. Bake at 400° for 10 minutes or until golden. Cool.
3. Combine cream cheese and dill, stirring well.

4. Combine tomato and next 4 ingredients in a small bowl, stirring well. Spread cream cheese mixture evenly over bread slices. Top evenly with tomato relish and salmon. Sprinkle evenly with pepper, and garnish with dill sprigs, if desired. **YIELD: 8 SERVINGS (SERVING SIZE: 2 BRUSCHETTA).**

PER SERVING: CAL 170 (27% from fat); FAT 5.1g (sat 2g); PRO 8g; CARB 22.3g; FIB 2.2g; CHOL 11mg; IRON 1.4mg; SOD 560mg; CALC 35mg

> ### SHALLOTS
> Shallots are small onions that taste like a cross between an onion and garlic. Their low water content means their flavor is more concentrated than that of onions. Use shallots when you want the full flavor of an onion without the bulk.

MINI PARTY BURGERS WITH CHEESE

POINTS value: 3

PREP: 18 minutes ■ **COOK:** 6 minutes
■ **OTHER:** 1 minute

    12 ounces ground sirloin
    1   (4-ounce) link lean turkey Italian sausage (such as Jennie-O), casing removed
    1   teaspoon Worcestershire sauce
    Cooking spray
    16 (0.4-ounce) dinner rolls (such as Rainbo)
    4   slices reduced-fat sharp Cheddar cheese, quartered
    3   tablespoons ketchup
    16 dill pickle slices
    16 baby spinach leaves

1. Preheat broiler.
2. Combine first 3 ingredients in a medium bowl. Divide mixture into 16 equal portions; flatten each into a 2-inch-wide patty. Place patties on a broiler pan coated with cooking spray. Broil in upper one-third of oven 3 minutes on each side or until done.
3. Cut rolls in half horizontally; place rolls, cut sides up, on a baking sheet. Turn off broiler, place rolls on bottom oven rack, and top each patty with cheese. Let rolls and patties stand in oven 1 minute or until cheese melts.
4. Top bottom half of each roll with a patty, about ½ teaspoon ketchup, 1 pickle, 1 spinach leaf, and top half of roll. **YIELD: 16 SERVINGS (SERVING SIZE: 1 MINI BURGER).**

PER SERVING: CAL 117 (44% from fat); FAT 5.7g (sat 2.4g); PRO 8.7g; CARB 7.5g; FIB 0.4g; CHOL 25mg; IRON 1.3mg; SOD 329mg; CALC 85mg

SPICY PORK SLIDERS WITH SWEET CHIPOTLE-PEACH SAUCE

POINTS value: 2

PREP: 7 minutes ■ **COOK:** 24 minutes
■ **OTHER:** 5 minutes

The small, flavorful dinner rolls used in this recipe can be found on the bread aisle of most supermarkets.

　　1　teaspoon chili powder
　　½　teaspoon ground cumin
　　¼　teaspoon ground cinnamon
　　¼　teaspoon salt
　　¼　teaspoon freshly ground black pepper
　　1　(1-pound) pork tenderloin, trimmed
　　Cooking spray
　　¼　cup peach fruit spread
　　1　chipotle chile, canned in adobo sauce
　　½　teaspoon adobo sauce
　　2　tablespoons light mayonnaise
　1½　teaspoons honey mustard
　12　(0.4-ounce) dinner rolls (such as Rainbo)

1. Preheat oven to 425°.
2. Combine first 5 ingredients in a small bowl; rub evenly over pork.
3. Heat a large nonstick skillet over medium-high heat; coat pan with cooking spray. Add pork; cook 2 minutes on each side or until browned. Transfer pork to a foil-lined jelly-roll pan. Bake at 425° for 19 minutes or until a thermometer registers 155°. Let pork stand 5 minutes or until thermometer reaches 160°. Slice tenderloin into 24 pieces.
4. While pork cooks, place peach fruit spread in a microwave-safe bowl. Microwave at HIGH 20 to 30 seconds or until spread melts slightly. Stir in chipotle chile and next 3 ingredients. Refrigerate until ready to serve. Serve pork on rolls with sauce. YIELD: 12 SERVINGS (SERVING SIZE: 2 SLICES PORK, 1 ROLL, AND ABOUT 1½ TEASPOONS SAUCE).

PER SERVING: CAL 105 (29% from fat); FAT 3.4g (sat 0.9g); PRO 8.8g; CARB 9.6g; FIB 0.2g; CHOL 25mg; IRON 0.8mg; SOD 168mg; CALC 24mg

CHICKEN LITTLES

POINTS value: 2

PREP: 6 minutes ■ **COOK:** 10 minutes

Both kids and adults will love these tender bites of chicken. Vitamin-rich wheat germ has a nutty flavor and contains most of the fat and oil found in wheat, making it highly perishable. Store your jar of wheat germ in the refrigerator or freezer to extend its life.

　　1　large egg white
　　⅔　cup toasted wheat germ
　　½　teaspoon salt
　　¼　teaspoon garlic powder
　　⅛　teaspoon freshly ground black pepper
　　½　pound skinless, boneless chicken breast, cut into bite-sized pieces
　　Cooking spray
　　⅓　cup light honey mustard dressing

1. Preheat oven to 400°.
2. Heat a large baking sheet in oven.
3. While pan heats, place egg white in a shallow dish; stir well with a whisk. Combine wheat germ and next 3 ingredients in a large zip-top plastic bag. Dip chicken in egg white; add chicken to bag, seal, and shake bag to coat chicken. Remove chicken from bag, shaking off excess wheat germ mixture.
4. Coat preheated baking sheet with cooking spray, and place chicken on pan. Bake at 400° for 10 minutes or until chicken is done and golden. Serve immediately with honey mustard dressing. YIELD: 6 SERVINGS (SERVING SIZE: ABOUT 4 CHICKEN PIECES AND ABOUT 1 TABLESPOON DRESSING).

PER SERVING: CAL 94 (29% from fat); FAT 3g (sat 0.4g); PRO 13.3g; CARB 5.8g; FIB 0.6g; CHOL 24mg; IRON 0.5mg; SOD 155mg; CALC 4mg

SPICY CHICKEN LETTUCE WRAPS

POINTS value: 2

PREP: 15 minutes ■ **COOK:** 5 minutes

　　1　pound ground chicken
　　⅓　cup chopped water chestnuts
　　2　tablespoons minced garlic
　　2　tablespoons minced peeled fresh ginger
　　1　tablespoon dark sesame oil
　　1　tablespoon red curry paste (such as Thai Kitchen)
　　1　teaspoon salt
　　Cooking spray
　　2　tablespoons hoisin sauce
　12　iceberg lettuce leaves, washed

1. Combine first 7 ingredients in a medium bowl, and stir well.

2. Heat a large nonstick skillet over medium-high heat; coat pan with cooking spray. Add chicken mixture; cook 5 minutes or until chicken is done. Stir in hoisin sauce.

3. Spoon ¼ cup chicken mixture onto each lettuce leaf, and roll up. Serve immediately. YIELD: 12 SERVINGS (SERVING SIZE: 1 WRAP).

PER SERVING: CAL 80 (51% from fat); FAT 4.5g (sat 1g); PRO 6.2g; CARB 2.8g; FIB 0.3g; CHOL 25mg; IRON 0.1mg; SOD 298mg; CALC 3mg

TURKEY AND GINGER WONTONS WITH ASIAN DIPPING SAUCE

POINTS value: 1

PREP: 21 minutes ■ COOK: 21 minutes

Lean ground pork works well as a substitute for turkey in these restaurant-style steamed dumplings. The *POINTS* value remains the same.

     4 ounces ground turkey
    ¼ cup finely chopped green onions
     1 teaspoon grated peeled fresh ginger
    ⅛ teaspoon crushed red pepper
    24 wonton wrappers
10½ cups plus 2 tablespoons water, divided
     3 tablespoons low-sodium soy sauce
     3 tablespoons sugar
     3 tablespoons cider vinegar
     2 tablespoons fresh lime juice

1. Combine first 4 ingredients; stir until blended.

2. Working with 1 wonton wrapper at a time (cover remaining wrappers with a damp towel to keep them from drying), spoon about 1 teaspoon turkey mixture into center of wrapper. Moisten edges of wrapper with water; bring 2 opposite corners to center, pinching points to seal. Bring remaining 2 corners to center, pinching points to seal. Pinch 4 edges together to seal. Place wonton, seam side up, on a platter. Repeat procedure with remaining wrappers and turkey mixture to form 24 wontons.

3. Add 2½ cups water to a 4-quart Dutch oven. Place a collapsible steamer basket in pan. Arrange wontons in a single layer on steamer basket (do not stack wontons on top of each other). Bring to a boil over medium-high heat. Cover and steam 13 minutes.

4. While wontons cook, combine soy sauce, next 3 ingredients, and 2 tablespoons water in a bowl, stirring until sugar dissolves.

5. Pour 2 quarts of water along 1 side of Dutch oven (this should be just enough to cover wontons). Bring to a boil, and boil 1 minute; remove from heat. Carefully remove steamer basket and wontons from Dutch oven. Place wontons on a serving platter and serve with dipping sauce. Serve warm or at room temperature. YIELD: 24 SERVINGS (SERVING SIZE: 1 WONTON AND 1½ TEASPOONS DIPPING SAUCE).

PER SERVING: CAL 39 (12% from fat); FAT 0.5g (sat 0.1g); PRO 1.9g; CARB 6.6g; FIB 0.2g; CHOL 4mg; IRON 0.3mg; SOD 125mg; CALC 7mg

STUFFED BABY PORTOBELLOS

POINTS value: 2

PREP: 9 minutes ■ COOK: 10 minutes
■ OTHER: 5 minutes

These easy-to-assemble mushroom morsels are like one-bite pizzas.

    14 baby portobello mushrooms (about 7 ounces), stems removed
     7 slices turkey pepperoni, quartered
     2 tablespoons pizza sauce
     1 tablespoon chopped fresh basil
     2 (1-ounce) reduced-fat mozzarella string cheese sticks, each cut crosswise into 7 pieces

1. Preheat oven to 425°.

2. Place mushrooms, tops down, on a foil-lined baking sheet. Place 2 pepperoni quarters in center of each mushroom. Combine pizza sauce and basil in a small bowl. Spoon sauce mixture evenly on top of each mushroom. Top each with a piece of cheese and press down to adhere.

3. Bake at 425° for 10 minutes or until cheese begins to brown. Remove from heat, and let stand 5 minutes. YIELD: 7 SERVINGS (SERVING SIZE: 2 MUSHROOMS).

Note: Be sure to press the cheese down into the center of each mushroom or the cheese could topple over and not melt evenly.

PER SERVING: CAL 101 (42% from fat); FAT 4.7g (sat 1.8g); PRO 12.2g; CARB 2.9g; FIB 0.4g; CHOL 41mg; IRON 1mg; SOD 625mg; CALC 128mg

SWEET POTATO FRIES WITH MAPLE-GINGER DIP

POINTS value: 2

PREP: 10 minutes ▪ **COOK:** 30 minutes

Sweet potatoes have a higher moisture content than white potatoes, so these flavorful fries won't be as crisp as traditional baked ones. On the plus side, sweet potatoes offer nutritional perks—they're a rich source of beta carotene and vitamin C.

>   3 sweet potatoes (about 1½ pounds), cut into
>   ½-inch-wide strips
>   Olive oil–flavored cooking spray
>   ½ teaspoon salt
>   ½ cup light sour cream
>   1 tablespoon maple syrup
>   ½ teaspoon grated peeled fresh ginger

1. Preheat oven to 450°.
2. Place potatoes in a single layer on a large shallow baking pan coated with cooking spray. Sprinkle potatoes evenly with salt. Bake at 450° for 30 minutes, turning once.
3. While potatoes cook, combine sour cream, syrup, and ginger in a small bowl. Serve potatoes immediately with dip. YIELD: 6 SERVINGS (SERVING SIZE: ½ CUP FRIES AND ABOUT 1½ TABLESPOONS DIP).

PER SERVING: CAL 106 (21% from fat); FAT 2.5g (sat 1.5g); PRO 1.9g; CARB 19.6g; FIB 2.5g; CHOL 8mg; IRON 0.6mg; SOD 247mg; CALC 48mg

SAUSAGE-STUFFED RED POTATOES

POINTS value: 1

PREP: 13 minutes ▪ **COOK:** 10 minutes

>   8 small red potatoes (about 1½ pounds)
>   Cooking spray
>   1 (4-ounce) link lean turkey Italian sausage (such as
>   Jennie-O), casing removed
>   ½ red bell pepper, finely chopped (about ¾ cup)
>   ¼ cup finely chopped green onions
>   2 tablespoons chopped fresh parsley
>   ½ cup (2 ounces) reduced-fat shredded extrasharp
>   Cheddar cheese
>   ⅛ teaspoon salt

1. Pierce potatoes with a fork; arrange on paper towels in microwave oven. Microwave at HIGH 8 minutes or until tender.
2. While potatoes cook, heat a large nonstick skillet over medium-high heat; coat pan with cooking spray.

Add sausage to pan; cook 4 minutes or until browned, stirring to crumble. Add bell pepper, and cook 2 minutes. Add onions and parsley, cook 30 seconds, and remove from heat. Sprinkle cheese over sausage mixture and toss gently to blend.
3. Cut potatoes in half lengthwise, and carefully scoop out 1 teaspoon potato pulp from each half, leaving the shells intact. Discard potato pulp. Sprinkle potato halves evenly with salt. Spoon 1 tablespoon sausage mixture onto each potato half; microwave at HIGH 2 minutes or until cheese melts. Serve warm. YIELD: 16 SERVINGS (SERVING SIZE: 1 STUFFED POTATO HALF).

PER SERVING: CAL 47 (31% from fat); FAT 1.6g (sat 0.8g); PRO 3g; CARB 5.3g; FIB 0.7g; CHOL 9mg; IRON 0.4mg; SOD 77mg; CALC 32mg

FRESH FIGS TOPPED WITH GOAT CHEESE AND HONEY

POINTS value: 2

PREP: 10 minutes ▪ **COOK:** 4 minutes ▪ **OTHER:** 5 minutes

A variety of flavored honey is available in supermarkets. The most common types are clover and orange blossom. We tested with summer flowers honey, but use whatever you prefer.

>   8 fresh figs
>   2 teaspoons balsamic vinegar
>   ½ cup (2 ounces) crumbled goat cheese
>   2 tablespoons flavored honey
>   1 tablespoon minced fresh mint

1. Preheat broiler.
2. Cut figs in half lengthwise. Arrange figs on a baking sheet, cut sides up, and brush with balsamic vinegar. Broil 4 minutes or until thoroughly heated. Place figs on a serving platter; cool 5 minutes.
3. Top each fig half with 1½ teaspoons goat cheese; drizzle evenly with honey, and sprinkle with mint. YIELD: 16 SERVINGS (SERVING SIZE: 1 FIG HALF).

PER SERVING: CAL 131 (10% from fat); FAT 1.4g (sat 0.9g); PRO 1.9g; CARB 30.9g; FIB 2.1g; CHOL 3mg; IRON 0.6mg; SOD 22mg; CALC 14mg

FRESH FIG AVAILABILITY

Fresh figs are available twice a year. The larger, more flavorful figs are usually available from June through July. The second crop usually arrives in early September and lasts through mid-October. Figs are highly perishable, so use them quickly, or store them in the refrigerator for no more than 2 to 3 days.

AMBROSIA SMOOTHIE

POINTS value: 2

pictured on page 50

PREP: 5 minutes

2 cups crushed ice
2 (6-ounce) cartons piña colada–flavored low-fat yogurt
1 (11-ounce) can mandarin oranges in light syrup, drained
½ teaspoon coconut extract

1. Combine all ingredients in a blender; process until smooth. Serve immediately. YIELD: 4 SERVINGS (SERVING SIZE: ABOUT ¾ CUP).

PER SERVING: CAL 120 (8% from fat); FAT 1.1g (sat 0.8g); PRO 2.7g; CARB 25.2g; FIB 0.4g; CHOL 5mg; IRON 0.2mg; SOD 51mg; CALC 104mg

MANGO LASSI

POINTS value: 2

PREP: 7 minutes

We prefer the more intense flavor of the mango nectar, but you can substitute 1⅓ cups pureed fresh mango (about 2 ripe fresh mangoes). The **POINTS** value remains the same.

2 cups ice
2 cups vanilla fat-free yogurt
1⅓ cups mango nectar
2 tablespoons honey
2 tablespoons fresh lemon juice
Mint sprigs (optional)

1. Combine first 5 ingredients in a blender; process until smooth. Garnish with mint, if desired. YIELD: 5 SERVINGS (SERVING SIZE: 1 CUP).

PER SERVING: CAL 106 (1% from fat); FAT 0.1g (sat 0g); PRO 4.2g; CARB 25.2g; FIB 0.5g; CHOL 2mg; IRON 0.1mg; SOD 56mg; CALC 124mg

LASSI—AN INDIAN TRADITION

Lassi is a traditional Indian yogurt drink often served to cool the heat of the spicy curries that are characteristic of Indian cuisine. Its consistency is similar to that of a thick milk shake, and it can be plain or flavored. A plain lassi can be served salted or sweetened, and cardamom may be added for extra flavor. Fruit is often the main ingredient in flavored lassi.

ICED MOCHA LATTE

POINTS value: 3

PREP: 5 minutes

A similar drink at your local coffee shop has a **POINTS** value of 8. By preparing this rich beverage at home, you'll save on calories and cash.

½ cup 1% chocolate low-fat milk
½ cup strong brewed coffee, cooled
1½ teaspoons "measures-like-sugar" calorie-free sweetener (such as Splenda)
½ cup crushed ice
¼ cup refrigerated fat-free dairy whipped topping (such as Reddi-wip)

1. Combine first 3 ingredients, stirring until sweetener dissolves. Pour over ice in a tall glass. Top with whipped topping. Serve immediately. YIELD: 1 SERVING (SERVING SIZE: 1¼ CUPS).

PER SERVING: CAL 120 (25% from fat); FAT 3.3g (sat 1.7g); PRO 4.1g; CARB 14.3g; FIB 0g; CHOL 11mg; IRON 0mg; SOD 111mg; CALC 150mg

POMEGRANATE-GINGER PUNCH

POINTS value: 2

PREP: 5 minutes ■ **COOK:** 3 minutes
■ **OTHER:** 30 minutes

Pomegranate juice contains much higher levels of antioxidants than other fruit juices. Antioxidants are thought to protect against heart disease and cancer.

½ cup water
½ cup sugar
2 tablespoons grated peeled fresh ginger
1 (24-ounce) bottle pomegranate juice, chilled
1 (25-ounce) bottle sparkling water, chilled
Lime wedges

1. Combine first 3 ingredients in a small saucepan; bring to a boil over medium heat, stirring until sugar dissolves. Cool to room temperature.
2. Strain ginger mixture through a fine sieve over a pitcher, pressing solids to extract remaining liquid; discard solids. Stir in pomegranate juice. Add sparkling water just before serving. Serve with lime wedges. YIELD: 7 SERVINGS (SERVING SIZE: 1 CUP).

PER SERVING: CAL 111 (0% from fat); FAT 0g (sat 0g); PRO 0.4g; CARB 28.3g; FIB 0g; CHOL 0mg; IRON 0.2mg; SOD 13mg; CALC 30mg

MADRAS SPRITZER

POINTS value: 1

PREP: 3 minutes

To make this drink ahead, combine the juice and liqueur, and then cover and chill. Add the sparkling water just before serving so the bubbles don't go flat. For a kid-friendly drink, substitute orange juice for the liqueur.

> 3 cups light cranberry juice cocktail, chilled
> ⅓ cup orange-flavored liqueur (such as Grand Marnier)
> 3 cups orange sparkling water (such as Poland Spring), chilled

1. Combine juice and liqueur in a pitcher; stir. Add sparkling water just before serving. YIELD: 6 SERVINGS (SERVING SIZE: ABOUT 1 CUP).

PER SERVING: CAL 67 (0% from fat); FAT 0g (sat 0g); PRO 0g; CARB 9.3g; FIB 0g; CHOL 0mg; IRON 0mg; SOD 38mg; CALC 0mg

FROZEN BLUEBERRY-LIME MARGARITAS

POINTS value: 1

PREP: 13 minutes

Prepare this margarita mix ahead, and freeze it in a freezer-safe container. Just before serving, thaw it slightly and scrape with a fork.

> 3 cups crushed ice
> 2¾ cups frozen blueberries
> 1 cup cold water
> ¾ cup "measures-like-sugar" calorie-free sweetener (such as Splenda)
> 2 teaspoons grated fresh lime rind
> ½ cup fresh lime juice (about 5 limes)
> ¼ cup orange-flavored liqueur (such as Grand Marnier)
> ¼ cup tequila

1. Combine all ingredients in a blender; process until smooth. Serve immediately. YIELD: 5 SERVINGS (SERVING SIZE: 1 CUP).

PER SERVING: CAL 68 (4% from fat); FAT 0.3g (sat 0g); PRO 0.3g; CARB 9g; FIB 1.3g; CHOL 0mg; IRON 0.1mg; SOD 1mg; CALC 6mg

POMEGRANATE MARTINI

POINTS value: 4

PREP: 5 minutes

If you happen to have lemon- or orange-flavored vodka on hand, use it as a flavorful alternative to plain vodka.

> 1 cup crushed ice
> ½ cup pomegranate juice
> 6 tablespoons chilled vodka
> 3 tablespoons orange-flavored liqueur (such as Grand Marnier)
> 1 tablespoon fresh lemon juice
> 2 (2-inch) fresh orange rind strips

1. Place crushed ice in a martini shaker. Add pomegranate juice and next 3 ingredients. Shake well; strain into 2 martini glasses.
2. Rub rim of each martini glass with inside of orange rind. Twist rind; drop into glasses. Serve immediately. YIELD: 2 SERVINGS (SERVING SIZE: ABOUT ⅔ CUP).

PER SERVING: CAL 213 (0% from fat); FAT 0g (sat 0g); PRO 0.3g; CARB 16.6g; FIB 0g; CHOL 0mg; IRON 0.1mg; SOD 8mg; CALC 11mg

BLOODY MARYS

POINTS value: 1

PREP: 4 minutes

If you prefer a nonalcoholic version, replace the vodka with additional tomato juice. The **POINTS** value remains the same.

> 4 cups reduced-sodium tomato juice (such as Campbell's Healthy Request)
> ½ cup vodka, chilled
> ¼ cup fresh lemon juice
> 1 tablespoon Worcestershire sauce
> 1 tablespoon hot sauce
> 1 tablespoon prepared horseradish
> Celery stalks (optional)
> Lemon wedges (optional)

1. Combine first 6 ingredients in a large pitcher. Serve over ice in glasses. Garnish with celery stalks and lemon wedges, if desired. YIELD: 6 SERVINGS (SERVING SIZE: ¾ CUP).

PER SERVING: CAL 82 (0% from fat); FAT 0g (sat 0g); PRO 0.8g; CARB 9.7g; FIB 0.8g; CHOL 0mg; IRON 0.7mg; SOD 371mg; CALC 19mg

Quick Cranberry Crescent Rolls, *page 32*

BLUEBERRY–BROWN SUGAR MUFFINS

POINTS value: 3

pictured on page 51

PREP: 10 minutes ■ COOK: 24 minutes

These brown sugar–topped muffins use fresh or frozen blueberries, which are ranked by the USDA as the fruit having the highest level of antioxidants.

- 1¾ cups all-purpose flour
- ½ cup granulated sugar
- 1½ teaspoons baking powder
- ½ teaspoon baking soda
- ¼ teaspoon salt
- 1 cup plain low-fat yogurt
- 2 tablespoons butter, melted
- 1 large egg
- 1 teaspoon grated fresh lemon rind
- 1 cup fresh blueberries or frozen unsweetened blueberries
- Cooking spray
- 1 tablespoon light brown sugar

1. Preheat oven to 350°.
2. Lightly spoon flour into dry measuring cups; level with a knife. Combine flour and next 4 ingredients in a large bowl; stir well. Set aside.
3. Combine yogurt and next 3 ingredients in a small bowl, stirring with a whisk until smooth. Add yogurt mixture to flour mixture, stirring just until moist. Gently fold in blueberries.
4. Place 12 paper muffin cup liners in muffin cups; coat liners with cooking spray. Spoon batter evenly into prepared cups. Sprinkle evenly with brown sugar. Bake at 350° for 24 minutes or until lightly browned and a wooden pick inserted in center comes out clean. YIELD: 12 SERVINGS (SERVING SIZE: 1 MUFFIN).

PER SERVING: CAL 144 (18% from fat); FAT 2.8g (sat 1.6g); PRO 3.4g; CARB 26.3g; FIB 0.8g; CHOL 24mg; IRON 1mg; SOD 196mg; CALC 74mg

PUMPKIN–CHOCOLATE CHIP MUFFINS

POINTS value: 4

PREP: 13 minutes ■ COOK: 18 minutes

Our Test Kitchens staff raved over the texture of these muffins and couldn't believe they were light. If you have any leftovers, store them in the freezer in zip-top plastic bags.

- 2 cups all-purpose flour
- ½ cup packed light brown sugar
- ¼ cup granulated sugar
- 1 tablespoon baking powder
- 1 teaspoon ground cinnamon
- ½ teaspoon salt
- ½ teaspoon ground ginger
- ½ teaspoon ground nutmeg
- ¼ teaspoon ground allspice
- 1 cup canned pumpkin
- ¾ cup 1% low-fat milk
- ¼ cup cinnamon-flavored applesauce
- 2 tablespoons canola oil
- 1 teaspoon vanilla extract
- 1 large egg, lightly beaten
- ⅓ cup semisweet chocolate minichips
- Cooking spray

1. Preheat oven to 400°.
2. Lightly spoon flour into dry measuring cups; level with a knife. Combine flour and next 8 ingredients in a medium bowl; stir well with a whisk.
3. Combine pumpkin and next 5 ingredients in a small bowl, stirring with a whisk until smooth. Add pumpkin mixture to flour mixture, stirring just until moist. Stir in minichips.
4. Spoon batter evenly into 12 muffin cups coated with cooking spray. Bake at 400° for 18 minutes or until muffins spring back when touched lightly in center. Remove muffins from pan immediately. Cool on a wire rack. YIELD: 12 SERVINGS (SERVING SIZE: 1 MUFFIN).

PER SERVING: CAL 195 (22% from fat); FAT 4.7g (sat 1.4g); PRO 3.6g; CARB 35.8g; FIB 1.8g; CHOL 18mg; IRON 2mg; SOD 238mg; CALC 112mg

GREEN ONION–DILL BISCUITS

POINTS value: 2

PREP: 9 minutes ■ **COOK:** 12 minutes

Cutting in the butter creates flaky biscuits, but make sure you stop the process when the mixture resembles coarse meal.

- 1½ **cups all-purpose flour**
- 1½ **teaspoons baking powder**
- ½ **teaspoon baking soda**
- ¼ **teaspoon salt**
- 3 **tablespoons chilled butter, cut into small pieces**
- 2 **tablespoons finely chopped green onions**
- 1 **tablespoon chopped fresh dill**
- ⅔ **cup low-fat buttermilk**

Cooking spray

- 1 **tablespoon grated fresh Parmesan cheese**

1. Preheat oven to 400°.
2. Lightly spoon flour into dry measuring cups; level with a knife. Combine flour and next 3 ingredients in a large bowl; cut in butter with a pastry blender or 2 knives until mixture resembles coarse meal. Stir in green onions and dill. Add buttermilk, and stir just until moist.
3. Turn dough out onto a lightly floured surface; knead lightly 5 times. Pat dough to ½-inch thickness; cut with a 1¾-inch biscuit cutter. Place biscuits on a baking sheet coated with cooking spray; sprinkle tops with Parmesan cheese.
4. Bake at 400° for 12 minutes or until lightly browned. Serve warm. **YIELD: 15 SERVINGS (SERVING SIZE: 1 BISCUIT).**

PER SERVING: CAL 72 (33% from fat); FAT 2.6g (sat 1.6g); PRO 1.8g; CARB 10.3g; FIB 0.4g; CHOL 7mg; IRON 0.7mg; SOD 163mg; CALC 47mg

SHELF LIFE OF BAKING POWDER

Before you bake, check the strength of your baking powder to make sure your baked products will rise properly. Add 1 teaspoon baking powder to ⅓ cup hot water. The fresher the baking powder, the more vigorously this mixture will bubble. If the reaction is weak or doesn't occur, you'll need to pick up a fresh can. Baking powder begins to lose its leavening ability when it comes in contact with moisture, so store it in a dry place and never dip a wet or damp measuring spoon into the can. Once the can is opened, the baking powder should last up to 6 months if stored properly.

SUNSHINE SCONES

POINTS value: 3

PREP: 10 minutes ■ **COOK:** 14 minutes

Cut into, but not completely through, the circles of dough to create wedges; do not separate. Keeping the wedges together allows them to bake as one large scone, making them moister than if they were baked separately. The wedges come apart easily after baking.

- 2 **cups all-purpose flour**
- ¼ **cup granulated sugar**
- 2 **teaspoons baking powder**
- ½ **teaspoon baking soda**
- ¼ **teaspoon salt**
- 2 **tablespoons chilled butter, cut into small pieces**
- ⅔ **cup light sour cream**
- ½ **cup low-fat buttermilk**
- 1 **tablespoon grated fresh lemon rind**

Cooking spray

- 2 **teaspoons turbinado sugar**

1. Preheat oven to 400°.
2. Lightly spoon flour into dry measuring cups; level with a knife. Combine flour and next 4 ingredients in a large bowl; cut in butter with a pastry blender or 2 knives until mixture resembles coarse meal.
3. Combine sour cream, buttermilk, and lemon rind in a small bowl; add to flour mixture, stirring just until moist.
4. Turn dough out onto a lightly floured surface; knead lightly 4 times. Divide dough in half, and pat each half into a 5½-inch circle on a baking sheet coated with cooking spray. Cut each circle into 6 wedges, cutting into, but not through, dough. Sprinkle with turbinado sugar. Bake at 400° for 14 minutes or until lightly browned. **YIELD: 12 SERVINGS (SERVING SIZE: 1 SCONE).**

PER SERVING: CAL 133 (26% from fat); FAT 3.8g (sat 2.3g); PRO 2.9g; CARB 21.9g; FIB 0.6g; CHOL 11mg; IRON 1.1mg; SOD 212mg; CALC 75mg

BANANA PANCAKES WITH PEANUT BUTTER–HONEY SYRUP

POINTS value: 4

PREP: 13 minutes
■ **COOK:** 3 minutes plus 6 minutes per batch

You can substitute honey wheat germ in place of regular wheat germ to add a little more sweetness to the pancakes.

- 1⅓ cups low-fat baking mix (such as Bisquick Heart Smart)
- ⅓ cup toasted wheat germ
- 1 tablespoon sugar
- ½ teaspoon ground cinnamon
- ¼ teaspoon salt
- 1 cup fat-free buttermilk
- 1 large egg, lightly beaten
- ½ teaspoon vanilla extract
- 1 large very ripe banana, mashed
- Cooking spray
- Peanut Butter–Honey Syrup

1. Combine first 5 ingredients in a large bowl; stir with a whisk. Combine buttermilk, egg, and vanilla in a medium bowl. Add buttermilk mixture to baking mix mixture; stir just until combined. Stir in banana.
2. Spoon 2 tablespoons batter per pancake onto a hot nonstick griddle or nonstick skillet coated with cooking spray. Cook 3 to 4 minutes or until tops are covered with bubbles and edges look cooked. Carefully turn pancakes over, and cook 3 to 4 minutes or until bottoms are lightly browned. Serve pancakes with Peanut Butter–Honey Syrup. YIELD: 9 SERVINGS (SERVING SIZE: 2 PANCAKES AND ABOUT 1 TABLESPOON SYRUP).

PER SERVING: CAL 217 (20% from fat); FAT 4.8g (sat 0.8g); PRO 6.3g; CARB 39.7g; FIB 1.8g; CHOL 24mg; IRON 1.5mg; SOD 350mg; CALC 111mg

Peanut Butter–Honey Syrup
POINTS value: 2

- ½ cup honey
- ¼ cup peanut butter
- 1 tablespoon fat-free buttermilk

1. Heat honey and peanut butter in a small saucepan over low heat 3 minutes or until smooth; remove from heat. Stir in buttermilk. YIELD: ⅔ CUP.

PER TABLESPOON: CAL 84 (32% from fat); FAT 3g (sat 0.6g); PRO 1.6g; CARB 14.5g; FIB 0.4g; CHOL 0mg; IRON 0.2mg; SOD 30mg; CALC 3mg

CHOCOLATE WAFFLES WITH DARK CHERRY SAUCE

POINTS value: 4

pictured on page 52
PREP: 7 minutes
■ **COOK:** 15 minutes plus 7 minutes per batch

The waffles will be soft when you first remove them from the waffle iron, but they will quickly firm up and become slightly crisp upon standing. You can freeze the waffles and reheat them in a toaster oven to the desired crispness.

- 1 cup low-fat baking mix (such as Bisquick Heart Smart)
- 1 tablespoon sugar
- ⅓ cup chocolate syrup
- ⅓ cup fat-free milk
- 1½ tablespoons canola oil
- 3 large egg whites
- Butter-flavored cooking spray
- Dark Cherry Sauce
- ½ cup frozen fat-free whipped topping, thawed

1. Combine baking mix and sugar in a medium bowl; stir with a whisk. Combine chocolate syrup, milk, and oil in a small bowl; stir with a whisk. Add chocolate mixture to baking mix mixture; stir just until moist.
2. Place egg whites in a medium bowl, and beat with a mixer at high speed until soft peaks form. Gently fold one-third of egg whites into batter. Fold remaining egg whites into batter.
3. Coat a waffle iron with cooking spray; preheat. Spoon 1 cup batter per waffle onto hot waffle iron, spreading batter to edges. Cook according to manufacturer's instructions until waffle iron stops steaming. Repeat procedure with remaining batter. Serve with Dark Cherry Sauce and whipped topping. YIELD: 9 SERVINGS (SERVING SIZE: 1 [4-INCH] WAFFLE, 2 TABLESPOONS SAUCE, AND ABOUT 1 TABLESPOON WHIPPED TOPPING).

PER SERVING: CAL 185 (16% from fat); FAT 3.2g (sat 0.3g); PRO 3.1g; CARB 35.8g; FIB 1g; CHOL 0mg; IRON 0.6mg; SOD 174mg; CALC 68mg

Dark Cherry Sauce
POINTS value: 1

This richly colored sauce can also be served over pancakes, angel food cake, or ice cream. Or try stirring some into a bowl of oatmeal.

- 1 (12-ounce) package frozen dark sweet cherries
- ⅔ cup seedless red raspberry fruit spread (such as Smucker's Simply Fruit)

1. Bring cherries and fruit spread to a boil in a medium skillet over medium-high heat; reduce heat, and cook, uncovered, 15 minutes or until thick, stirring often. Remove from heat. Serve warm. YIELD: 18 TABLESPOONS.

PER 2 TABLESPOONS: CAL 72 (0% from fat); FAT 0g (sat 0g); PRO 0.3g; CARB 17.3g; FIB 0.8g; CHOL 0mg; IRON 0mg; SOD 0mg; CALC 5mg

PARMESAN-PROSCIUTTO BISCOTTI

POINTS value: 1

PREP: 19 minutes ■ COOK: 1 hour and 8 minutes
■ OTHER: 20 minutes

Biscotti are crisp Italian cookies made by first baking a loaf of dough and then slicing it and baking the slices again. To get 18 slices from the loaf, discard the 2 end pieces.

  1¾ cups all-purpose flour
  ¼ cup grated fresh Parmesan cheese
  1 teaspoon baking powder
  ½ teaspoon salt
  ⅛ teaspoon freshly ground black pepper
  ¼ cup 2% reduced-fat milk
  2 large eggs
  2 garlic cloves, crushed
  2 ounces prosciutto, finely diced
  Cooking spray

1. Preheat oven to 350°.
2. Lightly spoon flour into dry measuring cups; level with a knife. Combine flour and next 4 ingredients in a large bowl, stirring well with a whisk. Combine milk, eggs, and garlic in a small bowl; stir with a whisk until smooth. Add milk mixture to flour mixture, stirring until well blended. Stir in prosciutto. Turn dough out onto a lightly floured surface, and knead lightly 8 times. Shape dough into a 12-inch-long roll. Place roll on a baking sheet coated with cooking spray; pat to 1-inch thickness.
3. Bake at 350° for 30 minutes or until top is lightly browned. Remove roll from baking sheet, and cool 20 minutes on a wire rack.
4. Reduce oven temperature to 325°.
5. Cut roll diagonally into 18 slices using a serrated knife. Place slices, cut sides down, on baking sheet. Bake at 325° for 20 minutes. Turn biscotti over; bake an additional 18 to 20 minutes or until lightly browned. Remove from baking sheet; cool completely on wire rack. YIELD: 18 SERVINGS (SERVING SIZE: 1 BISCOTTO).

PER SERVING: CAL 65 (18% from fat); FAT 1.3g (sat 0.5g); PRO 3.2g; CARB 9.7g; FIB 0.3g; CHOL 27mg; IRON 0.8mg; SOD 166mg; CALC 37mg

MAKING BISCOTTI

1. Use your hands to gently shape the dough into a roll.

2. Careful patting and forming allows you to flatten the dough to 1-inch thickness.

3. Cut the baked roll diagonally into slices of equal width. A sharp serrated knife is a must.

GREEN CHILE CORN BREAD

POINTS value: 4

PREP: 9 minutes ■ COOK: 28 minutes
■ OTHER: 5 minutes

This golden corn bread cooks in a baking pan, so you don't have to pull out your heavy cast-iron skillet.

  1 cup all-purpose flour
  1 cup stone-ground yellow cornmeal
  ¾ teaspoon baking powder
  ½ teaspoon salt
  ¼ teaspoon baking soda
  1 cup fat-free buttermilk
  2 tablespoons canola oil
  2 large eggs, lightly beaten
  1 large egg white
  1 (4.5-ounce) can chopped green chiles, drained
  ¼ cup (1 ounce) shredded 2% reduced-fat colby-Jack cheese
  Cooking spray

1. Preheat oven to 425°.
2. Lightly spoon flour into a dry measuring cup; level with a knife. Combine flour and next 4 ingredients. Combine buttermilk and next 3 ingredients, stirring with a whisk. Add buttermilk mixture to flour mixture, stirring just until moist. Gently fold in green chiles and cheese; pour batter into a 9-inch square baking pan coated with cooking spray.
3. Bake at 425° for 28 minutes or until golden. Let stand 5 minutes before cutting into squares. YIELD: 9 SERVINGS (SERVING SIZE: 1 SQUARE).

PER SERVING: CAL 170 (28% from fat); FAT 5.2g (sat 1.1g); PRO 6.3g; CARB 24.3g; FIB 1.5g; CHOL 49mg; IRON 1.6mg; SOD 499mg; CALC 162mg

TROPICAL TEA BREAD

POINTS value: 4

PREP: 9 minutes ■ **COOK:** 58 minutes
■ **OTHER:** 35 minutes

This flavorful, cakelike quick bread earned our Test Kitchens' highest rating. Since the tender loaf contains chunks of fruit, we recommend using a serrated knife to cut neat slices.

> 1 cup all-purpose flour
> ½ teaspoon baking powder
> ¼ teaspoon baking soda
> ¼ teaspoon salt
> ½ cup (4 ounces) ⅓-less-fat cream cheese, softened
> ¼ cup butter, softened
> ⅔ cup granulated sugar
> 1 large egg
> 2¼ teaspoons grated fresh orange rind, divided
> ¼ teaspoon coconut extract
> 1 (6-ounce) carton piña colada–flavored low-fat yogurt
> ⅓ cup flaked sweetened coconut, toasted
> ¼ cup canned crushed pineapple in juice, drained
> Cooking spray
> ⅓ cup powdered sugar
> 2 teaspoons fresh orange juice

1. Preheat oven to 325°.
2. Lightly spoon flour into a dry measuring cup; level with a knife. Combine flour and next 3 ingredients in a small bowl. Combine cream cheese and butter in a large bowl; beat with a mixer at medium speed until well blended. Gradually add granulated sugar, and beat until light and fluffy. Add egg, 2 teaspoons orange rind, and coconut extract, beating just until blended. Add flour mixture to butter mixture alternately with yogurt, beginning and ending with flour mixture. Stir in coconut and pineapple.
3. Spoon batter into an 8 x 4–inch loaf pan coated with cooking spray. Bake at 325° for 58 minutes or until a wooden pick inserted in center comes out clean. Cool in pan 5 minutes on a wire rack. Remove from pan; cool completely on wire rack over wax paper.
4. Combine powdered sugar, remaining ¼ teaspoon orange rind, and orange juice in a small bowl, stirring until smooth. Drizzle glaze over top of loaf. YIELD: 14 SERVINGS (SERVING SIZE: 1 SLICE).

PER SERVING: CAL 158 (35% from fat); FAT 6.2g (sat 4g); PRO 2.7g; CARB 23.5g; FIB 0.4g; CHOL 30mg; IRON 0.6mg; SOD 153mg; CALC 36mg

PURE VANILLA EXTRACT VS. IMITATION

Pure vanilla extract is made by steeping vanilla beans in an alcohol/water solution for several months. The FDA requires that pure vanilla extract contain 13.35 ounces of vanilla beans per gallon of liquid and 35% alcohol. This process produces a richly flavored, highly fragrant clear brown liquid. It costs more than imitation vanilla, but the flavor and quality are far superior. Imitation vanilla extract is made with synthetic vanilla and leaves a bitter aftertaste. Be sure to check the label to determine exactly what you are buying.

QUICK CRANBERRY CRESCENT ROLLS

POINTS value: 3

pictured on page 54

PREP: 7 minutes ■ **COOK:** 13 minutes

> ¼ cup packed brown sugar
> ½ teaspoon ground cinnamon
> 1 (8-ounce) can refrigerated reduced-fat crescent dinner roll dough
> ¼ cup cranberry-orange crushed fruit (such as Ocean Spray)
> 2 tablespoons chopped walnuts, toasted
> Cooking spray
> ¼ cup powdered sugar
> 1¼ teaspoons 1% low-fat milk
> ¼ teaspoon vanilla extract

1. Preheat oven to 375°.
2. Combine brown sugar and cinnamon in a small bowl; set aside.
3. Unroll dough, and separate into 8 triangles. Spread crushed fruit evenly over each triangle. Sprinkle triangles evenly with brown sugar mixture and walnuts. Roll crescents according to package directions, and pinch ends of crescents to seal.
4. Place rolls, point sides down, on a baking sheet coated with cooking spray. Bake at 375° for 13 to 15 minutes or until golden.
5. While rolls bake, combine powdered sugar, milk, and vanilla, stirring until smooth. Remove rolls from oven. Remove from pan, and cool slightly on a wire rack over wax paper. Spoon glaze evenly over warm rolls. YIELD: 8 SERVINGS (SERVING SIZE: 1 ROLL).

PER SERVING: CAL 153 (34% from fat); FAT 5.8g (sat 2.1g); PRO 2.3g; CARB 25g; FIB 0.4g; CHOL 0mg; IRON 0.9mg; SOD 227mg; CALC 8mg

HERB-GRILLED FLATBREAD

POINTS value: 2

PREP: 6 minutes ▪ **COOK:** 4 minutes

For the best flavor, use regular wheat flatbread rounds rather than the light variety.

  1 tablespoon olive oil
  3 garlic cloves, minced
  2 teaspoons chopped fresh rosemary
  2 teaspoons chopped fresh thyme
  ¼ teaspoon freshly ground black pepper
  ¼ teaspoon salt
  2 (6-inch) wheat flatbread rounds (such as Toufayan)
Cooking spray

1. Prepare grill.
2. Combine first 6 ingredients in a small bowl.
3. Spray both sides of bread with cooking spray. Place bread on grill rack; grill 2 minutes. Turn and spread olive oil mixture on grilled side of bread. Grill 2 minutes or until thoroughly heated. Cut each round into 8 wedges. YIELD: 4 SERVINGS (SERVING SIZE: 4 WEDGES).

PER SERVING: CAL 104 (29% from fat); FAT 3.4g (sat 0.5g); PRO 3.2g; CARB 16g; FIB 3.2g; CHOL 0mg; IRON 1.1mg; SOD 211mg; CALC 27mg

ROASTED PEPPER–FONTINA FLATBREAD

POINTS value: 2

PREP: 24 minutes ▪ **COOK:** 20 minutes ▪ **OTHER:** 2 hours and 5 minutes

This savory bread is perfect alongside Rustic Italian Tomato and Red Pepper Soup with Basil, found on page 160.

  1 package dry yeast (about 2¼ teaspoons)
  1 teaspoon sugar
  1 cup warm water (100° to 110°)
  1 tablespoon olive oil
  ¾ teaspoon salt
  1½ cups all-purpose flour, divided
  1 cup whole wheat flour
  1 tablespoon chopped fresh rosemary
Cooking spray
  ½ cup sliced bottled roasted red bell peppers
  ¾ cup (3 ounces) shredded fontina cheese

1. Dissolve yeast and sugar in 1 cup warm water in a large bowl; let stand 5 minutes. Stir in oil and salt.

2. Lightly spoon flours into dry measuring cups; level with a knife. Combine 1¼ cups all-purpose flour, whole wheat flour, and rosemary in a large bowl. Gradually add flour mixture to yeast mixture, stirring until a stiff dough forms. Turn dough out onto a lightly floured surface, and knead until smooth and elastic (about 8 minutes), adding enough of remaining ¼ cup all-purpose flour, 1 tablespoon at a time, to prevent dough from sticking to hands. Place dough in a large bowl coated with cooking spray, turning to coat top. Cover and let rise in a warm place (85°), free from drafts, 1 hour or until doubled in size. (Gently press two fingers into dough. If indentation remains, dough has risen enough.)
3. Punch dough down, and place in a 15 x 10–inch baking pan coated with cooking spray, pressing dough gently to reach all sides. Cover and let rise 1 hour or until doubled in size.
4. Preheat oven to 400°.
5. Arrange bell peppers evenly over top of dough; sprinkle evenly with cheese. Bake at 400° for 20 to 22 minutes or until edges of bread are lightly browned. Remove from pan; cool on a wire rack. Serve warm or at room temperature. YIELD: 16 SERVINGS (SERVING SIZE: 1 PIECE).

PER SERVING: CAL 98 (25% from fat); FAT 2.7g (sat 1.1g); PRO 3.7g; CARB 15.1g; FIB 1.3g; CHOL 6mg; IRON 0.9mg; SOD 164mg; CALC 33mg

FONTINA CHEESE

Fontina is a creamy, semisoft cow's milk cheese with a mild, nutty flavor. It has been produced in the Aosta Valley in Italy since the 12th century, but other countries, including Denmark, France, and the United States, produce their own versions. However, many of these fontinas tend to be softer and blander than the Italian original. It's a good melting cheese that works well in sauces, on pizzas and breads, and in casseroles.

ONION CARAWAY ROLLS

POINTS value: 2

PREP: 25 minutes ■ **COOK:** 25 minutes
■ **OTHER:** 1 hour and 40 minutes

These beautiful, golden rolls are at their best when served warm from the oven.

>   2 tablespoons canola oil
>   1 cup finely chopped onion
>   1 package dry yeast (about 2¼ teaspoons)
>   1 tablespoon sugar
>   1 cup warm water (100° to 110°)
> 2¼ cups bread flour, divided
>   1 cup rye flour
>   2 teaspoons caraway seeds
> 1½ teaspoons salt
> **Cooking spray**

1. Heat oil in a medium nonstick skillet over medium heat. Add onion, and cook, stirring occasionally, about 10 minutes or until onion is tender and lightly browned. Transfer to a bowl, and cool completely.
2. Dissolve yeast and sugar in 1 cup warm water in a large bowl; let stand 5 minutes. Lightly spoon flours into dry measuring cups; level with a knife. Combine 2 cups bread flour, rye flour, caraway seeds, salt, and onion in a large bowl. Gradually add flour mixture to yeast mixture, stirring until a stiff dough forms. Turn dough out onto a lightly floured surface, and knead until smooth and elastic (about 8 minutes), adding enough of remaining ¼ cup bread flour, 1 tablespoon at a time, to prevent dough from sticking to hands.
3. Place dough in a large bowl coated with cooking spray, turning to coat top. Cover and let rise in a warm place (85°), free from drafts, 1 hour or until doubled in size. (Gently press two fingers into dough. If indentation remains, dough has risen enough.)
4. Punch dough down. Divide dough into 16 equal portions; shape portions into balls. Place rolls on a large baking sheet coated with cooking spray. Cover and let rise 35 minutes or until doubled in size.
5. Preheat oven to 400°.
6. Bake at 400° for 13 minutes or until lightly browned. Remove from pan; cool on a wire rack. Serve warm or at room temperature. YIELD: 16 SERVINGS (SERVING SIZE: 1 ROLL).

PER SERVING: CAL 117 (18% from fat); FAT 2.3g (sat 0.2g); PRO 3.2g; CARB 20.9g; FIB 1.7g; CHOL 0mg; IRON 1.1mg; SOD 219mg; CALC 9mg

CRANBERRY-WALNUT BREAD

POINTS value: 3

PREP: 19 minutes ■ **COOK:** 30 minutes
■ **OTHER:** 1 hour and 35 minutes

Your whole house will smell like the holidays when this bread is baking.

>   1 package dry yeast (about 2¼ teaspoons)
>   ⅓ cup sugar
>   1 cup warm 2% reduced-fat milk (100° to 110°)
>   ½ teaspoon salt
>   2 tablespoons butter, melted
> 2¾ cups all-purpose flour, divided
>   ½ cup dried cranberries
>   ⅓ cup chopped walnuts
> **Cooking spray**

1. Dissolve yeast and sugar in warm milk in a large bowl; let stand 5 minutes. Add salt; stir to dissolve. Stir in butter.
2. Lightly spoon flour into dry measuring cups; level with a knife. Add 2½ cups flour to yeast mixture, stirring until a soft dough forms. Stir in cranberries and walnuts. Turn dough out onto a lightly floured surface. Knead until smooth and elastic (about 5 minutes), adding enough of remaining ¼ cup flour, 1 tablespoon at a time, to prevent dough from sticking to hands.
3. Place dough in a large bowl coated with cooking spray, turning to coat top. Cover and let rise in a warm place (85°), free from drafts, 1 hour or until doubled in size. (Gently press two fingers into dough. If indentation remains, dough has risen enough.)
4. Punch dough down; turn out onto a floured surface. Roll into a 10 x 6–inch rectangle. Starting with a short edge, roll up tightly, jelly-roll fashion, pressing firmly to eliminate air pockets; pinch seam and ends to seal. Place roll, seam side down, in a 9 x 5–inch loaf pan coated with cooking spray. Cover and let rise 30 minutes or until doubled in size.
5. Preheat oven to 375°.
6. Bake at 375° for 30 minutes or until top is golden and loaf sounds hollow when tapped. Remove from pan; cool completely on a wire rack. YIELD: 16 SERVINGS (SERVING SIZE: 1 SLICE).

PER SERVING: CAL 143 (22% from fat); FAT 3.5g (sat 1.2g); PRO 3.5g; CARB 24.5g; FIB 1g; CHOL 5mg; IRON 1.2mg; SOD 91mg; CALC 24mg

desserts

Sticky Toffee Pudding, *page 38*

BUTTERMILK BANANA CAKE WITH RUM-SOAKED STRAWBERRIES

POINTS value: 4

pictured on page 55

PREP: 8 minutes ■ **COOK:** 28 minutes
■ **OTHER:** 1 hour and 35 minutes

If you'd prefer a nonalcoholic version, substitute 1 teaspoon vanilla extract for the rum in the cake and simply omit adding it to the strawberries.

  4 cups strawberries, quartered
  ½ cup plus 2 tablespoons granulated sugar, divided
  3 tablespoons dark rum, divided
  1 cup all-purpose flour
  1 teaspoon baking powder
  ½ teaspoon baking soda
  ½ teaspoon ground cinnamon
  ¼ teaspoon salt
  1 large egg
  2 tablespoons butter, melted
  ½ cup low-fat buttermilk
  ½ cup mashed ripe banana (about 1 small)
Cooking spray
  ½ teaspoon powdered sugar

1. Combine strawberries, 2 tablespoons granulated sugar, and 1 tablespoon rum in a medium bowl, stirring well. Let stand 1 hour, stirring occasionally.
2. Preheat oven to 350°.
3. Lightly spoon flour into a dry measuring cup; level with a knife. Combine flour and next 4 ingredients in a medium bowl. Place egg, remaining ½ cup granulated sugar, and butter in a large bowl; beat with a mixer at medium speed until light and fluffy. Add flour mixture and buttermilk alternately to egg mixture, beginning and ending with flour mixture. Stir in banana and remaining 2 tablespoons rum.
4. Pour batter into an 8-inch round cake pan coated with cooking spray. Bake at 350° for 28 minutes or until a wooden pick inserted in center comes out clean. Cool in pan 5 minutes on a wire rack. Remove cake from pan; cool completely on wire rack.
5. Sprinkle cake with powdered sugar. Serve with strawberries. YIELD: 8 SERVINGS (SERVING SIZE: 1 SLICE CAKE AND ½ CUP STRAWBERRIES).

PER SERVING: CAL 205 (18% from fat); FAT 4g (sat 2.1g); PRO 3.6g; CARB 38g; FIB 2.5g; CHOL 35mg; IRON 1.4mg; SOD 259mg; CALC 74mg

BLUEBERRY–CREAM CHEESE CUPCAKES

POINTS value: 5

PREP: 16 minutes ■ **COOK:** 20 minutes
■ **OTHER:** 30 minutes

Instead of letting the cream cheese soften at room temperature, keep it in the refrigerator until you're ready to make the frosting. This helps create a spreadable frosting that's easier to work with.

  1 cup plus 1 tablespoon all-purpose flour, divided
  ½ teaspoon baking soda
  ¼ teaspoon salt
  5 tablespoons butter, softened
  ¾ cup granulated sugar
  1 large egg
  2 large egg whites
  2½ teaspoons vanilla extract, divided
  ½ cup fat-free milk
  ¾ cup blueberries
  1½ cups powdered sugar
  ½ cup (4 ounces) ⅓-less-fat cream cheese

1. Preheat oven to 350°.
2. Lightly spoon 1 cup flour into a dry measuring cup; level with a knife. Combine 1 cup flour, baking soda, and salt in a medium bowl. Place butter and granulated sugar in a large bowl; beat with a mixer at medium speed until light and fluffy. Add egg and egg whites, beating until blended. Stir in 2 teaspoons vanilla.
3. Add flour mixture and milk alternately to sugar mixture, beginning and ending with flour mixture. Toss blueberries in remaining 1 tablespoon flour. Fold blueberries into batter. Spoon batter evenly into 12 muffin cups lined with paper liners. Bake at 350° for 20 minutes or until a wooden pick inserted in center comes out clean. Cool in pan 10 minutes on a wire rack. Remove from pan; cool completely on wire rack.
4. While cupcakes cool, combine powdered sugar, cream cheese, and remaining ½ teaspoon vanilla in a medium bowl; beat with a mixer at medium speed just until blended (do not overbeat). Spread frosting over cooled cupcakes. YIELD: 12 SERVINGS (SERVING SIZE: 1 CUPCAKE).

PER SERVING: CAL 233 (28% from fat); FAT 7.3g (sat 4.5g); PRO 3.8g; CARB 38.2g; FIB 0.5g; CHOL 37mg; IRON 0.6mg; SOD 197mg; CALC 26mg

APPLE BUTTER POUND CAKE

POINTS value: 6

PREP: 16 minutes ■ **COOK:** 1 hour and 11 minutes
■ **OTHER:** 45 minutes

Cake flour has the least amount of gluten of all wheat flours, making it perfectly suited for light, delicate products, such as pastries and cakes.

Butter-flavored cooking spray
 1 tablespoon cake flour
 4½ cups sifted cake flour
 1½ teaspoons baking powder
 ½ teaspoon baking soda
 1 teaspoon ground cinnamon
 ½ teaspoon ground cloves
 ½ teaspoon salt
 ⅔ cup butter, softened
 2½ cups packed dark brown sugar
 ½ cup granulated sugar
 2¼ cups apple butter
 1 cup egg substitute
 1 tablespoon vanilla extract
 ¼ cup apple juice
 1½ tablespoons butter

1. Preheat oven to 325°.
2. Coat a 10-inch Bundt pan or tube pan with cooking spray. Dust with 1 tablespoon cake flour; set aside.
3. Combine 4½ cups sifted cake flour and next 5 ingredients in a large bowl. Place ⅔ cup butter in a large bowl; beat with a mixer at medium speed until creamy. Add sugars and apple butter, and beat until fluffy. Add egg substitute and vanilla; beat until blended. Gradually add flour mixture to butter mixture, beating just until combined.
4. Pour batter into prepared pan. Bake at 325° for 1 hour and 10 minutes or until a long wooden pick inserted in center comes out clean. Cool cake in pan 15 minutes on a wire rack.
5. While cake cools, combine apple juice and 1½ tablespoons butter in a small saucepan. Bring to a boil, stirring until butter melts. Invert cake onto a plate. Pierce cake liberally with a wooden pick. Brush cake with glaze, allowing cake to absorb glaze. Cool completely. YIELD: 24 SERVINGS (SERVING SIZE: 1 SLICE).

PER SERVING: CAL 275 (19% from fat); FAT 5.9g (sat 3.7g); PRO 2.7g; CARB 53.1g; FIB 0.8g; CHOL 15mg; IRON 2.1mg; SOD 181mg; CALC 49mg

UPSIDE-DOWN PINEAPPLE SPICE CAKE

POINTS value: 4

PREP: 11 minutes ■ **COOK:** 50 minutes
■ **OTHER:** 25 minutes

Adding mashed banana to a cake mix makes this dessert very moist. To mash the banana easily, place it in a zip-top plastic bag and squeeze until the banana is well mashed; then add it to the ingredients in the bowl as directed.

 1 (18.25-ounce) package spice cake mix
 1⅓ cups water
 ¾ cup egg substitute
 ¼ cup mashed ripe banana (about ½ medium)
 2 tablespoons canola oil
 1 (20-ounce) can pineapple slices in juice, undrained
Cooking spray
 2 tablespoons dark brown sugar
 1¼ teaspoons cornstarch
 1 tablespoon light butter
 1 teaspoon vanilla extract

1. Preheat oven to 325°.
2. Combine first 5 ingredients in a large bowl; beat with a mixer at medium speed until well blended. Set aside.
3. Drain pineapple slices into a bowl, reserving ¾ cup juice. Press pineapple slices between paper towels until barely moist; cut in half. Arrange prepared pineapple slices in a single layer in a 9½-inch nonstick springform pan coated with cooking spray.
4. Pour batter over pineapple slices. Bake at 325° for 48 minutes or until a wooden pick inserted in center comes out almost clean. Cool in pan 10 minutes on a wire rack. Invert cake onto wire rack, and cool completely.
5. While cake cools, combine reserved pineapple juice, sugar, and cornstarch in a medium saucepan, stirring constantly with a whisk until cornstarch dissolves. Place juice mixture over medium-high heat; bring to a boil. Boil 1 minute, stirring constantly. Remove from heat, and stir in butter and vanilla. Cool 15 minutes. Transfer cooled cake to a serving plate. Pour cooled sauce evenly over cake. YIELD: 16 SERVINGS (SERVING SIZE: 1 SLICE).

PER SERVING: CAL 196 (29% from fat); FAT 6.3g (sat 1.9g); PRO 3.3g; CARB 32g; FIB 1.1g; CHOL 1mg; IRON 0.9mg; SOD 249mg; CALC 28mg

STICKY TOFFEE PUDDING

POINTS value: 4

pictured on page 56

PREP: 13 minutes ■ **COOK:** 35 minutes
■ **OTHER:** 35 minutes

This ooey-gooey cake is sure to satisfy your craving for something sweet.

  Cooking spray
    1 cup chopped pitted dates
  1¾ cups water
  1½ cups self-rising flour
    ⅛ teaspoon salt
    ¼ cup butter, softened
    ⅔ cup packed dark brown sugar
    2 large eggs
    1 teaspoon vanilla extract
  Toffee Sauce
  Frozen fat-free whipped topping, thawed (optional)

1. Preheat oven to 350°.
2. Line bottom of a 9-inch square cake pan with wax paper. Coat wax paper with cooking spray; set aside.
3. Combine dates and water in a medium saucepan. Cover and simmer 5 minutes. Remove from heat; let stand, covered, 5 minutes. Mash with a potato masher until smooth.
4. Lightly spoon flour into dry measuring cups; level with a knife. Combine flour and salt in a small bowl. Place butter and sugar in a medium bowl; beat with a mixer at medium–high speed until light and fluffy. Add eggs and vanilla, beating just until blended. Gradually add flour mixture to butter mixture, stirring just until combined. Stir in date mixture. Pour batter into prepared pan.
5. Bake at 350° for 28 minutes or until a wooden pick inserted in center comes out clean. Cool in pan 15 minutes on a wire rack.
6. Invert cake onto a plate. Remove and discard wax paper. Pierce cake at 1-inch intervals with a wooden pick. Pour Toffee Sauce over cake; let stand 15 minutes. Serve with whipped topping, if desired. YIELD: 16 SERVINGS (SERVING SIZE: 1 SQUARE).

PER SERVING: CAL 169 (31% from fat); FAT 5.9g (sat 3.4g); PRO 2.3g; CARB 27.7g; FIB 1.2g; CHOL 40mg; IRON 1mg; SOD 213mg; CALC 51mg

Toffee Sauce

POINTS value: 2

    ½ cup packed dark brown sugar
    3 tablespoons butter
    3 tablespoons fat-free half-and-half
  1½ teaspoons vanilla extract

1. Combine all ingredients in a small saucepan; simmer 2 minutes. YIELD: ½ CUP.

PER TABLESPOON: CAL 77 (50% from fat); FAT 4.3g (sat 2.7g); PRO 0.2g; CARB 9.4g; FIB 0g; CHOL 12mg; IRON 0.2mg; SOD 42mg; CALC 14mg

PUMPKIN BUNDT CAKE WITH CIDER SAUCE

POINTS value: 4

PREP: 10 minutes ■ **COOK:** 44 minutes
■ **OTHER:** 15 minutes

    1 (18.25-ounce) package spice cake mix
    1 cup canned pumpkin
    ¾ cup egg substitute
    ½ cup golden raisins
    2 tablespoons canola oil
  Cooking spray
    ¾ cup apple cider
    2 tablespoons light brown sugar
    1 tablespoon cornstarch
    2 tablespoons light butter
    2 tablespoons dark rum
    2 teaspoons vanilla extract

1. Preheat oven to 325°.
2. Combine first 5 ingredients in a large bowl. Beat with a mixer at medium speed 2 minutes or until smooth. Spoon batter into a 10-inch nonstick Bundt pan coated with cooking spray. Bake at 325° for 42 minutes or until a long wooden pick inserted in center comes out almost clean. Cool cake in pan 15 minutes on a wire rack. Invert cake onto wire rack, and cool completely.
3. While cake cools, combine cider, brown sugar, and cornstarch in a small saucepan. Bring to a boil; cook 1 minute, stirring constantly. Remove from heat, and stir in butter, rum, and vanilla. Cool completely. Serve cake with sauce. YIELD: 16 SERVINGS (SERVING SIZE: 1 SLICE CAKE AND ABOUT 2 TEASPOONS SAUCE).

PER SERVING: CAL 208 (29% from fat); FAT 6.8g (sat 2.2g); PRO 3.5g; CARB 32.8g; FIB 1.4g; CHOL 2mg; IRON 1.1mg; SOD 253mg; CALC 30mg

VANILLA AND PEACH SHORTCAKES

POINTS value: 4

PREP: 10 minutes ■ **COOK:** 9 minutes

If any juice remains in the bowl after you've spooned the peaches over the shortcakes, drizzle it evenly on top of the desserts.

- 1 pound fresh or frozen peach slices, thawed
- ¼ cup sugar, divided
- 1½ teaspoons vanilla extract, divided
- 1 cup low-fat baking mix (such as Bisquick Heart Smart)
- ½ teaspoon ground cinnamon
- ⅓ cup fat-free buttermilk
- Cooking spray
- 1 cup frozen fat-free whipped topping, thawed

1. Preheat oven to 450°.
2. Combine peaches, 2 tablespoons sugar, and 1 teaspoon vanilla in a medium bowl, stirring well. Set aside.
3. Combine baking mix, remaining 2 tablespoons sugar, and cinnamon in a small bowl, stirring well. Add buttermilk and remaining ½ teaspoon vanilla; stir just until blended.
4. Spoon batter evenly onto a baking sheet coated with cooking spray, creating 4 equal mounds. Bake at 450° for 9 minutes or until lightly golden.
5. Carefully cut each shortcake in half crosswise. Spoon ¼ cup peach mixture and ¼ cup whipped topping over bottom half of each shortcake. Replace top halves of shortcakes, and top each serving with ¼ cup peach mixture. YIELD: 4 SERVINGS (SERVING SIZE: 1 SHORTCAKE).

PER SERVING: CAL 222 (9% from fat); FAT 2.2g (sat 0g); PRO 4.1g; CARB 47.4g; FIB 2.2g; CHOL 0mg; IRON 1.5mg; SOD 346mg; CALC 149mg

CHEESECAKE CRACKS

Some cracking on the top of a cheesecake is normal. The most common cause of this is a drastic change in temperature when the cheesecake is cooking or cooling. In general, the slower the cheesecake is cooked, the less chance there is of cracking. Use an oven thermometer to double-check the temperature after preheating. If the temperature registers higher than it should, adjust the setting and wait for the oven to cool to the proper temperature before placing the cheesecake in it. You can also prevent cracking by running a knife or small metal spatula around the edge of the cheesecake after removing it from the oven. This allows the sides of the cheesecake to contract freely.

WHITE CHOCOLATE–RASPBERRY CHEESECAKE

POINTS value: 6

pictured on cover

PREP: 20 minutes ■ **COOK:** 47 minutes
■ **OTHER:** 9 hours

The raspberry topping makes this cheesecake a showstopper.

- 10 sheets low-fat graham crackers, crumbled
- 1¼ cups sugar, divided
- 3 tablespoons butter, melted and cooled
- Cooking spray
- 2 (8-ounce) packages fat-free cream cheese, softened
- 1 (8-ounce) package ⅓-less-fat cream cheese, softened
- ½ cup light sour cream, at room temperature
- 1 (4-ounce) bar white chocolate (such as Ghirardelli), melted and cooled
- 3 tablespoons all-purpose flour
- 3 large eggs
- 1 teaspoon vanilla extract
- ⅓ cup seedless raspberry preserves
- 2½ cups raspberries

1. Preheat oven to 350°.
2. Place graham crackers and ¼ cup sugar in a food processor; process until finely ground. Transfer to a medium bowl, and add butter, stirring until well blended. Firmly press mixture into bottom and 1 inch up sides of a 9-inch springform pan coated with cooking spray. Bake at 350° for 10 minutes or until golden brown. Cool.
3. Reduce oven temperature to 325°.
4. While crust cools, place cream cheeses and sour cream in a large bowl; beat with a mixer at medium speed until smooth and fluffy. Gradually add chocolate; beat well. Add remaining 1 cup sugar and flour; beat well. Add eggs, 1 at a time, beating well after each addition. Stir in vanilla.
5. Pour cheese mixture into prepared crust; bake at 325° for 37 minutes or until cheesecake center barely moves when pan is touched. Turn oven off. Leave cheesecake in oven with door partially open for 1 hour. Remove cheesecake from oven; run a knife around outside edge. Cool completely on a wire rack. Cover and chill at least 8 hours.
6. Spread preserves over top of cheesecake; top with raspberries. YIELD: 16 SERVINGS (SERVING SIZE: 1 SLICE).

PER SERVING: CAL 272 (35% from fat); FAT 10.5g (sat 6g); PRO 8.5g; CARB 37g; FIB 1.6g; CHOL 62mg; IRON 0.7mg; SOD 310mg; CALC 144mg

CHOCOLATE MALT CRÈME BRÛLÉE

POINTS value: 5

PREP: 18 minutes ■ COOK: 1 hour and 16 minutes
■ OTHER: 4 hours

This version of crème brûlée—French for "burnt cream"—uses malted milk powder to give the smooth, creamy custard a rich flavor. This dessert earned our Test Kitchens' highest rating.

    2 cups 1% low-fat chocolate milk
    ¼ cup malted milk powder
    ½ teaspoon vanilla extract
    3 ounces milk chocolate, chopped
    4 large egg yolks
Cooking spray
    6 teaspoons sugar

1. Preheat oven to 300°.
2. Combine first 3 ingredients in a medium saucepan, and cook over medium heat 5 to 6 minutes or until tiny bubbles form around edge (do not boil). Remove from heat, and add chocolate, stirring until chocolate melts.
3. Place egg yolks in a large bowl, stirring with a whisk. Gradually add hot milk mixture to yolks, stirring with a whisk until well blended.
4. Pour chocolate mixture evenly into 6 (4-ounce) ramekins or custard cups coated with cooking spray. Place ramekins in a 13 x 9–inch baking dish; add hot water to pan to a depth of 1 inch. Bake, uncovered, at 300° for 1 hour and 5 minutes or until center barely moves when ramekin is touched. Remove ramekins from pan; cool completely on a wire rack. Cover and chill at least 4 hours or overnight.
5. Sprinkle 1 teaspoon sugar evenly over each custard. Holding a kitchen blowtorch about 2 inches from the top of 1 custard, heat the sugar, moving the torch back and forth, until sugar is completely melted and caramelized (about 1 minute). Repeat procedure with remaining custards. Serve immediately or within 1 hour. YIELD: 6 SERVINGS (SERVING SIZE: 1 CRÈME BRÛLÉE).
Note: If you don't have a kitchen blowtorch, you can prepare the sugar topping on the stovetop. Cook the sugar in a small saucepan over medium heat 5 to 8 minutes or until golden. Don't stir while the sugar is cooking. Doing so will allow the sugar to caramelize. Working quickly, evenly drizzle the sugar mixture over the cold custards, and spread into a thin layer using a rubber spatula. The caramel will harden quickly.

PER SERVING: CAL 241 (35% from fat); FAT 9.3g (sat 4.2g); PRO 7.5g; CARB 31.9g; FIB 0.6g; CHOL 146mg; IRON 0.7mg; SOD 146mg; CALC 181mg

A WATER BATH

A water bath (a shallow pan of warm water in which containers of food are cooked) insulates and protects custards from the heat of the oven so that they cook slowly and evenly. The depth of the water should be half the height of the custard container (ramekin, cake pan, etc.). If you're baking multiple custards, the pan must be large enough so that the containers don't touch.

PEACH MELBA PANNA COTTA

POINTS value: 4

PREP: 27 minutes ■ COOK: 5 minutes
■ OTHER: 8 hours and 40 minutes

Panna cotta—Italian for "cooked cream"—is a light, silky custard that originated in the Piedmont region of northern Italy. We replaced the traditional heavy cream with fat-free half-and-half to make a delicious lightened version.

  1½ cups 2% reduced-fat milk
    ½ teaspoon vanilla extract
    1 tablespoon unflavored gelatin
    ½ cup plus 3 tablespoons sugar, divided
  1½ cups fat-free half-and-half
Cooking spray
    3 peaches, peeled and sliced
    1 (12-ounce) package frozen unsweetened raspberries, thawed
    1 tablespoon fresh lemon juice

1. Combine milk and vanilla in a medium saucepan. Sprinkle gelatin over milk mixture; let stand 10 minutes. Cook over medium-low heat 3 minutes, stirring until gelatin dissolves. Increase heat to medium; add ½ cup sugar. Cook 2 minutes or until sugar dissolves, stirring constantly. Remove from heat; stir in half-and-half. Pour milk mixture evenly into 6 (6-ounce) ramekins or custard cups coated with cooking spray. Cover and chill at least 8 hours or overnight.
2. Combine peaches and 1 tablespoon sugar in a medium bowl; toss to coat. Let stand at least 30 minutes, stirring occasionally.
3. Place raspberries, lemon juice, and remaining 2 tablespoons sugar in a food processor; process until smooth. Strain raspberry mixture through a fine sieve into a bowl; discard seeds.

4. Loosen edges of custards with a knife or rubber spatula. Invert custards onto plates. Serve with peaches and raspberry sauce. YIELD: 6 SERVINGS (SERVING SIZE: 1 PANNA COTTA, ½ CUP PEACH SLICES, AND ABOUT 2½ TABLESPOONS RASPBERRY SAUCE).

PER SERVING: CAL 202 (10% from fat); FAT 2.2g (sat 1.2g); PRO 5.5g; CARB 41.4g; FIB 1.5g; CHOL 8mg; IRON 0.4mg; SOD 119mg; CALC 139mg

GINGERBREAD PUMPKIN CREAM TRIFLE

POINTS value: 4

PREP: 18 minutes ■ COOK: 30 minutes
■ OTHER: 8 hours and 30 minutes

This beautiful and easy-to-assemble dessert combines all the flavors of fall.

    1 (14.5-ounce) package gingerbread cake mix
    1 large egg white
 1½ cups butter pecan light ice cream, softened
    1 (3.4-ounce) package butterscotch instant pudding mix
 1¼ cups 1% low-fat milk
    1 cup canned pumpkin
    1 (8-ounce) container frozen fat-free whipped topping, thawed
    1 (1.4-ounce) chocolate toffee bar (such as Heath), chopped

1. Prepare gingerbread cake mix according to package directions using 1 egg white and a 9-inch square baking pan. Remove from oven, and cool completely. Cut into 1-inch cubes; set aside.
2. While cake cools, combine ice cream and pudding mix in a medium bowl; add milk and pumpkin, stirring until smooth.
3. Place half of gingerbread cubes in a 3-quart bowl or trifle dish. Top with half of pumpkin mixture and half of whipped topping. Repeat procedure with remaining gingerbread, pumpkin mixture, and whipped topping. Cover; chill at least 8 hours. Sprinkle with chopped toffee bar just before serving. YIELD: 16 SERVINGS (SERVING SIZE: ABOUT ⅔ CUP).

PER SERVING: CAL 196 (23% from fat); FAT 4.9g (sat 1.5g); PRO 2.8g; CARB 34.3g; FIB 1.1g; CHOL 2mg; IRON 1.4mg; SOD 459mg; CALC 72mg

BANANAS PEACH FOSTER WITH PECANS

POINTS value: 4

pictured on page 53

PREP: 3 minutes ■ COOK: 5 minutes

You can enjoy this traditional dessert with a peachy twist year-round by using refrigerated bottled peaches, which you can find in the produce department of your grocery store.

  ¼ cup chopped pecans
    1 tablespoon light butter
    2 ripe bananas, peeled and cut into 1-inch slices
  ¼ cup firmly packed dark brown sugar
  ½ teaspoon ground cinnamon
    2 cups refrigerated peach slices
  ½ teaspoon vanilla extract
    2 cups vanilla fat-free ice cream

1. Heat a large nonstick skillet over medium–high heat. Add pecans, and cook 2 minutes or until nuts begin to brown, stirring frequently. Remove from pan; set aside.
2. Add butter to pan, and cook over medium heat until butter melts. Stir in bananas, brown sugar, and cinnamon; cook 1 minute, tossing with 2 spoons until banana slices are coated with sugar mixture. Add peaches, and cook 1 to 2 minutes or just until banana slices are soft, stirring constantly. Remove from heat; stir in reserved pecans and vanilla.
3. Divide banana mixture evenly among 6 dessert bowls, and top evenly with ice cream. Serve immediately. YIELD: 6 SERVINGS (SERVING SIZE: ABOUT ½ CUP BANANA MIXTURE AND ⅓ CUP ICE CREAM).

PER SERVING: CAL 215 (20% from fat); FAT 4.8g (sat 1.1g); PRO 3.5g; CARB 42.5g; FIB 2.3g; CHOL 2mg; IRON 0.8mg; SOD 50mg; CALC 68mg

MOJITO'D MELON MIX-UP

POINTS value: 2

pictured on page 54
PREP: 7 minutes

The classic ingredients of the Cuban mojito cocktail are poured over watermelon cubes for a quick and refreshing dessert that earned our Test Kitchens' highest rating.

> 4 cups cubed seeded watermelon
> 1 teaspoon grated fresh lime rind
> 6 tablespoons fresh lime juice
> ¼ cup light rum or vodka
> ¼ cup "measures-like-sugar" calorie-free sweetener (such as Splenda)
> ¼ cup chopped fresh mint
> 1 cup diet tonic water, chilled

1. Combine first 6 ingredients in a large bowl; toss gently. Cover and chill until ready to serve.
2. Spoon watermelon mixture evenly into small serving dishes or parfait glasses. Pour ¼ cup tonic water over each serving. Serve immediately. YIELD: 4 SERVINGS (SERVING SIZE: 1 CUP WATERMELON CUBES, ABOUT 2½ TABLESPOONS RUM MIXTURE, AND ¼ CUP TONIC WATER).

PER SERVING: CAL 85 (3% from fat); FAT 0.3g (sat 0g); PRO 1.1g; CARB 13.7g; FIB 0.9g; CHOL 0mg; IRON 0.5mg; SOD 11mg; CALC 18mg

APRICOT SORBET

POINTS value: 1

PREP: 4 minutes ■ **OTHER:** 24 hours

This cool, fruity treat is made with only three ingredients and doesn't require specialty equipment. Release the frozen apricots from the freezer-safe container by briefly running the bottom of the container under warm water.

> 1 (16-ounce) can apricot halves in light syrup, undrained
> 2 tablespoons pineapple juice
> ½ teaspoon vanilla extract

1. Pour apricots into a freezer-safe container. Cover and freeze 24 hours or until solid.
2. Remove apricots from container, cut into large chunks, and place in a food processor. Add pineapple juice and vanilla; process until smooth. Serve immediately, or store in freezer until ready to serve. YIELD: 4 SERVINGS (SERVING SIZE: ABOUT ½ CUP).

PER SERVING: CAL 77 (1% from fat); FAT 0.1g (sat 0g); PRO 0.6g; CARB 19.8g; FIB 1.8g; CHOL 0mg; IRON 0.5mg; SOD 5mg; CALC 14mg

MANGO-GINGER SHERBET

POINTS value: 2

PREP: 11 minutes

Serve this refreshing dessert with a spoon to get all the chunks of fruit. You can substitute pineapple canned in water for the fresh, if you'd like. The **POINTS** value remains the same.

> 1 mango, peeled and chopped (about ⅓ pound)
> 1 cup chopped fresh pineapple
> 1 teaspoon grated peeled fresh ginger
> 1⅓ cups orange sherbet
> 1⅓ cups diet ginger ale

1. Combine first 3 ingredients in a medium bowl. Spoon sherbet evenly into 4 tall glasses or bowls. Spoon fruit mixture evenly over sherbet. Pour ginger ale evenly over each serving, and serve immediately. YIELD: 4 SERVINGS (SERVING SIZE: ⅓ CUP SHERBET, ABOUT ½ CUP FRUIT MIXTURE, AND ⅓ CUP GINGER ALE).

PER SERVING: CAL 124 (9% from fat); FAT 1.2g (sat 0.6g); PRO 1g; CARB 28.7g; FIB 3.1g; CHOL 0mg; IRON 0.3mg; SOD 44mg; CALC 37g

HOW TO CUT A MANGO

A mango can be tricky to cut because of the large seed that grows horizontally inside it. You must cut around it on both sides.

1. Hold the mango vertically on the cutting board. Using a sharp knife, slice the fruit lengthwise on each side of the flat seed.

2. Holding a mango half in the palm of your hand, score the pulp in square cross sections. Be sure that you slice to, but not through, the skin. Repeat with other half.

3. Turn the mango halves inside out, and cut the chunks from the skin.

COCONUT-PINEAPPLE SHERBET

POINTS value: 3

PREP: 32 minutes ■ **COOK:** 3 minutes
■ **OTHER:** 1 hour and 30 minutes

This piña colada–inspired frozen treat will transport you to the tropics with its creamy, coconutty base that's studded with chunky, sweet pineapple. Compared with a popular national brand, our version decreases the ***POINTS*** value per serving by 2.

   1 cup water
   ½ cup sugar
   1½ tablespoons crystallized ginger, minced
   1 cup light coconut milk
   ½ cup cream of coconut
   1 tablespoon fresh lime juice
   1 (15¼-ounce) can crushed pineapple in juice, undrained

1. Combine first 3 ingredients in a saucepan; bring to a boil. Cook, stirring constantly until sugar dissolves. Cool completely.
2. Add coconut milk and remaining ingredients to cooled sugar mixture, stirring to combine.
3. Pour mixture into the freezer can of a 2- to 3-quart ice-cream freezer, and freeze according to manufacturer's instructions. Spoon ice cream into a freezer-safe container. Cover and freeze 1 hour or until firm.
YIELD: 8 SERVINGS (SERVING SIZE: ¾ CUP).

PER SERVING: CAL 160 (23% from fat); FAT 4.1g (sat 3.4g); PRO 0.6g; CARB 32.6g; FIB 0.4g; CHOL 0mg; IRON 0.4mg; SOD 16mg; CALC 11mg

FROZEN BERRIES AND CREAM POPS

POINTS value: 1

PREP: 10 minutes ■ **OTHER:** 2 hours

These easy-to-make fruit pops are a cool summer treat the whole family can enjoy.

   2 cups sliced strawberries
   ½ cup evaporated fat-free milk
   3 tablespoons corn syrup
   3 tablespoons frozen cranberry juice concentrate
   1 tablespoon vanilla extract

1. Combine all ingredients in a blender; process until smooth. Pour mixture evenly into 8 (3-ounce) wax-coated paper cups. Place a wooden craft stick in center of each cup.

2. Place prepared cups on a baking sheet, and freeze at least 2 hours or until firm. To release pops from cups, dip cups into hot water almost to rims of cups. YIELD: 8 SERVINGS (SERVING SIZE: 1 POP).

PER SERVING: CAL 55 (3% from fat); FAT 0.2g (sat 0g); PRO 1.5g; CARB 11.8g; FIB 0.8g; CHOL 1mg; IRON 0.2mg; SOD 24mg; CALC 54mg

RASPBERRY-ORANGE SAUCE WITH ICE CREAM

POINTS value: 3

PREP: 3 minutes ■ **COOK:** 4 minutes
■ **OTHER:** 10 minutes

This luscious ruby-colored sauce can be served over ice cream as listed here or spooned over angel food or pound cake. A ¼-cup serving of the sauce has a ***POINTS*** value of 1.

   1 (12-ounce) package frozen unsweetened raspberries, thawed
   ⅓ cup sugar
   2 teaspoons cornstarch
   1 teaspoon vanilla extract
   ½ teaspoon grated fresh orange rind
   3 cups vanilla light ice cream

1. Combine first 3 ingredients in a saucepan; bring to a boil over medium-high heat. Boil 1 minute, stirring often, until thick. Remove from heat; add vanilla and orange rind. Let stand 10 minutes. Serve over ice cream. YIELD: 6 SERVINGS (SERVING SIZE: ½ CUP ICE CREAM AND ABOUT ¼ CUP SAUCE).

PER SERVING: CAL 177 (20% from fat); FAT 3.9g (sat 2g); PRO 3.4g; CARB 33.5g; FIB 2.6g; CHOL 0mg; IRON 0.3mg; SOD 45mg; CALC 69mg

RASPBERRY NUTRITION

These intensely flavored berries house an assortment of antioxidants—they have an almost 50% higher antioxidant activity than strawberries and ten times that of tomatoes. And the good news is that fresh and frozen berries contain similar amounts of antioxidants, so the health benefits aren't lost in the packaging.

CHOCOLATE-CHERRY BAKED ALASKAS

POINTS value: 4

PREP: 16 minutes ■ **COOK:** 1 minute ■ **OTHER:** 3 hours

A traditional baked Alaska consists of sponge cake topped with a layer of ice cream and covered in meringue. It is then baked in a very hot oven to brown the meringue, which acts as insulation and prevents the ice cream from melting. We used meringue powder rather than egg whites to make the meringue. Meringue powder is pasteurized and is safe to eat without cooking. Look for it in stores that carry cake-decorating supplies.

    6 fat-free devil's food cookie cakes (such as
      Snackwell's)
    3 cups chocolate light ice cream (such as Edy's),
      slightly softened
    ½ cup chopped frozen pitted dark sweet cherries
    ¼ cup sugar
    ¼ cup water
    1 tablespoon meringue powder

1. Place 1 cookie in bottom of 6 (6-ounce) custard cups. Combine ice cream and cherries; spoon evenly into custard cups. Cover and freeze 3 hours.
2. Preheat broiler.
3. Place sugar, water, and meringue powder in a medium bowl; beat with a mixer at high speed until stiff peaks form. Remove cups from freezer; spoon meringue evenly over each cup, spreading to edges. Place cups on a baking sheet. Broil 1 to 2 minutes or until meringue is golden. Serve immediately. YIELD: 6 SERVINGS (SERVING SIZE: 1 CUSTARD CUP).

PER SERVING: CAL 204 (16% from fat); FAT 3.7g (sat 2.1g); PRO 4.5g; CARB 38.8g; FIB 1.5g; CHOL 20mg; IRON 0.5mg; SOD 78mg; CALC 77mg

CHOCOLATE MALTED MARSHMALLOW PIE

POINTS value: 6

PREP: 7 minutes ■ **COOK:** 5 minutes ■ **OTHER:** 9 hours

Malted milk powder—a soluble powder made from dry milk, malted barley, and wheat flour—is used in this recipe to add flavor. You can find it in most supermarkets next to the dry milk powder.

    1 cup 1% low-fat chocolate milk
    ⅓ cup malted milk powder
    4 cups miniature marshmallows
    1 tablespoon butter
    ¼ cup fat-free chocolate syrup (such as Hershey's),
      divided
    ½ cup (4 ounces) ⅓-less-fat cream cheese, softened
    1 (8-ounce) container frozen fat-free whipped topping,
      thawed and divided
    1 (6-ounce) reduced-fat graham cracker crust
    20 malted milk balls, divided

1. Heat milk in a large saucepan over medium-high heat 3 minutes or until tiny bubbles form around edge (do not boil). Add malted milk powder, stirring with a whisk. Reduce heat to low; add marshmallows and butter, stirring well with a whisk. Stir in 3 tablespoons chocolate syrup. Cover and refrigerate 1 hour or until mixture is cool and thick.
2. Place cream cheese in a medium bowl; beat with a mixer at medium speed until smooth. Add ¼ of marshmallow mixture; beat at low speed until combined. Fold cream cheese mixture into remaining marshmallow mixture.
3. Place ¾ cup whipped topping in a small bowl; chill.
4. Fold remaining whipped topping into marshmallow mixture. Pour half of mixture into crust.
5. Place 10 malted milk balls in a zip-top plastic bag. Coarsely crush milk balls using a meat mallet or small heavy skillet. Sprinkle over marshmallow mixture in crust. Spread remaining half of marshmallow mixture over milk balls, and drizzle evenly with remaining 1 tablespoon chocolate syrup. Cover and chill overnight or until firm.
6. Dollop reserved whipped topping around edges of pie. Top each dollop with a malted milk ball. YIELD: 10 SERVINGS (SERVING SIZE: 1 SLICE).

PER SERVING: CAL 280 (28% from fat); FAT 8.6g (sat 4g); PRO 4.3g; CARB 46.8g; FIB 0.4g; CHOL 14mg; IRON 0.4mg; SOD 193mg; CALC 56mg

MOCHA ICE CREAM PIE

POINTS value: 6

PREP: 7 minutes ■ **OTHER:** 2 hours

1 (1-quart) container latte low-fat ice cream (such as Starbucks), softened
1 (6-ounce) chocolate cookie crust
1 (0.81-ounce) package chocolate cookie thin crisps (such as Oreo 100 Calorie Packs), crushed

1. Spread ice cream evenly over crust, and sprinkle with crushed crisps. Freeze 2 hours or until firm. **YIELD: 8 SERVINGS (SERVING SIZE: 1 SLICE).**

PER SERVING: CAL 289 (27% from fat); FAT 8.6g (sat 2.6g); PRO 5.9g; CARB 26.8; FIB 0.9g; CHOL 10mg; IRON 1.2mg; SOD 209mg; CALC 100mg

BUTTERMILK CUSTARD–APPLE PIE

POINTS value: 6

PREP: 15 minutes ■ **COOK:** 53 minutes

The filling is very moist, so we baked the pie on the lowest oven rack to prevent the crust from getting soggy.

1 (12-ounce) package frozen apples (such as Stouffer's Harvest Apples)
½ (15-ounce) package refrigerated pie dough (such as Pillsbury)
2 large eggs
1 large egg white
⅔ cup granulated sugar
1⅔ cups fat-free buttermilk
4½ tablespoons all-purpose flour, divided
3 tablespoons maple syrup
1 teaspoon vanilla extract
2½ tablespoons brown sugar
¼ teaspoon ground cinnamon
1½ tablespoons chilled butter, cut into small pieces
1 (1.5-ounce) package oat and honey granola bars, crushed

1. Remove plastic cover from apples, and microwave at HIGH 2 minutes or just until thawed. Place apples in a medium skillet over medium heat, and cook 6 minutes or until liquid evaporates, stirring often. Cool completely.
2. Move oven rack to lowest position. Preheat oven to 375°.
3. Unroll dough and fit into a 9-inch pie plate. Fold edges under and flute. Combine eggs and egg white in a medium bowl, stirring with a whisk. Add granulated

sugar, buttermilk, 2 tablespoons flour, maple syrup, and vanilla. Stir in apples. Pour apple mixture into prepared crust.
4. Bake at 375° for 15 minutes. Reduce oven temperature to 350°, and bake 15 minutes (edges of pie will be set, but center will not be).
5. While pie bakes, combine brown sugar, remaining 2½ tablespoons flour, and cinnamon in a small bowl. Cut in butter with a pastry blender or 2 knives until mixture resembles coarse meal, and stir in crushed granola bars.
6. Pull out oven rack carefully, but do not remove pie from rack. Quickly sprinkle granola mixture evenly over surface of filling.
7. Bake at 350° for 15 minutes or just until filling begins to rise above edges of crust and center is set. (Filling will settle back down into crust as pie cools.) Cool pie completely on a wire rack. **YIELD: 10 SERVINGS (SERVING SIZE: 1 SLICE).**

PER SERVING: CAL 290 (29% from fat); FAT 9.5g (sat 3.5g); PRO 4.5g; CARB 46.4g; FIB 0.8g; CHOL 50mg; IRON 0.6mg; SOD 177mg; CALC 64mg

BLUEBERRY-PINEAPPLE BUCKLE

POINTS value: 5

PREP: 12 minutes ■ **COOK:** 56 minutes

Cake mix is a time-saving tool in this cobblerlike dessert.

3 cups frozen blueberries
1 (20-ounce) can crushed pineapple in juice, undrained
½ cup "measures-like-sugar" calorie-free sweetener (such as Splenda)
¼ cup orange juice
2 teaspoons grated fresh lemon rind
Cooking spray
1 (18.25-ounce) package yellow cake mix (such as Duncan Hines)
¼ cup chilled butter, cut into small pieces

1. Preheat oven to 350°.
2. Combine first 5 ingredients in a large bowl. Spoon mixture into a 13 x 9–inch baking dish coated with cooking spray. Sprinkle cake mix over blueberry mixture; top evenly with butter.
3. Bake at 350° for 35 minutes. Press dry cake mix down with the back of a spoon. Bake an additional 21 minutes or until golden and bubbly. **YIELD: 14 SERVINGS (SERVING SIZE: 1/14 OF BUCKLE).**

PER SERVING: CAL 246 (20% from fat); FAT 5.4g (sat 2.6g); PRO 2.2g; CARB 49.2g; FIB 1.9g; CHOL 9mg; IRON 0.8mg; SOD 250mg; CALC 69mg

CRANAPPLE COBBLER

POINTS value: 5

pictured on page 57

PREP: 26 minutes ■ COOK: 45 minutes

Serve this tart cobbler with ¼ cup vanilla light ice cream. The **POINTS** value will be 6.

> 5 cups sliced peeled Granny Smith apples (about 1½ pounds)
> 1 cup fresh cranberries
> 1 tablespoon all-purpose flour
> 1 (12-ounce) container cranberry-orange crushed fruit (such as Ocean Spray)
> ¼ cup light cranberry juice
> 1 teaspoon grated fresh orange rind
> ½ teaspoon ground cinnamon
> Cooking spray
> 1½ cups all-purpose flour
> 3 tablespoons granulated sugar
> 1 teaspoon baking powder
> ¼ teaspoon baking soda
> ¼ teaspoon salt
> 5 tablespoons chilled butter, cut into small pieces
> 1 cup fat-free buttermilk
> 1½ tablespoons turbinado sugar
> 2½ cups vanilla light ice cream (optional)

1. Preheat oven to 400°.

2. Combine first 3 ingredients in a large bowl, tossing well. Stir in crushed fruit and next 3 ingredients. Spoon into a 12 x 8–inch baking dish coated with cooking spray. Bake at 400° for 20 minutes.

3. To prepare topping, lightly spoon flour into dry measuring cups; level with a knife. Combine flour and next 4 ingredients in a large bowl, stirring with a whisk. Cut in butter with a pastry blender or 2 knives until mixture resembles coarse meal. Stir in butter-milk to form a soft dough.

4. Remove dish from oven; drop dough by spoonfuls onto cranberry-apple filling to form 10 dumplings. Coat dumplings with cooking spray, and sprinkle with turbinado sugar. Bake at 400° for 25 minutes or until filling is bubbly and dumplings are lightly browned. Serve warm, and top each serving with ice cream, if desired. YIELD: 10 SERVINGS (SERVING SIZE: ABOUT ¾ CUP COBBLER AND 1 DUMPLING).

PER SERVING: CAL 244 (22% from fat); FAT 6g (sat 3.6g); PRO 3.2g; CARB 45.2g; FIB 2.9g; CHOL 15mg; IRON 1.1mg; SOD 209mg; CALC 68mg

LEMON DROP TARTLETS

POINTS value: 1

pictured on page 56

PREP: 11 minutes ■ COOK: 17 minutes
■ OTHER: 30 minutes

Lemon curd contains a higher proportion of lemon juice and rind than lemon filling, so it has a more intense lemon flavor. Its thick, smooth consistency provides a nice balance to the crisp phyllo shells.

> 1 (1.9-ounce) package frozen miniature phyllo shells
> ⅓ cup bottled lemon curd (such as Dickinson's)
> 2 tablespoons white chocolate morsels (such as Ghirardelli)
> 1 large egg white
> Dash of cream of tartar
> 2 tablespoons sugar
> 3 lemon-flavored drop candies

1. Preheat oven to 350°.

2. Place phyllo shells on a baking sheet. Bake at 350° for 3 minutes or until lightly browned and thoroughly heated.

3. Reduce oven temperature to 325°.

4. Combine lemon curd and white chocolate morsels in a small microwave-safe bowl. Microwave at HIGH 30 to 40 seconds (morsels will not look melted). Stir until morsels melt. Spoon lemon mixture evenly into phyllo shells.

5. Place egg white and cream of tartar in a small bowl; beat with a mixer at high speed until foamy. Gradually add sugar, 1 tablespoon at a time, beating until stiff peaks form. Spoon meringue over lemon mixture, spreading to edges. Bake at 325° for 13 minutes or until meringue is lightly browned.

6. While tartlets bake, place candies in a zip-top plastic bag; seal bag. Crush candies with a meat mallet or small heavy skillet. Remove tartlets from oven, and immediately sprinkle with crushed candies. Cool completely on wire racks. YIELD: 15 SERVINGS (SERVING SIZE: 1 TARTLET).

PER SERVING: CAL 59 (27% from fat); FAT 1.8g (sat 0.5g); PRO 0.3g; CARB 10.8g; FIB 0.7g; CHOL 6mg; IRON 0.2mg; SOD 23mg; CALC 3mg

STRAWBERRY-RHUBARB TURNOVERS

POINTS value: 2

PREP: 16 minutes ■ **COOK:** 24 minutes
■ **OTHER:** 20 minutes

If your strawberries don't render much juice after standing, add about 1 tablespoon of water to the rhubarb mixture.

- ⅓ cup granulated sugar, divided
- 1½ cups sliced strawberries
- 1 cup sliced fresh or frozen rhubarb
- 1 tablespoon uncooked quick-cooking tapioca
- ½ teaspoon grated fresh lemon rind
- 1½ teaspoons fresh lemon juice
- ⅛ teaspoon ground nutmeg
- 2 tablespoons butter, divided
- 18 (12 x 8–inch) sheets frozen phyllo dough, thawed and divided

Cooking spray

- ½ cup powdered sugar
- 2 teaspoons 1% low-fat milk
- ⅛ teaspoon vanilla extract

1. Sprinkle 2 tablespoons granulated sugar over strawberries; let stand 10 minutes.

2. Combine remaining granulated sugar, rhubarb, and next 4 ingredients in a small saucepan. Drain juice from strawberries, reserving juice. Set strawberries aside. Add strawberry juice to rhubarb mixture, stirring well. Let stand 5 minutes. Bring to a boil; reduce heat, and simmer 3 to 5 minutes or until rhubarb is tender, stirring constantly. Stir in strawberries and 1½ teaspoons butter. Cook 30 seconds to 1 minute or until strawberries begin to soften and butter melts; cool.

3. Preheat oven to 400°.

4. Melt remaining 4½ teaspoons butter; set aside. Place 1 phyllo sheet on a large cutting board or work surface (cover remaining dough to keep from drying); lightly coat with cooking spray. Repeat layers twice. Cut stack into 3 (4–inch–wide) strips.

5. Working with 1 strip at a time, place 1 tablespoon strawberry mixture onto 1 end of strip (keep remaining strips covered). Fold 1 corner over strawberry mixture, forming a triangle. Continue folding back and forth into a triangle to end of strip. Repeat procedure with remaining 2 phyllo strips and strawberry mixture. Place triangles, seam sides down, on a large baking sheet coated with cooking spray. Brush triangles with melted butter. Repeat procedure 5 times with remaining phyllo sheets, cooking spray, strawberry mixture, and melted butter.

6. Bake at 400° for 15 minutes or until golden. Cool on wire racks 5 minutes.

7. While turnovers cool, combine powdered sugar, milk, and vanilla, stirring until smooth. Drizzle sugar mixture evenly over turnovers. Serve warm. **YIELD:** 18 SERVINGS (SERVING SIZE: 1 TURNOVER).

PER SERVING: CAL 104 (22% from fat); FAT 2.5g (sat 1.1g); PRO 1.5g; CARB 19.1g; FIB 0.8g; CHOL 3mg; IRON 0.7mg; SOD 101mg; CALC 11mg

PHYLLO TIPS

- Look for the ultraflaky dough in the frozen-foods section of your grocery store.

- Thaw frozen phyllo in the refrigerator for at least 24 hours. Thawing it in the microwave or at room temperature doesn't produce even results, and it can also cause some of the sheets to stick together.

- After it's thawed, let the dough stand at room temperature for a couple of hours before unwrapping it. Remove only the dough sheets you need from the package.

- Tightly wrap the remaining dough in its original protective paper, and then cover the paper with plastic wrap. It will keep in the refrigerator up to 1 week. Do not refreeze the phyllo once it's thawed because it will become brittle and hard to work with.

- Handle phyllo sheets slowly and gently. Phyllo is thin and delicate and can break or tear if roughly handled.

- Phyllo can dry out quickly, so keep it covered with a damp cloth or paper towel and plastic wrap when you're not working with it. Make sure the cloth isn't too wet because that can make the dough soggy, causing the sheets to stick together.

OATMEAL, DRIED CHERRY, AND PECAN COOKIES

POINTS value: 2

PREP: 20 minutes ■ **COOK:** 12 minutes per batch
■ **OTHER:** 2 minutes

When these cookies are warm from the oven, they have slightly crisp edges and soft centers.

¼ cup butter, softened
½ cup granulated sugar
⅓ cup packed light brown sugar
⅓ cup apple butter
1 teaspoon vanilla extract
1 large egg
¾ cup all-purpose flour
1 cup quick-cooking oats
½ (3.4-ounce) package vanilla instant pudding mix
   (about 4½ tablespoons)
½ teaspoon baking soda
¼ teaspoon salt
½ cup dried cherries
¼ cup chopped pecans
Cooking spray

1. Preheat oven to 350°.
2. Place butter in a large bowl; beat with a mixer at medium speed until fluffy. Add sugars, beating until blended. Add apple butter, vanilla, and egg, beating just until blended.
3. Lightly spoon flour into a dry measuring cup; level with a knife. Combine flour and next 4 ingredients in a bowl.
4. Gradually add flour mixture to butter mixture, stirring just until combined; fold in cherries and pecans. Drop by level tablespoonfuls 1½ inches apart onto baking sheets coated with cooking spray.
5. Bake at 350° for 12 to 14 minutes or until lightly browned. Cool on pan 2 minutes or until firm. Remove cookies from pan; cool on wire racks. **YIELD: 32 SERVINGS (SERVING SIZE: 1 COOKIE).**

PER SERVING: CAL 82 (26% from fat); FAT 2.4g (sat 1g); PRO 1g; CARB 14.1g; FIB 0.7g; CHOL 10mg; IRON 0.4mg; SOD 61mg; CALC 8mg

RASPBERRY BLONDIES WITH WHITE CHOCOLATE AND PECANS

POINTS value: 4

PREP: 15 minutes ■ **COOK:** 33 minutes

We used dark brown sugar instead of light brown sugar because the dark variety has more molasses, which gives these blondies a richer flavor.

1½ cups all-purpose flour
½ cup regular oats
1 teaspoon baking powder
¼ teaspoon salt
1 cup packed dark brown sugar
½ cup butter, softened
¾ cup egg substitute
1 teaspoon vanilla extract
½ cup chopped pecans, toasted
½ cup white chocolate chips
1 cup raspberries
Cooking spray

1. Preheat oven to 350°.
2. Lightly spoon flour into dry measuring cups; level with a knife. Combine flour and next 3 ingredients in a medium bowl. Place brown sugar and butter in a large bowl; beat with a mixer at medium speed until blended. Add egg substitute and vanilla, beating just until blended. Add flour mixture to sugar mixture, beating just until combined. Fold in pecans and white chocolate chips. Gently fold in raspberries.
3. Pour batter into a 9-inch square baking pan coated with cooking spray. Bake at 350° for 33 minutes or until a wooden pick inserted in center comes out clean. **YIELD: 20 SERVINGS (SERVING SIZE: 1 BLONDIE).**

PER SERVING: CAL 166 (47% from fat); FAT 8.6g (sat 4.5g); PRO 2.5g; CARB 20.6g; FIB 1.1g; CHOL 12mg; IRON 1mg; SOD 114mg; CALC 30mg

BROWN SUGAR: LIGHT VS. DARK

Brown sugar owes its moist texture and caramel-like flavor to molasses, a small amount of which is added to granulated sugar to create brown sugar. Light brown sugar has a more delicate flavor. If you want a richer taste, use dark brown sugar, which has more molasses.

Smoked Salmon Bruschetta with
Sun-Dried Tomato Relish, *page 21*

Ambrosia Smoothie, *page 25*

Strawberry–Mango Salsa, *page 19*

Blueberry–Brown Sugar Muffins, *page 28*

Chocolate Waffles with Dark Cherry Sauce,
page 30

Bananas Peach Foster with Pecans,
page 41

Quick Cranberry Crescent Rolls,
page 32

Mojito'd Melon Mix-Up,
page 42

Buttermilk Banana Cake with
Rum-Soaked Strawberries, *page 36*

Sticky Toffee Pudding, *page 38*

Lemon Drop Tartlets, *page 46*

Cranapple Cobbler, *page 46*

Mahimahi with Pineapple–Green Onion Salsa, *page 67*

Seared Tuna Tacos, *page 71*

Pan-Seared Salmon with
Lemon-Garlic Spinach, *page 69*

Tabbouleh, *page 79*

Cumin'd Black Beans and Rice, *page 78*

Vegetable Nachos Grandes,
page 79

Seared Scallops with
Lemon-Butter Sauce, *page 73*

Top-Shelf Veggie Pizza,
page 84

fish & shellfish

Mahimahi with Pineapple–Green Onion Salsa,
page 67

SPICY THAI FISH

POINTS value: 4

PREP: 10 minutes ■ COOK: 10 minutes
■ OTHER: 30 minutes

The fiery marinade gives this fish a kick. It would also taste great on any other flaky white fish or shrimp.

⅓ cup chopped fresh cilantro
3 tablespoons rice vinegar
1 jalapeño pepper, seeded and minced
2 garlic cloves, minced
½ teaspoon grated fresh lime rind
2 tablespoons fresh lime juice
2 teaspoons canola oil
1 teaspoon minced peeled fresh ginger
½ teaspoon salt
½ teaspoon toasted sesame oil
½ teaspoon Sriracha (hot chili sauce; such as Huy Fong)
¼ teaspoon freshly ground black pepper
¼ teaspoon crushed red pepper
4 (6-ounce) grouper fillets
Cooking spray
Lime wedges

1. Combine first 13 ingredients in a small bowl, stirring well with a whisk. Reserve 4 teaspoons marinade. Pour remaining marinade into a large zip-top plastic bag; add fish, and seal bag. Chill 30 minutes, turning bag occasionally.
2. Prepare grill.
3. Remove fish from bag; discard marinade. Place fish on grill rack coated with cooking spray.
4. Grill 5 to 6 minutes on each side or until fish flakes easily when tested with a fork. Serve fish with lime wedges and reserved marinade. YIELD: 4 SERVINGS (SERVING SIZE: 1 FILLET AND 1 TEASPOON MARINADE).

PER SERVING: CAL 176 (18% from fat); FAT 3.5g (sat 0.6g); PRO 33.1g; CARB 1.4g; FIB 0.2g; CHOL 63mg; IRON 1.6mg; SOD 260mg; CALC 50mg

TAME THE HEAT OF CHILE PEPPERS

When using fresh chile peppers in a dish, control how much heat you add by removing the membrane and seeds, where most of the heat-inducing compound called capsaicin is found. When handling peppers, wear rubber gloves or wash your hands immediately afterward because skin unaccustomed to holding peppers can burn. If your mouth feels like it's on fire after eating a chile pepper, drink milk or eat bread to neutralize the burning sensation.

GRILLED GROUPER WITH MANGO SALSA

POINTS value: 4

PREP: 10 minutes ■ COOK: 6 minutes

If you can't find grouper, substitute a firm white fish, such as cod, snapper, or tilapia.

1 large mango, peeled and chopped (about 1 cup)
2 tablespoons chopped red onion
1 tablespoon fresh lime juice
2 teaspoons olive oil, divided
½ teaspoon chipotle chile, canned in adobo sauce, minced
¼ teaspoon salt, divided
4 (6-ounce) grouper fillets
⅛ teaspoon freshly ground black pepper
Cooking spray

1. Prepare grill.
2. Combine mango, red onion, lime juice, 1 teaspoon oil, chipotle chile, and ⅛ teaspoon salt. Set aside.
3. Brush fish with remaining 1 teaspoon oil, and sprinkle with remaining ⅛ teaspoon salt and pepper. Place fish on grill rack coated with cooking spray. Grill 3 to 4 minutes on each side or until fish flakes easily when tested with a fork. Serve with salsa. YIELD: 4 SERVINGS (SERVING SIZE: 1 FILLET AND ¼ CUP SALSA).

PER SERVING: CAL 207 (18% from fat); FAT 4.1g (sat 0.7g); PRO 33.3g; CARB 7.9g; FIB 0.9g; CHOL 63mg; IRON 1.6mg; SOD 243mg; CALC 52mg

GRILLED HALIBUT WITH PEACH SALSA

POINTS value: 6

PREP: 12 minutes ■ COOK: 12 minutes
■ OTHER: 30 minutes

1½ cups diced peeled peaches (about 2 peaches)
¾ cup diced red bell pepper
¾ cup chopped red onion
¼ cup chopped fresh cilantro
2 tablespoons chopped fresh mint
1 jalapeño pepper, diced
4 tablespoons fresh lime juice, divided
3 tablespoons honey, divided
½ teaspoon ground red pepper, divided
¼ teaspoon salt
4 (6-ounce) halibut fillets
Cooking spray

1. Combine first 6 ingredients, 2 tablespoons lime juice, 1 tablespoon honey, ¼ teaspoon ground red pepper, and salt; cover and chill at least 30 minutes.
2. Prepare grill.
3. Combine remaining 2 tablespoons lime juice, 2 tablespoons honey, and ¼ teaspoon ground red pepper; brush over fish. Place fish on grill rack coated with cooking spray. Grill 6 minutes on each side or until fish flakes easily when tested with a fork. Serve with peach salsa. YIELD: 4 SERVINGS (SERVING SIZE: 1 FILLET AND ½ CUP SALSA).

PER SERVING: CAL 290 (13% from fat); FAT 4.3g (sat 0.6g); PRO 36.9g; CARB 26.2g; FIB 2.6g; CHOL 54mg; IRON 2.6mg; SOD 241mg; CALC 105mg

MAHIMAHI WITH PINEAPPLE–GREEN ONION SALSA

POINTS value: 4

pictured on page 58

PREP: 8 minutes ■ COOK: 8 minutes

Mahimahi is a versatile fish that pairs well with this citrusy salsa. If you can't find mahimahi, substitute another firm white fish, such as grouper or orange roughy. Serve with wild rice to complete the meal. A ½ cup of wild rice has a **POINTS** value of 1.

    4 (6-ounce) mahimahi fillets
    1 tablespoon olive oil
    ½ teaspoon salt
    ¼ teaspoon freshly ground black pepper
Cooking spray
    4 (½-inch-thick) slices pineapple
    ½ cup thinly sliced green onions
    4 teaspoons grated fresh lime rind
    2 teaspoons fresh lime juice
    ½ teaspoon chili garlic sauce (such as Huy Fong)

1. Preheat grill.
2. Brush fish with oil; sprinkle with salt and pepper. Place fish on grill rack coated with cooking spray; grill 3 to 4 minutes on each side or until fish flakes easily when tested with a fork. While fish grills, grill pineapple 4 to 6 minutes on each side.
3. Chop pineapple, and place in a medium bowl. Add green onions and next 3 ingredients, stirring well. Serve fish with salsa. YIELD: 4 SERVINGS (SERVING SIZE: 1 FILLET AND ¼ CUP SALSA).

PER SERVING: CAL 206 (20% from fat); FAT 4.6g (sat 0.8g); PRO 31.8g; CARB 8.3g; FIB 1g; CHOL 124mg; IRON 2.5mg; SOD 450mg; CALC 37mg

CRAB-TOPPED ORANGE ROUGHY

POINTS value: 6

PREP: 20 minutes ■ COOK: 27 minutes

The citrus of the orange complements the sweetness of the crabmeat in this entrée that is easy enough for weeknights yet elegant enough for company.

    1 large navel orange
    2 tablespoons butter
    1 teaspoon olive oil
    ⅔ cup thinly sliced green onions
    1 (6-ounce) can crabmeat (such as Bumble Bee), drained
    ¼ teaspoon salt, divided
    ½ teaspoon freshly ground black pepper, divided
    2 teaspoons dried fines herbes
    2 large egg whites, lightly beaten
    ½ cup panko (Japanese breadcrumbs)
    4 (6-ounce) orange roughy fillets (¾ inch thick)

1. Preheat oven to 425°.
2. Grate rind from orange to measure ½ teaspoon. Cut orange in half, and cut 4 thin slices from 1 half; juice remaining half to measure 2 tablespoons.
3. Heat butter and oil in a 10-inch ovenproof skillet over medium heat until butter melts. Stir in green onions; cook 3 minutes or just until tender. Remove pan from heat.
4. Combine crabmeat, orange juice, and orange rind in a medium bowl. Add green onions, reserving drippings in pan. Add ⅛ teaspoon salt, ¼ teaspoon pepper, and next 3 ingredients to bowl. Toss gently with a fork until blended. Set aside.
5. Place orange slices in pan. Place fish on top of slices, and sprinkle with remaining ⅛ teaspoon salt and remaining ¼ teaspoon pepper. Spoon crab mixture evenly on fish, packing lightly to form a mound covering fish. Bake at 425° for 20 minutes.
6. Preheat broiler. Broil 3 minutes or until crab topping is golden and fish flakes easily when tested with a fork. YIELD: 4 SERVINGS (SERVING SIZE: 1 FILLET).

PER SERVING: CAL 293 (27% from fat); FAT 8.9g (sat 3.9g); PRO 40.1g; CARB 10.7g; FIB 1.9g; CHOL 155mg; IRON 2.5mg; SOD 506mg; CALC 96mg

MISO-GLAZED SALMON

POINTS value: 8

PREP: 11 minutes ■ **COOK:** 17 minutes
■ **OTHER:** 10 minutes

Miso, also called bean paste, is a staple in Japanese cuisine. It comes in a variety of colors and can be quite salty, so be sure to use low-sodium miso in this recipe. This is a wonderful glaze on poultry as well.

> 3 tablespoons low-sodium white miso
> 2 tablespoons mirin (sweet rice wine)
> 2 tablespoons honey
> 1 tablespoon low-sodium soy sauce
> 2 teaspoons minced peeled fresh ginger
> 1 teaspoon dark sesame oil
> 1 garlic clove, minced
> 4 (6-ounce) salmon fillets (1 inch thick)

1. Preheat oven to 450°.
2. Combine first 7 ingredients in a medium bowl; stir with a whisk.
3. Place fish in a shallow dish; add half of miso mixture, and turn to coat. Marinate 10 minutes. Remove fish from dish, reserving miso mixture.
4. Place fish on a foil-lined broiler pan; brush with half of remaining miso mixture. Bake at 450° in upper one-third of oven for 6 minutes or until glaze begins to lightly brown.
5. Brush fish with remaining miso mixture, and bake an additional 11 minutes or until fish flakes easily when tested with a fork. YIELD: 4 SERVINGS (SERVING SIZE: 1 FILLET).

PER SERVING: CAL 354 (36% from fat); FAT 14.2g (sat 3.3g); PRO 37.1g; CARB 14.5g; FIB 0.1g; CHOL 87mg; IRON 0.7mg; SOD 637mg; CALC 23mg

POACHED SALMON WITH CUCUMBER-YOGURT SAUCE

POINTS value: 8

PREP: 15 minutes ■ **COOK:** 11 minutes

This delicious sauce uses thick, rich Greek-style yogurt. You can substitute plain fat-free yogurt, but be sure to drain it first to thicken it to the desired consistency. You'll need 2 (8-ounce) cartons.

> ⅔ cup Greek-style plain fat-free yogurt
> ⅓ cup light sour cream
> 2 garlic cloves, minced
> 1 cup shredded seeded cucumber, patted dry
> 1 tablespoon white wine vinegar
> 2 tablespoons chopped fresh dill, divided
> ¾ teaspoon salt, divided
> ½ teaspoon black pepper
> 4 (6-ounce) skinless salmon fillets
> ½ cup dry white wine

1. Combine first 5 ingredients in a bowl. Stir in 1 tablespoon dill, ½ teaspoon salt, and pepper. Set aside.
2. Place fish in a large skillet. Add wine, remaining ¼ teaspoon salt, and enough water to cover fish (about 4 cups). Bring to a boil over high heat. Reduce heat and simmer, uncovered, 5 minutes. Gently remove fish from pan with a wide spatula; drain on paper towels.
3. Place 1 fillet on each of 4 plates; sprinkle with remaining 1 tablespoon dill. Serve with yogurt sauce. YIELD: 4 SERVINGS (SERVING SIZE: 1 FILLET AND ABOUT ¼ CUP SAUCE).

PER SERVING: CAL 328 (43% from fat); FAT 15.5g (sat 4.6g); PRO 40.4g; CARB 4.2g; FIB 0.3g; CHOL 95mg; IRON 0.9mg; SOD 444mg; CALC 77mg

HOW TO DRAIN YOGURT: QUICK-DRAIN METHOD

One 8-ounce carton of plain fat-free yogurt yields about ⅓ cup quick-drained yogurt. Use this method when you need just a small amount of soft yogurt.

1. Spoon yogurt onto several layers of heavy-duty paper towels; spread to ½-inch thickness.

2. Cover with additional paper towels; let stand 2 to 3 minutes.

3. Scrape yogurt into a bowl using a rubber spatula; cover and refrigerate.

PAN-SEARED SALMON WITH CUCUMBER-RADISH SALAD

POINTS value: 7

PREP: 15 minutes ■ **COOK:** 15 minutes

The tangy crunch of the Cucumber-Radish Salad goes well with the seared-in flavor of the salmon.

- 2 tablespoons rice wine vinegar
- 1 tablespoon low-sodium soy sauce
- 1½ teaspoons honey
- ½ teaspoon dark sesame oil
- ¼ teaspoon crushed red pepper
- ½ teaspoon freshly ground black pepper, divided
- 1 cup thinly sliced English cucumber, halved
- ½ cup thinly sliced radishes
- ¼ cup diagonally sliced green onions
- 1 teaspoon sesame seeds
- 4 (6-ounce) salmon fillets
- **Cooking spray**

1. Combine first 5 ingredients and ¼ teaspoon black pepper in a medium bowl, stirring with a whisk. Add cucumber, radishes, and green onions, tossing gently. Cover and chill until ready to serve.
2. Place sesame seeds in a large nonstick skillet over medium heat, and cook 5 minutes or until toasted and golden; remove from pan.
3. Sprinkle fish with remaining ¼ teaspoon black pepper; coat fish with cooking spray. Place fish in pan over medium-high heat. Cook 5 minutes on each side or until fish flakes easily when tested with a fork. Top fish with cucumber-radish salad and sesame seeds. YIELD: 4 SERVINGS (SERVING SIZE: 1 FILLET, ABOUT ⅓ CUP CUCUMBER-RADISH SALAD, AND ¼ TEASPOON SESAME SEEDS).

PER SERVING: CAL 302 (42% from fat); FAT 14g (sat 3.2g); PRO 36.9g; CARB 4.5g; FIB 0.8g; CHOL 87mg; IRON 1.9mg; SOD 240mg; CALC 34mg

PAN-SEARED SALMON WITH LEMON-GARLIC SPINACH ✓

POINTS value: 7

pictured on page 60

PREP: 6 minutes ■ **COOK:** 20 minutes

Three packages of fresh spinach may seem like too much, but the spinach will reduce in volume once it wilts, yielding the perfect amount.

- 1 teaspoon ground cumin, divided
- ½ teaspoon salt, divided
- ¼ teaspoon black pepper, divided
- 4 (6-ounce) salmon fillets
- 2 teaspoons olive oil, divided
- 2 garlic cloves, minced
- 3 (6-ounce) packages fresh baby spinach
- 1 teaspoon grated fresh lemon rind
- **Lemon wedges**

1. Combine ½ teaspoon cumin, ¼ teaspoon salt, and ⅛ teaspoon pepper; sprinkle evenly over fish. Heat 1 teaspoon oil in a large nonstick skillet over medium-high heat. Add fish, flesh sides down, and cook 4 minutes. Turn fish over, and cook 5 to 7 minutes or until fish flakes easily when tested with a fork. Remove fish from pan; keep warm. Wipe drippings from pan with a paper towel.
2. Add remaining 1 teaspoon oil to pan; heat over medium-high heat. Add garlic; sauté 1 minute. Add spinach, in batches, and cook until spinach wilts and liquid almost evaporates, stirring frequently. Stir in remaining ½ teaspoon cumin, ¼ teaspoon salt, ⅛ teaspoon pepper, and lemon rind. Serve fish over wilted spinach. Squeeze lemon wedges over fish and spinach before serving. YIELD: 4 SERVINGS (SERVING SIZE: 1 FILLET AND ABOUT ⅔ CUP SPINACH).

PER SERVING: CAL 328 (44% from fat); FAT 15.9g (sat 3.5g); PRO 40.1g; CARB 6g; FIB 3.1g; CHOL 87mg; IRON 4.3mg; SOD 473mg; CALC 155mg

SALMON MINI LOAVES WITH HOMEMADE TARTAR SAUCE

POINTS value: 5

PREP: 14 minutes ■ **COOK:** 27 minutes ■ **OTHER:** 1 hour

We discarded the skin and bones from the canned salmon, but they *are* edible. You can stir them in with the fish, if you'd like, to get some additional calcium and magnesium.

Cooking spray
½ cup finely chopped onion
½ cup finely chopped green bell pepper
1 garlic clove, minced
1 (14¾-ounce) can pink salmon, skin and bones discarded
1 cup fresh breadcrumbs (about 1 large bread slice)
½ cup egg substitute
1 teaspoon canola oil
¼ teaspoon black pepper
Homemade Tartar Sauce

1. Preheat oven to 350°.
2. Heat a medium nonstick skillet over medium-high heat; coat pan with cooking spray. Add onion, bell pepper, and garlic; sauté 2 minutes.
3. Combine onion mixture, fish, and next 4 ingredients in a large bowl, stirring gently.
4. Divide salmon mixture into 4 portions. Shape each portion into a 4 x 2–inch loaf, and place loaves in a 13 x 9–inch baking dish coated with cooking spray. Bake at 350° for 25 minutes or until lightly browned. Serve immediately with tartar sauce. YIELD: 4 SERVINGS (SERVING SIZE: 1 LOAF AND ¼ CUP TARTAR SAUCE).

PER SERVING: CAL 223 (32% from fat); FAT 8g (sat 1.8g); PRO 21g; CARB 16.4g; FIB 2g; CHOL 51mg; IRON 1.9mg; SOD 862mg; CALC 217mg

Homemade Tartar Sauce ☑.
POINTS value: 0

¾ cup fat-free mayonnaise
2 tablespoons dill pickle relish, drained
1 tablespoon finely grated onion
1 tablespoon Dijon mustard
1½ teaspoons fresh lemon juice
⅛ teaspoon salt
⅛ teaspoon hot sauce

1. Combine all ingredients in a small bowl. Cover and chill 1 hour. YIELD: 1 CUP.

PER TABLESPOON: CAL 10 (27% from fat); FAT 0.3g (sat 0.1g); PRO 0g; CARB 1.8g; FIB 0.3g; CHOL 1mg; IRON 0mg; SOD 165mg; CALC 1mg

ROASTED JALAPEÑO-APRICOT TILAPIA

POINTS value: 6

PREP: 9 minutes ■ **COOK:** 20 minutes

Tilapia fillets can vary in size. If you can't find 6-ounce fillets, use 4 (3-ounce) fillets.

1 tablespoon canola oil
2 tablespoons diced onion
2 tablespoons diced yellow bell pepper
2 tablespoons finely chopped seeded jalapeño pepper
2 garlic cloves, minced
⅓ cup white wine
½ cup sugar-free apricot preserves (such as Smucker's)
2 teaspoons honey Dijon mustard
2 (6-ounce) tilapia fillets
¼ teaspoon salt
¼ teaspoon freshly ground black pepper

1. Preheat oven to 400°.
2. Heat oil in a small saucepan over medium-high heat. Add onion and bell pepper; sauté 2 minutes or until tender. Add jalapeño; cook 1 minute. Add garlic; cook 1 minute or until golden. Add wine to pan, and cook until liquid evaporates, scraping pan to loosen browned bits. Stir in preserves and mustard. Bring to a boil; reduce heat, and simmer 4 minutes or until thick. Set aside.
3. Sprinkle fish evenly with salt and pepper. Place fish on a baking sheet lined with parchment paper. Spoon apricot mixture evenly over fish. Bake at 400° for 8 minutes or until fish flakes easily when tested with a fork. Serve immediately. YIELD: 2 SERVINGS (SERVING SIZE: 1 FILLET).

PER SERVING: CAL 289 (31% from fat); FAT 10g (sat 1.5g); PRO 34.9g; CARB 25.3g; FIB 0.7g; CHOL 85mg; IRON 1.3mg; SOD 440mg; CALC 30mg

TILAPIA WITH CAPER SAUCE

POINTS value: 5

PREP: 6 minutes ■ **COOK:** 17 minutes

1 tablespoon olive oil
4 (6-ounce) tilapia fillets
⅛ teaspoon salt
⅛ teaspoon freshly ground black pepper
1 cup white wine
¼ cup minced shallots
2 tablespoons capers, drained
1 tablespoon chilled butter, cut into small pieces
1 tablespoon chopped fresh parsley

1. Heat oil in a large nonstick skillet over medium-high heat. Sprinkle fish evenly with salt and pepper. Add fish to pan, and cook 3 to 4 minutes on each side or until fish flakes easily when tested with a fork. Remove fish from pan, and keep warm.

2. Add wine and shallots to pan, and cook 10 minutes or until reduced by half. Stir in capers and butter.

3. Place 1 fillet on each of 4 plates. Drizzle evenly with sauce, and sprinkle with parsley. YIELD: 4 SERVINGS (SERVING SIZE: 1 FILLET AND 3 TABLESPOONS SAUCE).

PER SERVING: CAL 230 (36% from fat); FAT 9.2g (sat 3.3g); PRO 34.7g; CARB 2.8g; FIB 0.3g; CHOL 93mg; IRON 1.5mg; SOD 315mg; CALC 29mg

SEARED TUNA TACOS

POINTS value: 6

pictured on page 59

PREP: 13 minutes ■ COOK: 6 minutes
■ OTHER: 5 minutes

Serve these vibrant tacos with Green Chile Rice on page 154.

    1½ cups shredded angel hair cabbage
    ½   cup fresh salsa, divided
    3   tablespoons chopped fresh cilantro, divided
    2   tablespoons light mayonnaise
    1   cup chopped seeded yellow tomato
    1   cup chopped seeded green tomato
    ¼   cup thinly sliced red onion
    4   hard taco shells
        Cooking spray
    1   (8-ounce) tuna steak
    ¼   teaspoon freshly ground black pepper
    ⅛   teaspoon salt

1. Combine cabbage, 1 tablespoon salsa, 1 tablespoon cilantro, and mayonnaise in a bowl, tossing to coat.

2. Combine tomato, onion, and remaining 2 tablespoons cilantro in a small bowl; set aside.

3. Heat taco shells according to package directions; keep warm.

4. Heat a small nonstick skillet over medium-high heat; coat pan with cooking spray. Sprinkle fish evenly with pepper and salt. Cook fish 2 to 3 minutes on each side or until desired degree of doneness; let stand 5 minutes. Cut crosswise into thin slices.

5. Fill taco shells evenly with coleslaw mixture, fish, and tomato mixture. Serve with remaining salsa. YIELD: 2 SERVINGS (SERVING SIZE: 2 TACOS AND ABOUT ¼ CUP SALSA).

PER SERVING: CAL 317 (29% from fat); FAT 10.1g (sat 2.2g); PRO 28.6g; CARB 24.4g; FIB 3.6g; CHOL 58mg; IRON 2.6mg; SOD 562mg; CALC 75mg

HOT AND SOUR MUSSELS

POINTS value: 6

PREP: 6 minutes ■ COOK: 11 minutes

We really liked the addition of green onions and cilantro as the finishing touches to this dish—they add both color and flavor.

    1¼ cups water
    1   tablespoon tomato paste
    1   tablespoon rice vinegar
    1   teaspoon dark sesame oil
    1   teaspoon chili garlic sauce (such as Huy Fong)
    ⅛   teaspoon salt
    2   pounds mussels (about 32), scrubbed and debearded
    1   tablespoon thinly sliced green onions
    1   tablespoon chopped fresh cilantro

1. Combine first 6 ingredients in a large Dutch oven; bring to a boil. Reduce heat, and simmer, uncovered, 5 minutes or until liquid reduces slightly. Add mussels; cover and cook 4 minutes or until shells open. Remove from heat; discard any unopened shells.

2. Using a slotted spoon, spoon mussels evenly into 2 bowls. Stir green onions and cilantro into remaining liquid. Pour broth evenly over mussels, and serve immediately. YIELD: 2 SERVINGS (SERVING SIZE: ABOUT 16 MUSSELS AND ¾ CUP BROTH).

PER SERVING: CAL 249 (29% from fat); FAT 8g (sat 1.4g); PRO 30.7g; CARB 11.7g; FIB 0.6g; CHOL 72mg; IRON 10.3mg; SOD 921mg; CALC 69mg

BUYING AND STORING MUSSELS

Always buy fresh mussels, and use them within a day. Choose only those that have tightly closed shells or that are slightly open but snap shut when tapped. These are signs that a mussel is alive; an open shell that doesn't close if tapped means the mussel is dead or dehydrated. Discard mussels with broken shells (as well as those that stay closed after they've been cooked). To store mussels, remove them from the packaging, and refrigerate them wrapped in a moist towel. Don't store them in plastic because this prevents them from breathing.

CRAB CAKES WITH ROASTED YELLOW PEPPER–CURRY SAUCE

POINTS value: 8

PREP: 33 minutes ■ COOK: 36 minutes
■ OTHER: 55 minutes

These soft and tender crab cakes, served with curry sauce and tomato relish, are reminiscent of a dish you'd find at an upscale restaurant—this is definitely a recipe to impress dinner guests! Each of the components can be made ahead if you need to simplify the meal planning.

 2 teaspoons butter
Cooking spray
 ¼ cup finely chopped red bell pepper
 ¼ cup finely chopped green onions
 1½ teaspoons minced jalapeño pepper
 1 garlic clove, minced
 1 pound lump crabmeat, drained and shell pieces removed
 ¼ cup light mayonnaise
 2 tablespoons chopped fresh cilantro, divided
 ¼ teaspoon grated fresh lime rind
 1 tablespoon fresh lime juice
 2 teaspoons Dijon mustard
 ¼ teaspoon black pepper
 ⅛ teaspoon salt
 1 cup panko (Japanese breadcrumbs), divided
 1 tablespoon butter
 1 garlic clove, crushed
 2 tablespoons canola oil
Roasted Yellow Pepper–Curry Sauce
Tomato-Lime Relish

1. Heat 2 teaspoons butter in a small nonstick skillet coated with cooking spray over medium-high heat. Add red bell pepper, green onions, jalapeño, and minced garlic; sauté 2 minutes or until tender.
2. Combine sautéed vegetables, crabmeat, mayonnaise, next 6 ingredients, and ¼ cup breadcrumbs in a bowl, stirring gently to combine. Shape mixture into 8 patties. Cover and chill 30 minutes.
3. Preheat oven to 450°.
4. Melt 1 tablespoon butter in a small skillet over medium heat. Add crushed garlic and remaining ¾ cup breadcrumbs; cook 2 to 3 minutes or until breadcrumbs are lightly browned, stirring frequently. Place breadcrumbs in a shallow plate or dish. Dredge patties in breadcrumb mixture, coating all sides.
5. Place a rimmed baking sheet coated with 2 tablespoons oil in preheated oven for 3 minutes. Place patties on hot pan, and bake at 450° for 8 minutes on each side or until lightly browned. Serve with Roasted Yellow Pepper–Curry Sauce and Tomato-Lime Relish. YIELD: 4 SERVINGS (SERVING SIZE: 2 CRAB CAKES, 2 TABLESPOONS SAUCE, AND 2 TABLESPOONS RELISH).

PER SERVING: CAL 348 (50% from fat); FAT 19.3g (sat 5.2g); PRO 24g; CARB 19.3g; FIB 2.2g; CHOL 106mg; IRON 1.6mg; SOD 714mg; CALC 127mg

Roasted Yellow Pepper–Curry Sauce
POINTS value: 0

 1 large yellow bell pepper, halved and seeded
 2 tablespoons light coconut milk
 ½ teaspoon curry powder
 ¼ teaspoon honey
 ⅛ teaspoon grated fresh lime rind
 ¼ teaspoon fresh lime juice
 ⅛ teaspoon ground coriander
 ⅛ teaspoon ground red pepper

1. Preheat broiler.
2. Place bell pepper halves, skin sides up, on a foil-lined baking sheet, and flatten with hand. Broil 10 to 15 minutes or until blackened. Place bell peppers in a large zip-top plastic bag; seal. Let stand 15 minutes. Remove peppers from bag; peel and discard skins.
3. Place peeled peppers in a food processor or blender. Process 1 minute or until smooth. Place puree in a microwave-safe bowl; add coconut milk and remaining ingredients, stirring well. Cover with wax paper, and microwave at HIGH 1 minute or until thoroughly heated. YIELD: ½ CUP.

PER TABLESPOON: CAL 10 (27% from fat); FAT 0.3g (sat 0.2g); PRO 0.3g; CARB 1.9g; FIB 0.3g; CHOL 0mg; IRON 0.2mg; SOD 2mg; CALC 3mg

Tomato-Lime Relish
POINTS value: 0

 ½ cup chopped seeded plum tomato
 ¼ cup chopped green onions
 2 tablespoons chopped fresh cilantro
 2 teaspoons fresh lime juice
 ⅛ teaspoon salt

1. Combine all ingredients in a small bowl. Let stand 10 minutes. YIELD: ½ CUP.

PER TABLESPOON: CAL 5 (0% from fat); FAT 0g (sat 0g); PRO 0.3g; CARB 1.2g; FIB 0.4g; CHOL 0mg; IRON 0.1mg; SOD 38mg; CALC 5mg

CRISPY COCONUT SCALLOPS WITH MANGO SAUCE

POINTS value: 7

PREP: 15 minutes ■ **COOK:** 12 minutes

Often used as a dipping sauce for egg rolls or spring rolls, sweet chili sauce adds zip to fresh mango and lime, complementing the sweetness of both the coconut and scallops. Look for it in the Asian-foods section of the supermarket.

¼ cup cornstarch
⅛ teaspoon salt
⅛ teaspoon garlic powder
1 large egg white, lightly beaten
6 tablespoons panko (Japanese breadcrumbs)
¼ cup flaked sweetened coconut
¾ pound small sea scallops (about 16)
Cooking spray
1 ripe mango, peeled and chopped
¼ teaspoon grated fresh lime rind
2 tablespoons fresh lime juice
1 tablespoon mild sweet chili sauce (such as Maggi Taste of Asia)

1. Preheat oven to 450°.
2. Combine first 3 ingredients in a small bowl. Place egg white in another bowl. Combine panko and coconut in a shallow dish.
3. Heat a large baking sheet in preheated oven for about 5 minutes.
4. While pan heats, dredge scallops in cornstarch mixture. Dip in egg white; dredge in panko mixture, pressing gently to coat. Place scallops on a wire rack over wax paper. Coat scallops with cooking spray. Remove hot pan from oven; coat pan with cooking spray. Place scallops in a single layer on pan. Bake at 450° for 12 minutes or until scallops are done and coating is crisp.
5. While scallops bake, place mango and next 3 ingredients in a food processor, and pulse 3 to 4 times or until sauce is slightly chunky. Serve scallops with mango sauce. YIELD: 2 SERVINGS (SERVING SIZE: ABOUT 8 SCALLOPS AND 6 TABLESPOONS MANGO SAUCE).

PER SERVING: CAL 343 (15% from fat); FAT 5.6g (sat 3.5g); PRO 32.5g; CARB 39.6g; FIB 2.1g; CHOL 56mg; IRON 0.9mg; SOD 632mg; CALC 53mg

SEARED SCALLOPS WITH LEMON-BUTTER SAUCE

POINTS value: 5

pictured on page 63

PREP: 6 minutes ■ **COOK:** 8 minutes

Succulent scallops and citrusy butter sauce make this light dish unexpectedly indulgent.

1½ pounds sea scallops
¼ teaspoon salt
¼ teaspoon pepper
½ cup sweet white wine
2 tablespoons chopped fresh parsley
1 tablespoon minced shallots
2 teaspoons grated fresh lemon rind
2 tablespoons butter

1. Pat scallops dry with paper towels; sprinkle with salt and pepper. Heat a large nonstick skillet over medium-high heat. Add scallops; cook 2 to 3 minutes on each side or until browned. Remove scallops from pan; keep warm.
2. Add wine and next 3 ingredients to pan, scraping pan to loosen browned bits. Add butter; cook 2 minutes or until butter melts and sauce is slightly thick. Return scallops to pan; cook 2 minutes. Serve scallops with sauce. YIELD: 4 SERVINGS (SERVING SIZE: 4 OUNCES SCALLOPS AND 2 TEASPOONS SAUCE).

PER SERVING: CAL 205 (31% from fat); FAT 7g (sat 3.7g); PRO 28.8g; CARB 5.2g; FIB 0.2g; CHOL 71mg; IRON 0.8mg; SOD 463mg; CALC 50mg

ADOBO-RUM GRILLED SHRIMP

POINTS value: 4

PREP: 15 minutes ■ COOK: 6 minutes
■ OTHER: 30 minutes

    2 pounds large shrimp, peeled and deveined
    2 teaspoons grated fresh lime rind
    2 teaspoons grated fresh orange rind
    ¼ cup fresh lime juice
    ¼ cup fresh orange juice
    ¼ cup dark rum
    3 tablespoons light brown sugar
    1 tablespoon canola oil
    ½ teaspoon adobo seasoning (such as Goya)
  Cooking spray
  Lime wedges

1. Place shrimp in a large zip-top plastic bag. Combine lime rind and next 7 ingredients in a bowl; pour over shrimp. Seal bag; shake well to coat. Chill 30 minutes.
2. Prepare grill.
3. Remove shrimp from bag; discard marinade. Thread shrimp onto 8 (8-inch) metal skewers. Place kebabs on grill rack coated with cooking spray. Grill 3 minutes on each side or until shrimp are done. Serve with lime wedges. YIELD: 4 SERVINGS (SERVING SIZE: 2 KEBABS).

PER SERVING: CAL 197 (13% from fat); FAT 2.8g (sat 0.6g); PRO 36.1g; CARB 2.9g; FIB 0.1g; CHOL 336mg; IRON 5.4mg; SOD 431mg; CALC 71mg

CRUNCHY GARLIC SHRIMP

POINTS value: 6

PREP: 15 minutes ■ COOK: 18 minutes

    2 large egg whites
    3 tablespoons cornstarch
    6 large garlic cloves, pressed
    2 tablespoons finely chopped fresh flat-leaf parsley
    2 teaspoons grated fresh lemon rind
    ¼ teaspoon salt
    ¼ teaspoon freshly ground black pepper
  1½ pounds jumbo shrimp (about 28), peeled
       and deveined
  1½ cups panko (Japanese breadcrumbs)
  Olive oil–flavored cooking spray

1. Preheat oven to 450°.
2. Heat a large baking sheet in oven for 5 minutes.
3. While pan heats, place egg whites in a medium bowl; stir with a whisk until foamy. Add cornstarch and next 5 ingredients; stir until blended. Add shrimp, stirring to coat.

4. Place breadcrumbs in a shallow dish. Dredge shrimp, 3 or 4 at a time, in breadcrumbs, and set aside on a separate plate. When shrimp are breaded, remove hot pan from oven, and coat pan well with cooking spray. Place shrimp in a single layer on pan. Coat shrimp with cooking spray. Bake at 450° for 18 minutes or until crisp and golden. Serve immediately. YIELD: 4 SERVINGS (SERVING SIZE: ABOUT 7 SHRIMP).

PER SERVING: CAL 289 (12% from fat); FAT 3.7g (sat 0.6g); PRO 38.8g; CARB 22.1g; FIB 1g; CHOL 259mg; IRON 4.4mg; SOD 474mg; CALC 102mg

GARLIC SHRIMP WITH RICE

POINTS value: 7

PREP: 7 minutes ■ COOK: 9 minutes

Be careful when you sauté garlic because it cooks quickly, and burnt garlic can add a bitter flavor to the finished dish.

    ½ cup fat-free, less-sodium chicken broth
    2 tablespoons low-sodium soy sauce
    2 tablespoons orange marmalade
    1 tablespoon cornstarch
    1 teaspoon grated peeled fresh ginger
    ½ teaspoon dark sesame oil
    ¼ teaspoon crushed red pepper
  Cooking spray
    1 red bell pepper, cut into 1-inch pieces
    ½ cup (1-inch) diagonally cut green onions
    1 teaspoon canola oil
    5 garlic cloves, minced
    2 pounds medium shrimp, peeled and
       deveined
    2 cups hot cooked brown rice

1. Combine first 7 ingredients in a medium bowl, stirring with a whisk; set aside.
2. Heat a large nonstick skillet over medium-high heat; coat pan with cooking spray. Add bell pepper to pan, and sauté 3 minutes or until browned. Add green onions; cook 1 minute or until green onions wilt. Remove from pan; set aside, and keep warm.
3. Heat oil in pan over medium-high heat. Add garlic; sauté 1 minute or until lightly toasted. Add shrimp; sauté 2 to 3 minutes or just until done. Add soy sauce mixture and bell pepper mixture to pan. Bring to a boil; cook, uncovered, 1 to 2 minutes or until shrimp are done and sauce thickens slightly. Serve over rice. YIELD: 4 SERVINGS (SERVING SIZE: 1 CUP SHRIMP AND ½ CUP RICE).

PER SERVING: CAL 360 (14% from fat); FAT 5.6g (sat 1g); PRO 38.3g; CARB 37.2g; FIB 2.6g; CHOL 259mg; IRON 5.2mg; SOD 634mg; CALC 111mg

SHRIMP AND PANCETTA PASTA

POINTS value: 7

PREP: 9 minutes ▪ **COOK:** 24 minutes

We chose penne rigate (with its ridged sides) over smooth penne because the ridges help trap the sauce.

  9 ounces uncooked penne rigate
Cooking spray
  4 ounces pancetta, finely chopped
  1 cup chopped onion
  4 garlic cloves, minced
  1 (28-ounce) can crushed tomatoes, undrained
  ¼ cup dry white wine
  1 tablespoon chopped fresh parsley
  2 teaspoons minced fresh rosemary
  1 teaspoon sugar
  ¼ teaspoon crushed red pepper
  ⅛ teaspoon black pepper
  1¼ pounds medium shrimp, peeled and deveined
  ¼ cup grated fresh Parmesan cheese

1. Cook pasta according to package directions, omitting salt and fat. Drain.
2. While pasta cooks, heat a large nonstick skillet over medium-high heat; coat pan with cooking spray. Add pancetta, and cook 4 minutes or until crisp and browned, stirring often. Add onion and garlic, and cook until onion is almost tender, stirring often. Stir in tomatoes and next 6 ingredients. Bring to a boil; reduce heat, and simmer 10 minutes. Add shrimp, and cook over medium-high heat 5 minutes or until shrimp are done.
3. Combine pasta and shrimp mixture in a large bowl, stirring to coat pasta. Sprinkle with Parmesan cheese. Serve warm. YIELD: 6 SERVINGS (SERVING SIZE: 1½ CUPS).

PER SERVING: CAL 370 (22% from fat); FAT 9g (sat 3.6g); PRO 26.9g; CARB 44.5g; FIB 3.8g; CHOL 156mg; IRON 4.7mg; SOD 700mg; CALC 122mg

DEVEINING SHRIMP

Recipes often call for shrimp to be deveined, but the edible "vein" (actually the digestive tract) is fine to leave in all shrimp except larger shrimp and prawns, where it can be gritty.

1. Using a deveining tool or sharp knife, remove the dark vein.

2. Peel back the shell.

CREAMY SHRIMP AND CHEESE GRITS

POINTS value: 8

PREP: 5 minutes ▪ **COOK:** 28 minutes

You'll love these creamy triple-cheese grits smothered with savory sautéed shrimp.

  3¼ cups fat-free, less-sodium chicken broth, divided
  1½ cups fat-free milk
  ¾ cup uncooked quick-cooking grits
  ½ cup (4 ounces) ⅓-less-fat cream cheese
  ½ cup (2 ounces) reduced-fat shredded sharp Cheddar cheese
  ¼ cup grated fresh Parmesan cheese
  ⅛ teaspoon ground red pepper (optional)
  2 teaspoons olive oil, divided
  1 (8-ounce) package sliced mushrooms
  ½ cup chopped red bell pepper
  2 teaspoons bottled minced garlic
  2¾ pounds medium shrimp, peeled and deveined
  2 tablespoons all-purpose flour
  ¼ teaspoon freshly ground black pepper
  ¼ cup chopped green onions

1. Bring 1¾ cups broth and milk to a boil in a medium saucepan; gradually add grits, stirring with a whisk. Reduce heat to medium-low, and simmer 10 minutes or until thick, stirring occasionally. Stir in cheeses and, if desired, ground red pepper. Remove from heat; cover and keep warm.
2. Heat 1 teaspoon oil in a large nonstick skillet over medium-high heat. Add mushrooms, red bell pepper, and garlic; sauté 5 minutes or until tender, stirring frequently. Remove from pan, and keep warm.
3. Heat remaining 1 teaspoon oil in pan over medium-high heat. Add shrimp, and cook 2 minutes or until shrimp are lightly browned. Add shrimp to reserved vegetables; keep warm.
4. Combine flour and ½ cup broth in a small bowl. Add remaining 1 cup broth to pan, scraping pan to loosen browned bits. Add flour mixture to pan, and cook over medium-high heat 3 minutes or until thick. Return cooked vegetables and shrimp to mixture in pan; stir in black pepper and green onions. Cook 1 minute or until thoroughly heated. Serve over cheese grits. YIELD: 6 SERVINGS (SERVING SIZE: 1 CUP SHRIMP MIXTURE AND ¾ CUP GRITS).

PER SERVING: CAL 388 (25% from fat); FAT 10.7g (sat 5.4g); PRO 44.6g; CARB 25.7g; FIB 1.3g; CHOL 319mg; IRON 5.9mg; SOD 893mg; CALC 262mg

SHRIMP CREOLE ☑

POINTS value: 5

PREP: 20 minutes ■ **COOK:** 27 minutes

Creole cookery reflects the influences of French, Spanish, Mediterranean, Caribbean, and African cuisines. It is characterized by the use of the "holy trinity" of chopped bell pepper, onion, and celery. Creole cuisine is generally not as spicy as its Cajun cousin.

> 2 teaspoons olive oil
> 1 cup chopped onion
> 1 cup chopped green bell pepper
> 1 cup chopped celery
> 2 garlic cloves, minced
> 1 (14.5-ounce) can stewed tomatoes, undrained and chopped
> 1 (8-ounce) can tomato sauce
> ¼ teaspoon dried thyme
> ¼ teaspoon crushed red pepper
> 2 pounds medium shrimp, peeled and deveined
> 3 cups hot cooked brown rice

1. Heat oil in a Dutch oven over medium heat. Add onion and next 3 ingredients; sauté 6 minutes or until crisp-tender. Stir in tomatoes and next 3 ingredients; cover and cook 12 minutes or until vegetables are tender.
2. Stir in shrimp; cover and cook over medium heat 8 minutes or until shrimp are done, stirring occasionally. Serve over rice. YIELD: 6 SERVINGS (SERVING SIZE: ABOUT 1 CUP SHRIMP AND ½ CUP RICE).

PER SERVING: CAL 286 (12% from fat); FAT 3.7g (sat 0.8g); PRO 28.1g; CARB 33.5g; FIB 4.7g; CHOL 224mg; IRON 5.5mg; SOD 625mg; CALC 101mg

CRISPY CALAMARI WITH CITRUS AÏOLI

POINTS value: 4

PREP: 16 minutes ■ **COOK:** 6 minutes

Serve this as a main course with a baked potato and a green salad or as an appetizer before a meal of steak or seafood.

> 2 large egg whites, lightly beaten
> 2 tablespoons cornstarch
> 2 tablespoons water
> 1 pound squid (tubes only), cut into thin strips
> 1 cup panko (Japanese breadcrumbs)
> 2 tablespoons dehydrated onion flakes
> ¼ teaspoon salt
> Cooking spray
> Citrus Aïoli

1. Preheat oven to 450°.
2. Heat a large baking sheet in preheated oven for about 5 minutes.
3. While pan heats, place egg whites in a medium bowl, stirring with a whisk until foamy. Add cornstarch and water; stir until blended. Add squid, stirring to coat.
4. Combine panko, onion flakes, and salt in a shallow dish. Dredge squid, in 3 batches, in panko mixture. Place on a shallow plate. When all pieces of squid are breaded, remove hot pan from oven, and coat well with cooking spray. Place squid in a single layer on pan. Coat squid with cooking spray. Bake at 450° for 6 minutes or until crisp and lightly golden. Serve immediately with aïoli. YIELD: 4 SERVINGS (SERVING SIZE: 4 OUNCES SQUID AND 2½ TABLESPOONS AÏOLI).

PER SERVING: CAL 217 (11% from fat); FAT 2.7g (sat 0.5g); PRO 21.8g; CARB 24.1g; FIB 1.2g; CHOL 266mg; IRON 0.9mg; SOD 651mg; CALC 46mg

Citrus Aïoli

POINTS value: 0

One serving of this aïoli has a **POINTS** value of 0; ¼ cup has a **POINTS** value of 1.

> ⅓ cup fat-free mayonnaise
> 2½ tablespoons honey Dijon mustard
> ½ teaspoon finely grated fresh lemon rind
> ¼ teaspoon finely grated fresh orange rind
> 1 tablespoon fresh lemon juice
> ½ tablespoon fresh orange juice
> 1 garlic clove, minced

1. Combine all ingredients in a small bowl, stirring well. YIELD: 10 TABLESPOONS.

PER TABLESPOON: CAL 11 (16% from fat); FAT 0.2g (sat 0g); PRO 0.1g; CARB 2.2g; FIB 0.2g; CHOL 1mg; IRON 0mg; SOD 154mg; CALC 1mg

ABOUT CALAMARI

Calamari—Italian for "squid"—have 10 tentacles that are edible. However, a squid's body is the prime location for meat. It can be stuffed whole, cut into strips, or sliced crosswise into rings. The white meat is firm, with a mild, slightly sweet flavor. It's available fresh, frozen, canned, dried, and pickled.

meatless main dishes

Top-Shelf Veggie Pizza, *page 84*

ARTICHOKE QUESADILLAS

POINTS value: 5

PREP: 10 minutes ■ **COOK:** 13 minutes

These flavor-packed quesadillas rival any restaurant's version.

2 cups commercial tomato trinity (chopped tomato, green bell pepper, and onion; such as Incredible Fresh)
1 (7.5-ounce) jar marinated artichoke hearts, drained and chopped
3 tablespoons chopped fresh basil
1 tablespoon balsamic vinegar
2 garlic cloves, minced
1 teaspoon chopped banana pepper or jalapeño pepper
⅛ teaspoon salt
⅛ teaspoon freshly ground black pepper
½ cup (2 ounces) shredded light 6-cheese Italian blend cheese
6 tablespoons fat-free ricotta cheese
Olive oil–flavored cooking spray
4 (8-inch) 96% fat-free flour tortillas
1 cup refrigerated fresh salsa

1. Combine first 8 ingredients in a medium bowl, and stir well.
2. Combine Italian blend cheese and ricotta cheese in a small bowl; set aside.
3. Heat a large nonstick skillet over medium–high heat; coat pan with cooking spray. Add tomato mixture to pan; cook 5 minutes or until thoroughly heated. Remove from heat; set aside.
4. Spread cheese mixture evenly on one side of each tortilla. Sprinkle tomato mixture evenly over cheese. Fold tortillas in half.
5. Heat pan over medium heat; coat pan with cooking spray. Place 2 tortillas, folded edges together, in pan. Cook 2 to 3 minutes on each side or until lightly browned and cheese melts. Remove from pan, and keep warm. Repeat procedure with remaining tortillas. Cut each quesadilla into 4 wedges, and serve immediately with salsa. YIELD: 4 SERVINGS (SERVING SIZE: 4 WEDGES AND ¼ CUP SALSA).

PER SERVING: CAL 251 (16% from fat); FAT 4.4g (sat 1g); PRO 12.4g; CARB 36.6g; FIB 4.4g; CHOL 9mg; IRON 0.4mg; SOD 814mg; CALC 152mg

CUMIN'D BLACK BEANS AND RICE

POINTS value: 5

pictured on page 61

PREP: 13 minutes ■ **COOK:** 11 minutes
■ **OTHER:** 8 minutes

Top with a tablespoon of light sour cream for added flavor and richness. The **POINTS** value remains the same.

Cooking spray
1 cup sliced carrot
1 cup chopped seeded poblano chile pepper (about 3 medium)
½ cup chopped onion
¾ cup water
½ cup instant brown rice
1 (15-ounce) can black beans, rinsed and drained
½ cup (2 ounces) part-skim mozzarella cheese, cut into ¼-inch cubes
1½ tablespoons extravirgin olive oil
¾ teaspoon ground cumin
½ teaspoon salt
3 tablespoons chopped fresh cilantro
4 lime wedges
4 tablespoons light sour cream (optional)

1. Heat a Dutch oven over medium–high heat; coat pan with cooking spray. Add carrot, chile pepper, and onion; sauté 5 minutes or until onion is tender, stirring often.
2. Add water and rice. Cover, reduce heat, and simmer over low heat 5 minutes. Remove from heat, and stir. Cover; let stand 5 minutes or until liquid is absorbed.
3. Add beans and next 4 ingredients; remove from heat. Cover; let stand 3 minutes. Spoon into bowls. Sprinkle evenly with cilantro; top each with a lime wedge and sour cream, if desired. YIELD: 4 SERVINGS (SERVING SIZE: 1 CUP).

PER SERVING: CAL 249 (32% from fat); FAT 8.9g (sat 2.3g); PRO 8.6g; CARB 35.5g; FIB 6.6g; CHOL 8mg; IRON 1.5mg; SOD 588mg; CALC 140mg

POBLANO PEPPERS

This dark green (sometimes almost black) heart-shaped chile pepper varies from mild to medium heat, with the darkest poblanos having the richest flavor. They're large—about 3 inches wide and 4 to 5 inches long—and they taper from top to bottom. Fresh poblanos are available year-round at supermarkets and Mexican markets. As poblanos ripen, they turn a reddish brown and become sweeter. You can also find these peppers canned or dried. Dried poblanos are known as ancho chiles.

VEGETABLE NACHOS GRANDES

POINTS value: 6

pictured on page 62

PREP: 10 minutes ■ **COOK:** 28 minutes

To decrease the sodium in these casserole-style nachos, use organic or low-sodium refried beans.

    1 (16-ounce) can fat-free refried beans
    ½ cup bottled salsa
    2 teaspoons canola oil
    Cooking spray
    2 cups diced zucchini
    ½ cup chopped red onion
    1 garlic clove, minced
    1 cup frozen whole-kernel corn, thawed
    ¼ cup water
    2 tablespoons 40%-less-sodium taco seasoning
    5 cups baked tortilla chips (such as Guiltless Gourmet)
    ¼ cup sliced black olives
    1 cup (4 ounces) preshredded reduced-fat 4-cheese
        Mexican blend cheese
    ¼ cup chopped fresh cilantro
    Toppings: salsa, chopped avocado, light sour cream,
        shredded lettuce

1. Preheat oven to 350°.
2. Combine beans and salsa in a medium bowl; set aside.
3. Heat oil in a large nonstick skillet coated with cooking spray over medium-high heat. Add zucchini, onion, and garlic; sauté 5 minutes or until vegetables are crisp-tender. Add corn, water, and taco seasoning; cook until zucchini is tender and water evaporates.
4. Layer chips in a 13 x 9–inch baking dish coated with cooking spray. Spoon bean mixture evenly over chips. Top with zucchini mixture, olives, and cheese. Bake at 350° for 15 minutes. Sprinkle with cilantro; serve immediately. Serve with toppings, if desired. YIELD: 6 SERVINGS (SERVING SIZE: ⅙ OF CASSEROLE).

PER SERVING: CAL 299 (30% from fat); FAT 10g (sat 3.3g); PRO 13g; CARB 45.8g; FIB 6.7g; CHOL 13mg; IRON 1mg; SOD 990mg; CALC 163mg

TABBOULEH

POINTS value: 6

pictured on page 61

PREP: 15 minutes ■ **COOK:** 14 minutes ■ **OTHER:** 1 hour

You can vary this recipe by substituting ricotta salata or any other sharp-tasting cheese for the feta or by using cannellini, kidney, or black beans in place of the chickpeas.

    1½ cups water
    1 cup uncooked bulgur
    1 (15½-ounce) can chickpeas (garbanzo beans),
        rinsed and drained
    1½ cups grape tomatoes, halved
    1 cup diced cucumber
    ½ cup thinly sliced green onions
    ½ cup (2 ounces) crumbled feta cheese
    ⅓ cup chopped fresh parsley
    2 tablespoons finely chopped fresh mint
    ½ teaspoon salt
    ¼ cup fresh lemon juice
    1 tablespoon olive oil

1. Bring 1½ cups water to a boil in a medium saucepan over medium-high heat. Add bulgur; cover, reduce heat, and simmer 13 to 15 minutes or until water is absorbed. Transfer to a large bowl; cool completely.
2. Add chickpeas and next 7 ingredients to bulgur. Combine lemon juice and oil in a small bowl, stirring with a whisk. Pour over bulgur mixture; toss gently to coat. YIELD: 4 SERVINGS (SERVING SIZE: ABOUT 1½ CUPS).

PER SERVING: CAL 312 (26% from fat); FAT 9g (sat 3.5g); PRO 11.7g; CARB 49.9g; FIB 11.1g; CHOL 17mg; IRON 2.9mg; SOD 648mg; CALC 155mg

GOLDEN VEGETABLE CURRY

POINTS value: 6

PREP: 14 minutes ■ **COOK:** 24 minutes

Take a trip to India with this veggie-inspired curry that's loaded with authentic flavor.

- 2 cups cubed Yukon gold potato (about 1 pound)
- 3 cups cauliflower florets
- 1 (5.5-ounce) extralarge bag boil-in-bag brown rice
- 1 tablespoon butter
- 1 cup chopped onion
- 1 tablespoon minced peeled fresh ginger
- 1 garlic clove, minced
- 1 tablespoon all-purpose flour
- 1 tablespoon curry powder
- 1 teaspoon ground turmeric
- 1 teaspoon ground cumin
- 1½ cups organic vegetable broth (such as Swanson Certified Organic)
- ½ cup golden raisins
- 1 (15½-ounce) can chickpeas (garbanzo beans), drained
- ½ teaspoon salt
- ¼ teaspoon ground red pepper
- 1 (5.3-ounce) container Greek-style yogurt with honey
- 1½ tablespoons chopped fresh cilantro

1. Place potato in a large saucepan, and add water to cover. Bring to a boil; reduce heat, and simmer 5 minutes or until tender. Add cauliflower, and simmer 3 minutes or until crisp-tender. Drain; set aside.

2. Cook rice according to package directions, omitting salt and fat. Set aside.

3. While rice cooks, melt butter in a large nonstick skillet over medium-high heat. Add onion, ginger, and garlic; sauté 5 minutes or until onion is tender. Add flour and next 3 ingredients; cook 30 seconds or until fragrant, stirring constantly. Add potato mixture, broth, raisins, and chickpeas. Bring to a boil; reduce heat, and simmer 6 minutes, stirring until thick. Stir in salt, red pepper, and yogurt. Sprinkle with cilantro. Serve curry over rice. YIELD: 6 SERVINGS (SERVING SIZE: 1 CUP CURRY AND ½ CUP RICE).

PER SERVING: CAL 341 (15% from fat); FAT 5.7g (sat 3g); PRO 9.2g; CARB 65.5g; FIB 7.5g; CHOL 8mg; IRON 2.8mg; SOD 525mg; CALC 79mg

MOUSSAKA

POINTS value: 4

PREP: 17 minutes ■ **COOK:** 1 hour and 5 minutes
■ **OTHER:** 10 minutes

Moussaka is an eggplant-based dish enjoyed throughout Greece, Turkey, the Balkans, and the Middle East. It's traditionally prepared with lamb or red meat. This tasty meatless version can be assembled several hours ahead or the night before. Remember to allow additional baking time if the dish is cold when it's placed in the oven.

- 1 (1½-pound) eggplant, cut into ¼-inch-thick slices
- Cooking spray
- 2 teaspoons olive oil
- 1 cup minced onion
- 3 garlic cloves, minced
- 1 (12-ounce) package meatless crumbles (such as Morningstar Farms)
- 1 (14½-ounce) can diced tomatoes, drained
- ¼ cup dry red wine
- 1 teaspoon dried oregano
- ¼ teaspoon salt
- ¼ teaspoon ground cinnamon
- ¼ teaspoon freshly ground black pepper
- 1½ cups 1% low-fat milk
- 3 tablespoons all-purpose flour
- ¼ teaspoon salt
- ⅛ teaspoon ground nutmeg
- 1 large egg
- 5 tablespoons grated Parmigiano-Reggiano cheese, divided

1. Preheat broiler.

2. Place eggplant slices in a single layer on a large baking sheet coated with cooking spray. Broil 5 to 6 minutes on each side or until lightly browned. Repeat with remaining eggplant slices, if needed.

3. Reduce oven temperature to 400°.

4. Heat oil in a large nonstick skillet over medium-high heat. Add onion and garlic; sauté 4 minutes or until tender. Add meatless crumbles and next 6 ingredients; sauté 5 minutes or until thoroughly heated and liquid evaporates.

5. Arrange half of eggplant slices in an 8-inch square baking dish coated with cooking spray. Spoon meatless crumbles mixture over eggplant. Top with remaining eggplant slices.

6. Combine milk and next 3 ingredients in a saucepan over medium heat, stirring with a whisk. Bring to a boil; reduce heat, and simmer 6 minutes or until thick.

Remove pan from heat. Place egg in a small bowl, stirring with a whisk. Add ½ cup milk mixture to egg in a thin stream, stirring constantly. Add egg mixture to milk mixture, stirring with a whisk. Add ¼ cup cheese, stirring until cheese melts. Pour sauce over eggplant slices, and sprinkle with remaining 1 tablespoon cheese. Bake at 400° for 20 minutes or until bubbly.

7. Preheat broiler. Broil 5 minutes or until golden. Let stand 10 minutes before serving. YIELD: 6 SERVINGS (SERVING SIZE: ⅙ OF CASSEROLE).

PER SERVING: CAL 216 (30% from fat); FAT 7.1g (sat 1.7g); PRO 17.3g; CARB 23.2g; FIB 7.3g; CHOL 41mg; IRON 3mg; SOD 606mg; CALC 179mg

ROASTED MUSHROOM AND GARLIC PASTA BAKE

POINTS value: 6

PREP: 30 minutes ■ COOK: 1 hour and 5 minutes

If you'd like a less saucy version, use half of the 10-ounce jar of light Alfredo sauce. The **POINTS** value will be 5.

- 2 (3.5-ounce) packages shiitake mushrooms, stems removed and quartered
- 2 (3.5-ounce) packages oyster mushrooms, stems removed and coarsely chopped
- 1 (8-ounce) package baby portobello mushrooms, stems removed and quartered
- 12 garlic cloves, crushed
- 2 tablespoons extravirgin olive oil
- ½ teaspoon salt
- ½ teaspoon freshly ground black pepper
- 1 (13.25-ounce) package whole wheat penne rigate pasta (such as Ronzoni Healthy Harvest)
- 1 (6-ounce) package fresh baby spinach, chopped
- 1 (10-ounce) container refrigerated light Alfredo sauce
- Cooking spray
- ½ cup (2 ounces) grated fresh Parmigiano-Reggiano cheese

1. Preheat oven to 400°.
2. Combine first 7 ingredients on a large foil-lined baking sheet, tossing well. Spread mushroom mixture into a single layer. Bake at 400° for 25 minutes in top one-third of oven until lightly browned.
3. Cook pasta in a large Dutch oven according to package directions until al dente, omitting salt and fat. Drain well, and return to pan. Add mushroom mixture, spinach, and Alfredo sauce; stir well.
4. Spoon pasta mixture into a 13 x 9–inch baking dish coated with cooking spray. Cover and bake at 400° for

20 minutes; uncover and sprinkle with cheese. Bake an additional 10 minutes or until golden. YIELD: 8 SERVINGS (SERVING SIZE: 1 CUP).

PER SERVING: CAL 288 (30% from fat); FAT 9.5g (sat 3.4g); PRO 12.2g; CARB 44.4g; FIB 7g; CHOL 15mg; IRON 2.9mg; SOD 486mg; CALC 161mg

BAKED POTATOES WITH MUSHROOM STROGANOFF

POINTS value: 5

PREP: 12 minutes ■ COOK: 1 hour and 12 minutes

You can find small baking potatoes sold in bulk 5-pound bags at your supermarket.

- 4 (6-ounce) baking potatoes
- 1 tablespoon butter
- 1 cup chopped onion
- 1 garlic clove, minced
- 8 ounces presliced exotic mushroom blend (such as shiitake, cremini, and oyster)
- 1½ cups organic vegetable broth (such as Swanson Certified Organic)
- ½ cup dry sherry
- 1 tablespoon tomato paste
- 2 teaspoons Worcestershire sauce
- ¼ teaspoon salt
- ¼ teaspoon pepper
- 2½ tablespoons water
- 2 tablespoons all-purpose flour
- ½ cup light sour cream
- 2 tablespoons chopped fresh parsley

1. Preheat oven to 400°.
2. Rinse potatoes; pierce several times with a fork. Bake at 400° for 1 hour or until tender. Set aside.
3. Melt butter in a large nonstick skillet over medium heat. Add onion and garlic; cook until tender, stirring constantly. Add mushrooms, and cook 2 to 3 minutes or until tender. Stir in broth and next 5 ingredients.
4. Combine water and flour, stirring well with a whisk. Add mixture to pan. Bring to a boil, and cook until thick, stirring constantly. Stir in sour cream. Cook 30 seconds or until thoroughly heated.
5. Cut a lengthwise slit in each potato. Press ends of each potato towards center, pushing up pulp. Top potatoes evenly with mushroom mixture. Sprinkle evenly with parsley. YIELD: 4 SERVINGS (SERVING SIZE: 1 POTATO AND ¾ CUP MUSHROOM MIXTURE).

PER SERVING: CAL 287 (18% from fat); FAT 5.8g (sat 3.9g); PRO 8.1g; CARB 50.9g; FIB 5.4g; CHOL 8mg; IRON 2.4mg; SOD 460mg; CALC 40mg

SPANISH POTATO TORTILLA

POINTS value: 6

PREP: 3 minutes ■ **COOK:** 39 minutes

This Southwestern version of an Italian frittata is good served hot or at room temperature.

- 3 cups peeled, thinly sliced baking potato (about 1¼ pounds)
- 1 tablespoon olive oil, divided
- 1 cup thinly sliced onion
- ½ teaspoon salt, divided
- ½ teaspoon black pepper, divided
- 4 large eggs
- 2 large egg whites
- ¼ teaspoon smoked paprika or regular paprika
- ¼ cup (1 ounce) grated fresh Parmesan cheese
- 2 tablespoons minced fresh parsley

1. Place potato in a large nonstick skillet. Add just enough water to cover (about 2½ cups). Bring water to a boil over medium-high heat. Reduce heat; simmer 9 minutes, uncovered, just until potato is tender, stirring occasionally. Drain and transfer to a large bowl.

2. Heat 1 teaspoon oil in pan over medium heat. Add onion, ¼ teaspoon salt, and ¼ teaspoon pepper. Sauté 5 minutes or until lightly browned, stirring occasionally.

3. Combine eggs, egg whites, paprika, remaining ¼ teaspoon salt, and remaining ¼ teaspoon pepper in a large bowl, stirring with a whisk. Add potato and onion, stirring gently to combine.

4. Preheat oven to 350°.

5. Heat remaining 2 teaspoons oil in a 10- to 11-inch ovenproof skillet over medium heat. Add potato mixture, smoothing into an even layer. Cook 1 minute without stirring. Bake at 350° for 20 minutes or until lightly browned and center is set. Remove from oven.

6. Preheat broiler.

7. Sprinkle tortilla with cheese. Broil 2 minutes or until cheese melts and is lightly browned. Invert tortilla onto a serving plate, and sprinkle evenly with parsley. YIELD: 4 SERVINGS (SERVING SIZE: 1 WEDGE).

PER SERVING: CAL 270 (33% from fat); FAT 10g (sat 2.9g); PRO 13.1g; CARB 32.7g; FIB 3.4g; CHOL 216mg; IRON 2.8mg; SOD 476mg; CALC 105mg

BUTTERNUT SQUASH LASAGNA

POINTS value: 7

PREP: 17 minutes ■ **COOK:** 1 hour and 15 minutes ■ **OTHER:** 15 minutes

This creamy lasagna earned our Test Kitchens' highest rating. If the squash is too large for your microwave, cook one half for 7½ minutes, and then repeat with the other half.

- 1 teaspoon ground coriander
- 1 teaspoon salt, divided
- ¼ teaspoon ground red pepper
- 1 (3-pound) butternut squash, halved and seeded
- 2 tablespoons butter
- 2 cups chopped leek
- 1 garlic clove, minced
- 1 tablespoon chopped fresh sage
- ⅓ cup all-purpose flour
- 4½ cups 2% reduced-fat milk, divided
- ½ teaspoon ground nutmeg
- Cooking spray
- 9 no-boil lasagna noodles
- 1½ cups (6 ounces) shredded light 6-cheese Italian blend cheese, divided

1. Preheat oven to 350°.

2. Combine coriander, ½ teaspoon salt, and red pepper in a small bowl. Place squash, cut sides down, in an 11 x 8–inch baking dish. Microwave at HIGH 15 minutes; cool. Scoop out pulp; cut into chunks. Place squash in a medium bowl; sprinkle with coriander mixture.

3. Melt butter in a large nonstick skillet over medium heat. Add leek and garlic; sauté 4 minutes or until leek is tender. Add sage; cook 30 seconds. Add leek mixture to squash mixture, stirring gently.

4. Combine flour and ½ cup milk in a small bowl, stirring until smooth. Place remaining 4 cups milk in a large saucepan over medium heat. Gradually add flour mixture to milk, stirring constantly with a whisk. Cook 15 minutes or until thick, stirring frequently. Stir in remaining ½ teaspoon salt and nutmeg. Reserve ½ cup milk mixture. Add remaining milk mixture to squash mixture.

5. Spread 2 cups squash mixture in an 11 x 8–inch baking dish coated with cooking spray. Arrange 3 lasagna noodles over squash mixture; top with 2 cups squash mixture and ½ cup cheese. Repeat layers. Top with remaining lasagna noodles. Pour reserved milk mixture over noodles.

6. Cover with nonstick foil. Bake at 350° for 30 minutes. Uncover and top with remaining ½ cup cheese.

Bake an additional 10 minutes or until golden. Let stand 15 minutes before serving. YIELD: 8 SERVINGS (SERVING SIZE: ⅛ OF CASSEROLE).

PER SERVING: CAL 332 (24% from fat); FAT 8.9g (sat 5.1g); PRO 16.7g; CARB 48.2g; FIB 4.3g; CHOL 25mg; IRON 2.7mg; SOD 540mg; CALC 407mg

BUTTERNUT SQUASH RISOTTO

POINTS value: 6

PREP: 8 minutes ■ COOK: 48 minutes

Arborio rice is an Italian-grown rice characterized by short, fat grains with a high starch content. The increased starch content is responsible for the creamy texture for which risotto is famous.

1 (12-ounce) package frozen butternut squash (such as McKenzie's)
3 cups fat-free, less-sodium chicken broth
2 teaspoons olive oil
1 onion, diced
2 garlic cloves, minced
1 cup Arborio rice
½ cup dry white wine
1 tablespoon chopped fresh sage
½ cup (2 ounces) grated fresh Parmesan cheese
⅛ teaspoon freshly ground black pepper

1. Cook squash according to package directions, and set aside.
2. Pour chicken broth into a 4-cup glass measure or microwave-safe bowl; microwave at HIGH 4 minutes. Set aside.
3. While broth heats, heat oil in a large saucepan over medium heat; add onion and garlic. Sauté 5 minutes or until onion is tender. Stir in rice. Add wine, and cook 1 to 2 minutes or until wine is absorbed, stirring constantly. Add hot broth, ½ cup at a time, stirring constantly until each portion of broth is absorbed before adding the next (about 33 minutes total). Stir in cooked squash, sage, cheese, and pepper; cook 1 to 2 minutes or until thoroughly heated and cheese melts. YIELD: 4 SERVINGS (SERVING SIZE: ABOUT 1 CUP).

PER SERVING: CAL 311 (23% from fat); FAT 8g (sat 2.4g); PRO 11.3g; CARB 50.1g; FIB 3.3g; CHOL 9mg; IRON 1mg; SOD 782mg; CALC 140mg

Pumpkin Risotto: Substitute 1 cup canned pumpkin for the butternut squash.

POINTS value: 5

PER SERVING: CAL 280 (19% from fat); FAT 6g (sat 2.1g); PRO 11.6g; CARB 47.3g; FIB 5g; CHOL 9mg; IRON 0.8mg; SOD 587mg; CALC 135mg

MEDITERRANEAN ONION AND TOMATO TART

POINTS value: 6

PREP: 19 minutes ■ COOK: 26 minutes

Refrigerated pizza dough generally makes a soft crust. However, if you prebake the crust on a pan in a superhot oven, add the toppings, and then place the pizza directly on the oven rack to finish baking, you'll get a crispy crust with a soft interior.

1 (13.8-ounce) refrigerated pizza crust dough
Cooking spray
2 teaspoons olive oil, divided
3 onions, thinly sliced (about 1 pound)
1 teaspoon sugar
5 large plum tomatoes, cut into ¼-inch-thick slices
2 large garlic cloves, minced
1 teaspoon dried herbes de Provence, crumbled
2 teaspoons sherry vinegar
¾ cup (3 ounces) grated fresh Parmesan cheese, divided
⅓ cup coarsely chopped kalamata olives
Chopped fresh basil (optional)

1. Preheat oven to 425°.
2. Roll out pizza dough to a 14 x 11–inch rectangle on a large baking sheet coated with cooking spray. Bake on bottom rack of oven at 425° for 9 minutes.
3. While pizza dough bakes, heat 1 teaspoon oil in a large nonstick skillet over medium heat. Add onion and sugar; cook 10 minutes or until tender, stirring frequently. While onion cooks, arrange tomato slices in a single layer between several layers of paper towels; pat gently to remove excess moisture.
4. When onion is tender, stir in garlic and herbes de Provence; cook 5 minutes, stirring constantly. Stir in vinegar, and remove from heat.
5. Sprinkle prebaked crust with 2 tablespoons cheese, and top with onion mixture. Sprinkle with olives and remaining 10 tablespoons cheese. Drizzle with remaining 1 teaspoon oil.
6. Remove pizza from baking sheet, and place pizza directly on bottom rack of oven. Bake at 425° for 11 minutes or until cheese is golden. Sprinkle with basil, if desired. YIELD: 6 SERVINGS (SERVING SIZE: 1 PIECE).

PER SERVING: CAL 302 (27% from fat); FAT 9g (sat 2.3g); PRO 11.4g; CARB 43.9g; FIB 3.5g; CHOL 9mg; IRON 2.4mg; SOD 725mg; CALC 145mg

TOP-SHELF VEGGIE PIZZA

POINTS value: 6

pictured on page 64

PREP: 16 minutes ■ **COOK:** 22 minutes
■ **OTHER:** 45 minutes

Look for fresh pizza dough in your supermarket's bakery, or purchase it from your local pizza parlor.

    16 ounces pizza dough
    Olive oil–flavored cooking spray
     1 (1-ounce) package dried porcini mushrooms
     1 tablespoon olive oil, divided
     1 tablespoon yellow cornmeal
     1 garlic clove, minced
     1 red bell pepper, cut into thin strips
     1 (12-ounce) jar marinated quartered artichoke hearts, drained
     1 cup (4 ounces) shredded part-skim mozzarella cheese
    ¼ cup chopped fresh basil (optional)

1. Place dough in a large bowl coated with cooking spray; turn to coat top. Cover and let rise in a warm place (85°), free from drafts, 45 minutes or until doubled in size. (Gently press two fingers into dough. If indentation remains, dough has risen enough.)
2. Preheat oven to 425°.
3. Rinse mushrooms with cold water; drain. Place mushrooms in water to cover in a saucepan. Bring to a boil, and cook 2 to 5 minutes. Drain mushrooms in a colander, discarding liquid. Chop mushrooms, and set aside.
4. Brush a 15-inch round pizza pan with 1 teaspoon oil; sprinkle with cornmeal. Roll dough into a 15-inch circle on a floured surface; place on prepared pan. Brush dough with remaining 2 teaspoons oil, and sprinkle with garlic. Pierce surface liberally with a fork (do not allow dough to rise). Bake on bottom rack of oven at 425° for 15 minutes or until lightly browned.
5. While pizza dough bakes, heat a large nonstick skillet over medium-high heat; coat pan with cooking spray. Add bell pepper, and sauté 4 minutes. Add prepared mushrooms and artichokes; sauté 1 minute.
6. Top pizza crust with bell pepper mixture, leaving a ½-inch border, and sprinkle with cheese. Remove pizza from pizza pan, and place pizza directly on bottom rack of oven. Bake at 425° for 4 minutes or until cheese melts. Sprinkle with basil, if desired. YIELD: 6 SERVINGS (SERVING SIZE: 1 SLICE).

PER SERVING: CAL 324 (26% from fat); FAT 9.4g (sat 3g); PRO 14.2g; CARB 45g; FIB 4.9g; CHOL 15mg; IRON 3.9mg; SOD 749mg; CALC 118mg

PITA PIZZAS

POINTS value: 6

PREP: 10 minutes ■ **COOK:** 6½ minutes

For an appetizer, use kitchen shears to cut each pita pizza into 6 wedges after baking. Each wedge has a **POINTS** value of 1.

     4 (6-inch) whole wheat pitas
    ¾ cup tomato-basil pasta sauce (such as Classico)
    ¼ teaspoon crushed red pepper
     2 cups packed baby spinach, coarsely chopped
     8 sun-dried tomato halves, chopped (¼ cup)
     8 pitted kalamata olives, chopped
     1 cup (4 ounces) shredded part-skim mozzarella cheese

1. Preheat broiler.
2. Place pitas on a foil-lined broiler pan. Broil 2½ minutes or until browned, turning once. Remove from oven.
3. Reduce oven temperature to 475°.
4. Spread 3 tablespoons pasta sauce on each pita; top evenly with remaining ingredients. Bake at 475° for 4 minutes or until cheese melts. Serve immediately. YIELD: 4 SERVINGS (SERVING SIZE: 1 PITA PIZZA).

PER SERVING: CAL 281 (26% from fat); FAT 8.2g (sat 3.9g); PRO 15.3g; CARB 39g; FIB 4.6g; CHOL 15mg; IRON 2.9mg; SOD 563mg; CALC 303mg

PARMESAN POLENTA WEDGES WITH RATATOUILLE

POINTS value: 7

PREP: 25 minutes ■ **COOK:** 37 minutes

Polenta is made from corn and is a delicious staple in Italian cuisine. This fat-free, cholesterol-free, high-fiber food helps bring the fiber content of this dish to 10 grams per serving, which is more than a third of the recommended daily intake.

     3 cups water
     1 cup instant polenta
    ⅔ cup grated fresh Parmesan cheese, divided
    ¾ teaspoon salt, divided
    Cooking spray
     1 (1-pound) eggplant, cut into ½-inch cubes
     1 large red bell pepper, seeded and cut into ½-inch cubes
     1 large zucchini, cut into ¾-inch cubes
     2 tablespoons minced fresh or 2 teaspoons dried thyme or rosemary
     1 tablespoon olive oil
     2 cups reduced-sodium marinara sauce (such as L.E. Roselli's)
     3 garlic cloves, minced

1. Bring 3 cups water to a boil in a heavy saucepan. Add polenta, stirring with a whisk; cook 2 to 3 minutes over medium-low heat or until mixture is slightly thick, stirring constantly. Stir in ⅓ cup Parmesan cheese and ¼ teaspoon salt. Spoon polenta into a pie plate coated with cooking spray. Cool.

2. Preheat oven to 450°.

3. Combine eggplant and next 4 ingredients in a large bowl, tossing to coat. Add remaining ½ teaspoon salt.

4. Arrange vegetables in a single layer in a roasting pan coated with cooking spray. Bake at 450° for 20 minutes or until vegetables are tender.

5. Transfer vegetables to a Dutch oven; add marinara sauce and garlic. Bring to a simmer, and cook over medium heat 10 minutes.

6. Preheat broiler.

7. Sprinkle polenta evenly with remaining ⅓ cup cheese. Broil 3 minutes or until lightly browned. Serve polenta with ratatouille. YIELD: 4 SERVINGS (SERVING SIZE: 2 POLENTA WEDGES AND 1 CUP RATATOUILLE).

PER SERVING: CAL 339 (31% from fat); FAT 11.5g (sat 2.8g); PRO 11.6g; CARB 40.3g; FIB 10g; CHOL 12mg; IRON 0.8mg; SOD 894mg; CALC 169mg

CHEESE RAVIOLI LASAGNA

POINTS value: 8

PREP: 7 minutes ■ COOK: 49 minutes ■ OTHER: 10 minutes

Convenience products make this family-friendly dish easy to assemble, leaving you time to relax while it bakes.

- 2 (9-ounce) packages spinach and cheese ravioli (such as Monterey Pasta Company)
- ¾ cup matchstick-cut carrot
- 1½ cups chunky marinara sauce with mushrooms (such as Barilla)
- Cooking spray
- 1 cup part-skim ricotta cheese, divided
- 1 cup (4 ounces) shredded part-skim mozzarella cheese, divided

1. Preheat oven to 350°.

2. Cook ravioli according to package directions, omitting salt and fat. After ravioli has cooked for 3 minutes, add carrot; cook 1 minute. Drain. Combine ravioli mixture with marinara sauce in a medium bowl.

3. Layer one-third of pasta mixture in an 8 x 4–inch loaf pan coated with cooking spray; top with ⅓ cup ricotta cheese and ⅓ cup mozzarella cheese. Repeat layers twice.

4. Cover and bake at 350° for 35 minutes. Let stand 10 minutes before serving. YIELD: 6 SERVINGS (SERVING SIZE: ⅙ OF CASSEROLE).

PER SERVING: CAL 365 (32% from fat); FAT 12.9g (sat 7.4g); PRO 21.9g; CARB 41.5g; FIB 2.1g; CHOL 52mg; IRON 2.4mg; SOD 783mg; CALC 379mg

INDIVIDUAL ASPARAGUS QUICHES

POINTS value: 6

PREP: 19 minutes ■ COOK: 36 minutes ■ OTHER: 5 minutes

Move one oven rack to the second-from-the-top position before preheating your oven. This will prevent you from having to move a hot oven rack when you're ready to broil the quiches.

- ¼ pound asparagus, trimmed and cut into ⅓-inch-thick pieces (1 cup)
- 1 large egg
- 2 large egg whites
- ⅓ cup plus 2 tablespoons grated fresh Parmesan cheese, divided
- ⅓ cup light sour cream
- 3 tablespoons all-purpose flour
- ½ teaspoon salt
- 1½ cups 1% low-fat milk
- 2 teaspoons olive oil
- ½ cup chopped onion
- Cooking spray
- ½ cup shredded reduced-fat sharp Cheddar cheese

1. Preheat oven to 350°.

2. Cook asparagus in boiling water to cover in a medium saucepan 3 minutes or until crisp-tender; drain. Rinse under cold water, drain well, and set aside.

3. While asparagus cooks, combine egg and egg whites in a large bowl, stirring with a whisk. Add ⅓ cup Parmesan cheese, sour cream, flour, and salt; stir. Add milk, stirring until blended.

4. Heat oil over medium heat in pan. Add onion, and sauté 3 minutes. Add asparagus, and sauté 1 minute.

5. Divide asparagus mixture evenly among 4 (10-ounce) custard cups coated with cooking spray. Place cups on a jelly-roll pan. Sprinkle each custard cup evenly with Cheddar cheese. Pour egg mixture evenly over cheese; sprinkle evenly with remaining 2 tablespoons Parmesan cheese. Bake at 350° for 23 minutes.

6. Preheat broiler. Broil 5 minutes or until puffed and golden. Let stand 5 minutes before serving. YIELD: 4 SERVINGS (SERVING SIZE: 1 QUICHE).

PER SERVING: CAL 238 (48% from fat); FAT 12.7g (sat 6.5g); PRO 15.9g; CARB 14g; FIB 1.2g; CHOL 85mg; IRON 1.4mg; SOD 656mg; CALC 369mg

ASPARAGUS AND TOMATO FRITTATA

POINTS value: 4

PREP: 12 minutes ■ COOK: 17 minutes

2 small plum tomatoes, thinly sliced
1 (8-ounce) carton egg substitute
3 large eggs, lightly beaten
2 tablespoons 1% low-fat milk
2 tablespoons chopped fresh basil
¼ teaspoon salt
¼ teaspoon pepper
¾ cup (3 ounces) grated fresh Parmesan cheese, divided
1 teaspoon olive oil
Olive oil–flavored cooking spray
¾ cup chopped onion
½ pound asparagus, trimmed and cut into 2-inch pieces (about 1½ cups)
1 garlic clove, minced

1. Arrange tomato slices in a single layer between several layers of paper towels; pat gently to remove moisture.
2. Preheat broiler.
3. Combine egg substitute and next 5 ingredients in a bowl, stirring well with a whisk. Stir in ½ cup cheese.
4. Heat oil in a medium ovenproof skillet coated with cooking spray over medium–high heat. Add onion; cook 3 minutes or until onion is crisp-tender, stirring constantly. Add asparagus and garlic; cook 4 minutes or until vegetables are tender, stirring often. Pour egg mixture over vegetables in pan. Reduce heat to medium-low; cook 5 minutes or until edges are set.
5. Top with tomato slices; sprinkle with remaining ¼ cup cheese. Broil 4 minutes or until set and lightly browned. YIELD: 4 SERVINGS (SERVING SIZE: 1 WEDGE).

PER SERVING: CAL 193 (44% from fat); FAT 9.4g (sat 4g); PRO 18.3g; CARB 8.8g; FIB 2.2g; CHOL 172mg; IRON 3.3mg; SOD 551mg; CALC 242mg

ABOUT ASPARAGUS

While green is the most common variety of asparagus in supermarkets, you may be able to find white and purple varieties at farmers' markets and specialty stores. White asparagus has a mild flavor because it's harvested before the vegetable begins to develop chlorophyll, which is what gives asparagus its green color. The white variety is more fibrous but has fewer phytonutrients and less vitamins A and C than green. Purple asparagus is a tender, slightly sweet variety that is a good option for those who don't like the grassier flavor of green asparagus.

TOFU, CORN, AND BLACK BEAN ENCHILADAS

POINTS value: 5

PREP: 12 minutes ■ COOK: 18 minutes ■ OTHER: 5 minutes

To properly drain tofu, slice it, and lay each slice flat between paper towels. Place a heavy skillet or cutting board on top; let it sit for 10 minutes, pressing occasionally. Draining off excess moisture allows the tofu to absorb more flavor while cooking.

1 (14-ounce) package firm tofu, drained and cut into 1-inch cubes
2 tablespoons reduced-sodium taco seasoning, divided
1 tablespoon canola oil, divided
⅓ cup ⅓-less-fat cream cheese, softened
1 tablespoon fat-free milk
1 cup chopped onion
1 teaspoon bottled minced garlic
1 cup frozen whole-kernel corn
1 (15-ounce) can no-salt-added black beans, rinsed and drained
½ cup loosely packed cilantro leaves
8 (8-inch) whole wheat tortillas
Cooking spray
1 cup refrigerated fresh salsa
⅔ cup reduced-fat shredded sharp Cheddar cheese
Light sour cream (optional)

1. Preheat oven to 400°.
2. Combine tofu and 1 tablespoon taco seasoning in a small bowl; toss to coat.
3. Heat 2 teaspoons oil in a large skillet over medium-high heat. Add tofu; cook 2 to 3 minutes or until browned. Remove from pan; keep warm.
4. While tofu cooks, combine cream cheese and milk in a small bowl; stir until creamy. Set aside.
5. Add remaining 1 teaspoon oil to pan; add onion and garlic. Cook 2 to 3 minutes or until onion is tender. Remove pan from heat. Add remaining 1 tablespoon taco seasoning to pan; stir in corn, black beans, cilantro, and cream cheese mixture. Gently stir in tofu.
6. Spoon about ½ cup tofu mixture down center of each tortilla; roll up. Arrange enchiladas, seam sides down, in a 13 x 9–inch baking dish coated with cooking spray. Top evenly with salsa; sprinkle with cheese.
7. Bake at 400° for 8 to 10 minutes or until cheese melts and is bubbly. Serve with sour cream, if desired.
YIELD: 8 SERVINGS (SERVING SIZE: 1 ENCHILADA).

PER SERVING: CAL 250 (51% from fat); FAT 14.2g (sat 3.3g); PRO 15.1g; CARB 21.8g; FIB 6.1g; CHOL 14mg; IRON 2.2mg; SOD 622mg; CALC 266mg

Steak Diane, *page 91*

meats

BEEF MOUSSAKA

POINTS value: 7

PREP: 17 minutes ■ **COOK:** 1 hour and 49 minutes
■ **OTHER:** 15 minutes

This dish, with its light béchamel sauce, is a healthier version
of the traditional creamy, rich Greek recipe. Serve with a simple
green salad and crusty bread.

>   1 large eggplant (about 1¾ pounds)
> **Cooking spray**
>   1½ pounds ground round
>   1 teaspoon olive oil
>   1½ cups chopped onion
>   2 garlic cloves, minced
>   1 (28-ounce) can diced tomatoes, undrained
>   ¾ cup dry red wine
>   1 teaspoon salt
>   1 teaspoon dried oregano
>   ¼ teaspoon ground cinnamon
>   ¼ teaspoon freshly ground black pepper
>   2 cups 1% low-fat milk, divided
>   ¼ cup all-purpose flour
>   ⅛ teaspoon ground nutmeg
>   ¼ cup (1 ounce) grated fresh Parmesan cheese, divided
>   ½ teaspoon salt
>   1 large egg, lightly beaten

1. Preheat broiler.

2. Cut eggplant into ½-inch-thick slices; cut slices in
half. Arrange eggplant on a baking sheet coated with
cooking spray. Broil 7 minutes on each side or until
browned; set aside.

3. Heat a large nonstick skillet over medium-high heat.
Add beef; cook 7 minutes or until browned, stirring to
crumble. Drain. Set aside, and keep warm.

4. Heat oil in pan over medium-high heat. Add onion
and garlic; sauté 4 minutes or until tender. Return beef
to pan; add tomatoes and next 5 ingredients. Bring to
a boil; reduce heat to medium, and cook 20 minutes or
until liquid almost evaporates.

5. Reduce oven temperature to 350°.

6. Gradually combine 1 cup milk with flour in a
medium saucepan over medium heat, stirring with a
whisk. Add remaining 1 cup milk and nutmeg, stirring
with a whisk. Cook 8 minutes or until mixture thickens, stirring constantly with a whisk. Remove from
heat; add 3 tablespoons cheese and ½ teaspoon salt.
Gradually add ½ cup hot milk mixture to egg, stirring
constantly with a whisk. Return milk mixture to pan;
stir well.

7. Arrange eggplant in a 13 x 9–inch baking dish coated
with cooking spray. Spread half of beef mixture over
eggplant; repeat layers. Spread béchamel sauce evenly
over beef mixture. Sprinkle remaining 1 tablespoon
cheese on top. Bake at 350° for 45 minutes or until
lightly browned. Let stand 15 minutes before serving.
YIELD: 8 SERVINGS (SERVING SIZE: ⅛ OF CASSEROLE).

PER SERVING: CAL 306 (46% from fat); FAT 15.6g (sat 6.2g); PRO 22.2g;
CARB 20g; FIB 5.7g; CHOL 89mg; IRON 3mg; SOD 701mg; CALC 158mg

CHIPOTLE MEAT LOAF

POINTS value: 6

PREP: 20 minutes ■ **COOK:** 1 hour ■ **OTHER:** 5 minutes

>   1 slice whole wheat double-fiber bread (such as Arnold)
>   ½ cup finely chopped onion
>   ½ cup finely chopped red bell pepper
>   ¼ cup chopped fresh cilantro
>   ¼ cup egg substitute
>   1 teaspoon salt
>   ½ teaspoon ground cumin
>   ½ teaspoon dried oregano
>   ½ teaspoon black pepper
>   1 cup ketchup, divided
>   2 teaspoons chipotle chiles, canned in adobo sauce,
>   chopped and divided
>   1 teaspoon adobo sauce
>   2 pounds ground sirloin
> **Cooking spray**
>   1 tablespoon honey
>   ½ teaspoon ground cumin

1. Preheat oven to 350°.

2. Place bread in a food processor; pulse 10 times or
until coarse crumbs measure ½ cup.

3. Combine breadcrumbs, onion, and next 7 ingredients. Stir in ½ cup ketchup, 1½ teaspoons chipotle chiles,
and adobo sauce in a large bowl. Add beef; stir until
blended. Shape beef mixture into an 8 x 4–inch loaf,
and place on a broiler pan coated with cooking spray.
Bake at 350° for 45 minutes.

4. While meat loaf bakes, combine remaining ½ cup
ketchup, honey, ½ teaspoon cumin, and remaining ½
teaspoon chipotle chiles in a small bowl; set aside.

5. Spread ketchup mixture over meat loaf. Bake an
additional 15 minutes or until a thermometer registers
160°. Let stand 5 minutes before slicing. **YIELD:** 8 SERV-
INGS (SERVING SIZE: 1 SLICE).

PER SERVING: CAL 261 (41% from fat); FAT 11.8g (sat 4.6g); PRO 24.8g;
CARB 14.2g; FIB 1.4g; CHOL 74mg; IRON 3.3mg; SOD 760mg; CALC 42mg

SWEET POTATO–TOPPED SHEPHERD'S PIE

POINTS value: 6

PREP: 32 minutes ■ **COOK:** 1 hour and 12 minutes

We combined Yukon Gold and sweet potatoes to create a topping that adds flavor and extra vitamins to your meal.

    1½ pounds ground sirloin
    1 cup chopped onion
    1 cup chopped carrot
    1 garlic clove, minced
    1 (14-ounce) can fat-free, less-sodium beef broth
    ¼ cup tomato paste
    1 tablespoon Worcestershire sauce
    ¾ teaspoon salt
    ½ teaspoon dried thyme
    1½ tablespoons all-purpose flour
    1½ tablespoons water
    ½ cup frozen chopped spinach, thawed and drained
    Cooking spray
    Sweet Potato Topping

1. Preheat oven to 375°.
2. Cook first 4 ingredients in a large nonstick skillet over medium–high heat 10 minutes, stirring to crumble beef. (Drain, if necessary, and return beef mixture to pan.) Add broth and next 4 ingredients. Bring to a boil; cover, reduce heat, and simmer 10 minutes.
3. Combine flour and 1½ tablespoons water in a small bowl. Stir flour mixture into beef mixture. Cook 2 minutes or until mixture thickens, stirring constantly. Stir in spinach.
4. Spoon beef mixture into a shallow 2-quart casserole dish coated with cooking spray. Top with Sweet Potato Topping. Bake at 375° for 30 minutes or until beef mixture is hot and potatoes begin to brown. Serve warm. YIELD: 8 SERVINGS (SERVING SIZE: ⅛ OF CASSEROLE).

PER SERVING: CAL 300 (35% from fat); FAT 11.7g (sat 5.4g); PRO 20.9g; CARB 27.8g; FIB 4.2g; CHOL 63mg; IRON 3mg; SOD 602mg; CALC 73mg

Sweet Potato Topping

POINTS value: 2

    3 cups cubed peeled Yukon Gold potato (about 1½ pounds)
    3 cups cubed peeled sweet potato
    ⅓ cup 1% low-fat milk
    2 tablespoons butter
    ½ teaspoon salt
    ⅛ teaspoon ground cinnamon (optional)

1. Place potato in a large saucepan; add water to cover. Bring to a boil; reduce heat, and simmer 10 to 15 minutes or until tender; drain. Place potato, milk, butter, salt, and, if desired, cinnamon in a large bowl. Beat with a mixer at medium speed until smooth. YIELD: 4 CUPS.

PER ½ CUP: CAL 115 (24% from fat); FAT 3.1g (sat 1.9g); PRO 2.2g; CARB 20.3g; FIB 2.3g; CHOL 8mg; IRON 0.5mg; SOD 187mg; CALC 31mg

SWEET POTATO NUTRITION

Sweet potatoes are rich in beta carotene and vitamins A, C, and E. One cup has more than six times the recommended amount of beta carotene, more than twice your daily vitamin A needs, and 50 percent of the Recommended Dietary Allowance (RDA) for vitamin C.

KOREAN BEEF

POINTS value: 4

PREP: 10 minutes ■ **COOK:** 12 minutes ■ **OTHER:** 2 hours

    ½ cup low-sodium soy sauce
    ½ cup finely chopped green onions
    ¼ cup rice wine vinegar
    2 tablespoons brown sugar
    2 teaspoons grated peeled fresh ginger
    2 teaspoons dark sesame oil
    1 garlic clove, minced
    ½ teaspoon crushed red pepper
    1 pound flank steak, trimmed
    Cooking spray

1. Combine first 8 ingredients in a bowl. Reserve ⅓ cup soy sauce mixture; set aside. Pour remaining soy sauce mixture into a large zip-top plastic bag. Add steak; seal bag, and refrigerate 2 to 4 hours.
2. Preheat broiler.
3. Remove steak from marinade, discarding marinade. Place steak on rack of a broiler pan coated with cooking spray. Broil 3 inches from heat 6 minutes on each side or until desired degree of doneness. Cut steak diagonally across grain into thin slices, and drizzle with reserved soy sauce mixture. YIELD: 4 SERVINGS (SERVING SIZE: 3 OUNCES STEAK AND ABOUT 1½ TABLESPOONS SAUCE).

PER SERVING: CAL 179 (38% from fat); FAT 7.5g (sat 2.9g); PRO 23.2g; CARB 2.6g; FIB 0.2g; CHOL 45mg; IRON 1.6mg; SOD 447mg; CALC 17mg

CARNE ASADA TACOS

POINTS value: 8

PREP: 27 minutes ■ **COOK:** 16 minutes
■ **OTHER:** 1 hour and 5 minutes

Carne asada is a Mexican recipe of marinated skirt or flank steak that is grilled, thinly sliced, and served on tortillas. This flavorful steak is delicious in burritos and salads or by itself.

- ⅓ cup chopped fresh cilantro
- ¼ cup sliced green onions
- ¼ cup fresh lime juice
- 3 garlic cloves, halved
- 1 jalapeño pepper, seeded and chopped
- 2 tablespoons white vinegar
- 1 tablespoon olive oil
- ¼ teaspoon salt
- ¼ teaspoon freshly ground black pepper
- 1 pound flank steak, trimmed
- 12 (6-inch) fat-free flour tortillas, warmed
- 2 cups shredded iceberg lettuce
- ¾ cup fresh salsa
- ¾ cup chopped avocado
- ¾ cup (3 ounces) shredded Monterey Jack cheese

1. Place first 9 ingredients in a blender; process until smooth. Transfer mixture to a large zip-top plastic bag. Add steak; seal bag, and marinate in refrigerator 1 to 5 hours, turning bag occasionally.
2. Prepare grill.
3. Remove steak from bag, discarding marinade. Place on grill rack, and grill 8 minutes on each side or until desired degree of doneness. Let steak stand 5 minutes. Cut steak diagonally across grain into thin slices.
4. Divide steak evenly among tortillas. Top each tortilla evenly with lettuce and remaining ingredients. YIELD: 6 SERVINGS (SERVING SIZE: 2 TACOS).

PER SERVING: CAL 395 (34% from fat); FAT 14.8g (sat 5.2g); PRO 25.2g; CARB 40.1g; FIB 3.3g; CHOL 42mg; IRON 1.4mg; SOD 795mg; CALC 120mg

SLICING FLANK STEAK

The secret to serving tender, juicy flank steak is in how you slice the steak. First, transfer the cooked steak to a cutting board, and let it stand about 5 minutes to redistribute the juices. Use a very sharp knife, and cut the steak diagonally (at an angle) across the grain into thin slices, about ¼ inch thick. Flank steak tends to toughen as it stands, so you'll want to slice the entire steak immediately after it has finished cooking.

STEAK AU POIVRE

POINTS value: 5

PREP: 2 minutes ■ **COOK:** 20 minutes

This classic French dish's name is easily translated to mean "pepper steak."

- 4 (4-ounce) beef tenderloin steaks, trimmed (about 1½ inches thick)
- 2 teaspoons coarsely ground black pepper
- ½ teaspoon salt
- 2 teaspoons olive oil
- ⅓ cup minced shallots (about 6 medium)
- 1 garlic clove, minced
- 2 teaspoons all-purpose flour
- 1 cup fat-free, less-sodium beef broth
- ¼ cup light sour cream

1. Sprinkle both sides of steaks with pepper and salt.
2. Heat oil in a large nonstick skillet over medium-high heat. Add steaks, and cook 3 to 4 minutes on each side or until desired degree of doneness. Transfer steaks to a serving plate; cover and keep warm.
3. Add shallots and garlic to pan. Cook 2 minutes over medium heat, stirring constantly. Sprinkle flour over shallot mixture, and cook 2 minutes, stirring often. Gradually add broth, stirring constantly. Bring to a simmer, and cook 5 minutes.
4. Add sour cream, stirring with a whisk. Simmer 2 minutes or until thoroughly heated. Spoon sauce over steaks. YIELD: 4 SERVINGS (SERVING SIZE: 1 STEAK AND ABOUT ¼ CUP SAUCE).

PER SERVING: CAL 198 (49% from fat); FAT 10.8g (sat 4g); PRO 19.5g; CARB 4.8g; FIB 0.4g; CHOL 59mg; IRON 2.7mg; SOD 448mg; CALC 31mg

FILET MIGNON WITH SHERRIED SHIITAKES

POINTS value: 5

PREP: 10 minutes ■ **COOK:** 13 minutes

- Cooking spray
- 2 (3½-ounce) packages shiitake mushrooms, stems removed and sliced
- 1 large shallot, diced
- ½ cup dry sherry, divided
- 4 teaspoons light butter
- ½ teaspoon salt, divided
- 4 (4-ounce) beef tenderloin steaks (about ¾ to 1 inch thick), trimmed
- ½ teaspoon coarsely ground black pepper

1. Heat a large nonstick skillet over medium–high heat; coat pan with cooking spray. Add mushrooms and shallots; coat vegetables with cooking spray. Sauté 3 minutes or until mushrooms are tender. Add ¼ cup sherry; cook 10 seconds or until liquid almost evaporates. Remove from heat; stir in butter and ¼ teaspoon salt. Place in a small bowl, and keep warm.

2. Sprinkle steaks evenly with remaining ¼ teaspoon salt and pepper. Heat pan over medium–high heat; coat pan with cooking spray. Add steaks, and cook 2 to 3 minutes on each side or until desired degree of doneness. Remove steaks from pan; keep warm.

3. Add remaining ¼ cup sherry to pan, scraping pan to loosen browned bits. Pour evenly over steaks, and serve with mushrooms. YIELD: 4 SERVINGS (SERVING SIZE: 1 STEAK, ¼ CUP MUSHROOMS, AND ABOUT ½ TABLESPOON PAN JUICES).

PER SERVING: CAL 227 (45% from fat); FAT 11.4g (sat 4.8g); PRO 24.9g; CARB 4.2g; FIB 0.6g; CHOL 75mg; IRON 4.1mg; SOD 384mg; CALC 15mg

STEAK DIANE

POINTS value: 4

pictured on page 129

PREP: 13 minutes ■ COOK: 12 minutes

  1 tablespoon butter
  6 (4-ounce) beef tenderloin steaks (about 1 inch thick)
  ½ teaspoon salt, divided
  ¼ teaspoon freshly ground black pepper
  ⅓ cup minced shallots (about 6 medium)
  1 garlic clove, minced
  1 tablespoon Worcestershire sauce
  2 tablespoons fresh lemon juice
  2 tablespoons brandy
  2 tablespoons fat-free, less-sodium beef broth
  1 teaspoon Dijon mustard
  2 tablespoons chopped fresh parsley (optional)

1. Melt butter in a large nonstick skillet over medium–high heat. Sprinkle steaks with ¼ teaspoon salt and pepper. Add steaks to pan; cook 4 to 5 minutes on each side or until desired degree of doneness. Remove steaks from pan; keep warm.

2. Add shallots and garlic to pan. Reduce heat to medium, and cook 2 minutes or until soft, stirring occasionally.

3. Combine Worcestershire sauce and next 4 ingredients in a bowl, stirring with a whisk. Add Worcestershire mixture to shallot mixture; reduce heat, and simmer 2 minutes or until slightly thick. Stir in remaining ¼ teaspoon salt. Spoon sauce evenly over steaks.

Sprinkle evenly with parsley, if desired. YIELD: 6 SERVINGS (SERVING SIZE: 1 STEAK AND 1⅓ TABLESPOONS SAUCE).

PER SERVING: CAL 178 (47% from fat); FAT 9.3g (sat 4g); PRO 18.3g; CARB 2.9g; FIB 0.2g; CHOL 59mg; IRON 2.8mg; SOD 306mg; CALC 15mg

PORT AND SPICE–BRAISED BEEF ROAST

POINTS value: 5

PREP: 12 minutes ■ COOK: 2 hours and 58 minutes

  1 tablespoon ground coriander
  1 tablespoon ground cumin
  ½ teaspoon salt
  ½ teaspoon black pepper
  ⅛ teaspoon ground red pepper
  1 (2-pound) boneless chuck roast, trimmed
  2 teaspoons olive oil
  2 carrots, chopped
  2 celery stalks, chopped
  1 onion, chopped
  6 garlic cloves, minced
  1 cup ruby port or other sweet red wine
  1 cup fat-free, less-sodium beef broth
  1½ tablespoons cold water
  1 tablespoon all-purpose flour

1. Preheat oven to 325°.

2. Combine first 5 ingredients in a small bowl. Rub 1 tablespoon spice mixture on both sides of roast. Set remaining spice mixture aside.

3. Heat oil in a large nonstick skillet over medium–high heat. Add roast, and cook 8 minutes on each side or until browned. Place roast in a large Dutch oven.

4. Add carrot, celery, and onion to pan; sauté 5 minutes. Stir in garlic and remaining spice mixture; sauté 1 minute. Add port and broth; bring to a boil, scraping pan to loosen browned bits. Pour mixture over roast. Cover and bake at 325° for 2½ to 3 hours or until roast is very tender.

5. Remove roast from Dutch oven; keep warm. Strain cooking liquid into a measuring cup, discarding solids. Skim off fat. Place liquid in a small saucepan, and bring to a boil over medium–high heat. Combine 1½ tablespoons water and flour in a small bowl, stirring with a whisk until smooth. Slowly add flour mixture to cooking liquid. Reduce heat to medium, and simmer 2 minutes or until thick. Serve roast with gravy. YIELD: 8 SERVINGS (SERVING SIZE: 3 OUNCES ROAST AND 1 TABLESPOON GRAVY).

PER SERVING: CAL 223 (46% from fat); FAT 11.5g (sat 3.5g); PRO 22.6g; CARB 6.2g; FIB 1.4g; CHOL 70mg; IRON 3.3mg; SOD 300mg; CALC 34mg

MOROCCAN CINNAMON BEEF

POINTS value: 7

PREP: 12 minutes ■ **COOK:** 1 hour and 20 minutes
■ **OTHER:** 5 minutes

1 (14½-ounce) can fat-free, less-sodium beef
   broth
1 cup water
3 tablespoons tomato paste
1½ teaspoons ground cinnamon
½ teaspoon ground cumin
½ teaspoon curry powder
⅛ teaspoon ground cloves
2 teaspoons canola oil, divided
1 cup coarsely chopped onion
½ cup chopped celery
3 garlic cloves, minced
1½ pounds lean boneless top sirloin, trimmed
   and cut into 1-inch cubes
2 tablespoons all-purpose flour
½ cup raisins
½ teaspoon salt
¼ teaspoon freshly ground black pepper
1½ cups water
1 cup uncooked couscous
⅓ cup sliced green onions

1. Combine first 7 ingredients in a medium bowl, stirring well with a whisk.
2. Heat 1 teaspoon oil in a Dutch oven over medium-
high heat. Add onion, celery, and garlic; sauté 5 to 6
minutes or until tender, stirring frequently. Remove
from pan, and set aside.
3. Heat remaining 1 teaspoon oil in pan over medium-
high heat; add beef. Cook 8 to 9 minutes or until
browned on all sides, stirring occasionally.
4. Sprinkle flour over beef, stirring until coated. Gradually add broth mixture, stirring until smooth. Add
reserved vegetables, raisins, salt, and pepper. Bring to a
boil; cover, reduce heat, and simmer 1 hour, stirring
occasionally.
5. While beef mixture simmers, bring 1½ cups water
to a boil in a medium saucepan. Stir in couscous.
Remove from heat; cover and let stand 5 minutes or
until liquid is absorbed. Fluff with a fork; keep warm.
Serve beef mixture over couscous. Sprinkle each serving with green onions. **YIELD: 6 SERVINGS (SERVING SIZE:
ABOUT ¾ CUP BEEF MIXTURE, ½ CUP COUSCOUS, AND ABOUT 1
TABLESPOON GREEN ONIONS).**

PER SERVING: CAL 371 (22% from fat); FAT 9.1g (sat 2.8g); PRO 31.6g;
CARB 39.9g; FIB 3.6g; CHOL 65mg; IRON 3.8mg; SOD 460mg; CALC 47mg

MUSTARD AND MINT–CRUSTED LAMB CHOPS ☑

POINTS value: 8

PREP: 8 minutes ■ **COOK:** 12 minutes ■ **OTHER:** 1 hour

These tender chops go well with asparagus and mashed
potatoes to make an elegant meal any day of the week.

3 tablespoons Dijon mustard
2 tablespoons fresh lemon juice
1 tablespoon chopped fresh mint
2 teaspoons olive oil
½ teaspoon salt
¼ teaspoon garlic powder
¼ teaspoon black pepper
8 (4-ounce) lamb loin chops, trimmed
Cooking spray

1. Combine first 7 ingredients in a large zip-top plastic
bag. Add lamb, and seal bag. Marinate in refrigerator
1 hour.
2. Prepare grill.
3. Remove lamb from bag, reserving marinade. Place
lamb on grill rack coated with cooking spray. Grill 6
to 7 minutes on each side or until desired degree of
doneness, basting frequently with reserved marinade.
YIELD: 4 SERVINGS (SERVING SIZE: 2 CHOPS).

PER SERVING: CAL 325 (42% from fat); FAT 15.3g (sat 5g); PRO 40.4g;
CARB 3.2g; FIB 0.1g; CHOL 128mg; IRON 2.8mg; SOD 674mg; CALC 28mg

MOROCCAN LAMB WITH TOMATO CHUTNEY

POINTS value: 5

pictured on page 131

PREP: 13 minutes ■ **COOK:** 45 minutes
■ **OTHER:** 8 hours and 10 minutes

Garam masala, which can contain up to 12 spices, gives this
lamb a warm flavor that pairs well with the mild sweetness of
the chutney.

1 (2½-pound) rolled boneless leg of lamb
1½ tablespoons olive oil
2 tablespoons garam masala
2 teaspoons sugar
2 teaspoons grated fresh orange rind
½ teaspoon salt
3 garlic cloves, thinly sliced
Cooking spray
Tomato Chutney

1. Unroll lamb, and trim fat. Brush both sides of lamb with oil. Combine garam masala and next 3 ingredients in a small bowl. Rub spice mixture on both sides of lamb. Reroll lamb; secure at 1-inch intervals with twine. Make several small slits in lamb, and stuff each slit with garlic slices. Cover and refrigerate 8 hours or overnight.
2. Preheat oven to 425°.
3. Place roast on rack of a broiler pan coated with cooking spray. Bake at 425° for 15 minutes. Reduce oven temperature to 325°, and bake 30 to 40 minutes or until desired degree of doneness. Let stand 10 minutes before slicing. Serve with Tomato Chutney. YIELD: 10 SERVINGS (SERVING SIZE: 3 OUNCES LAMB AND ABOUT 1½ TABLESPOONS CHUTNEY).

PER SERVING: CAL 246 (35% from fat); FAT 9.6g (sat 2.8g); PRO 22.5g; CARB 17.9g; FIB 2.5g; CHOL 64mg; IRON 2.8mg; SOD 392mg; CALC 46mg

Tomato Chutney
POINTS value: 0

- 1 tablespoon canola oil
- 2 teaspoons mustard seeds
- ¾ cup chopped onion
- 1 tablespoon minced peeled fresh ginger
- 2 garlic cloves, minced
- 2 (14.5-ounce) cans diced tomatoes, undrained
- ½ cup golden raisins
- ⅓ cup packed brown sugar
- ½ teaspoon salt
- ¼ teaspoon ground red pepper
- ¼ cup chopped fresh mint
- ½ teaspoon garam masala (optional)

1. Heat oil in a large nonstick skillet over medium-high heat. Add mustard seeds, and cook 1 minute or until seeds begin to pop. Add onion, ginger, and garlic, and cook 3 minutes. Add tomatoes and next 4 ingredients; bring to a boil. Reduce heat, and simmer 20 minutes or until mixture is slightly thick. Stir in mint and, if desired, garam masala. Serve warm or at room temperature. YIELD: 2 CUPS.

PER TABLESPOON: CAL 24 (19% from fat); FAT 0.5g (sat 0.1g); PRO 0.4g; CARB 5g; FIB 0.6g; CHOL 0mg; IRON 0.3mg; SOD 69mg; CALC 9mg

VEAL SCALLOPINI WITH SUN-DRIED TOMATO SAUCE
POINTS value: 7

PREP: 5 minutes ■ COOK: 14 minutes

If you use veal cutlets instead of scallopini, place the cutlets between 2 sheets of plastic wrap or wax paper; pound them with a meat mallet or small heavy skillet to ⅛-inch thickness.

- ⅔ cup fat-free, less-sodium chicken broth
- ½ cup dry white wine
- ⅓ cup julienne-cut sun-dried tomatoes, packed with oil
- 1 pound veal scallopini
- ½ teaspoon salt
- ½ teaspoon freshly ground black pepper
- ⅓ cup all-purpose flour
- 1 tablespoon extravirgin olive oil, divided
- 2 tablespoons finely chopped fresh parsley
- 2 teaspoons drained capers

1. Combine broth and wine in a 2-cup glass measure. Microwave at HIGH 1 minute or until hot; add sun-dried tomatoes. Set aside. Cut veal into 4 (4-ounce) pieces; flatten to ⅛-inch thickness, if necessary. Sprinkle veal evenly with salt and pepper; dredge in flour.
2. Heat 1½ teaspoons oil in a large nonstick skillet over medium-high heat. Add half of veal to pan; cook 45 to 60 seconds on each side or until browned. Transfer to a plate; keep warm. Repeat with remaining oil and veal.
3. Add broth mixture to pan; bring mixture to a boil over medium heat, scraping pan to loosen browned bits. Reduce heat, and simmer 6 minutes or until tomatoes are plump. Remove pan from heat; stir in parsley and capers. YIELD: 4 SERVINGS (SERVING SIZE: ABOUT 4 OUNCES VEAL AND 1 TABLESPOON SAUCE).

PER SERVING: CAL 272 (52% from fat); FAT 15.7g (sat 4.9g); PRO 21g; CARB 11g; FIB 1g; CHOL 74mg; IRON 1.7mg; SOD 506mg; CALC 30mg

ABOUT VEAL

Veal is the meat of a calf up to 3 months of age. The meat is very lean and tends to be tough if overcooked.

- Milk-fed veal is the most tender and flavorful. It is creamy pink and has a fine-grained texture.
- Formula-fed veal is also tender and pale, but it does not have as much flavor as milk-fed veal.
- Free-range veal is from a calf that has been weaned and fed on grass and grains. This veal is redder and has a meatier flavor.

COFFEE-MARINATED GRILLED PORK CHOPS

POINTS value: 4

PREP: 17 minutes ■ **COOK:** 8 minutes ■ **OTHER:** 8 hours

   1 cup freshly brewed coffee, chilled
   3 tablespoons dark brown sugar
   3 tablespoons molasses
   1 jalapeño pepper, seeded and minced
   1 tablespoon finely ground coffee beans
   1 tablespoon olive oil
   1 tablespoon fresh lime juice
   1 garlic clove, minced
 1½ teaspoons minced peeled fresh ginger
  ¾ teaspoon salt
  ¼ teaspoon black pepper
   4 (6-ounce) bone-in center-cut pork chops (about ¾ inch thick)
    Cooking spray

1. Combine first 11 ingredients in a small bowl. Place marinade and pork chops in a large zip-top plastic bag; seal bag. Marinate in refrigerator at least 8 hours.
2. Prepare grill.
3. Remove pork chops from bag, discarding marinade. Place pork chops on grill rack coated with cooking spray. Grill 4 to 5 minutes on each side or until desired degree of doneness. **YIELD: 4 SERVINGS (SERVING SIZE: 1 CHOP).**

PER SERVING: CAL 188 (35% from fat); FAT 7.4g (sat 2.6g); PRO 25.5g; CARB 3.2g; FIB 0g; CHOL 69mg; IRON 0.9mg; SOD 126mg; CALC 33mg

PORK CHOPS WITH GINGER-PEAR SAUCE

POINTS value: 6

PREP: 2 minutes ■ **COOK:** 20 minutes

A simple rice pilaf, such as Brown Rice and Onion Pilaf on page 154, is a nice companion for this saucy skillet entrée.

   1 teaspoon dried thyme
  ½ teaspoon salt
  ½ teaspoon ground sage
  ¼ teaspoon black pepper
   4 (4-ounce) boneless center-cut loin pork chops (1 inch thick)
   2 teaspoons olive oil
  ¾ cup pear nectar
   2 tablespoons ginger preserves (such as Duerr's)
   2 firm, ripe pears, cored and chopped
  ½ cup dried cranberries

1. Combine first 4 ingredients in a small bowl, and sprinkle over both sides of pork chops.
2. Heat oil in a large nonstick skillet over medium-high heat. Add pork chops, and cook 2 minutes on each side or just until browned. Add pear nectar and ginger preserves. Bring to a boil; cover, reduce heat, and simmer 3 minutes.
3. Add chopped pear and cranberries to pan. Bring to a boil; cover, reduce heat, and simmer 3 minutes or until pears are tender. Uncover and simmer 2 to 3 minutes or until liquid is slightly thick. **YIELD: 4 SERVINGS (SERVING SIZE: 1 CHOP AND ½ CUP SAUCE).**

PER SERVING: CAL 326 (25% from fat); FAT 9g (sat 2.7g); PRO 24.3g; CARB 37.1g; FIB 3.9g; CHOL 65mg; IRON 1.4mg; SOD 341mg; CALC 41mg

SICILIAN PORK CHOPS

POINTS value: 6

PREP: 10 minutes ■ **COOK:** 24 minutes

Sweet raisins, tart vinegar, and buttery pine nuts come together to make a sweet-and-sour chutney for the pork.

   5 teaspoons olive oil, divided
  ½ cup finely chopped shallots
  ½ cup white wine vinegar
  ¼ cup water
  ¼ cup golden raisins
   2 tablespoons brown sugar
   1 bay leaf
  ¾ teaspoon salt, divided
  ½ teaspoon freshly ground black pepper, divided
 1½ teaspoons toasted pine nuts
   1 teaspoon chopped fresh oregano
   4 (4-ounce) boneless loin pork chops (about 1 inch thick)

1. Heat 2 teaspoons oil in a large nonstick skillet over medium heat. Add shallots; sauté 4 minutes or until soft. Stir in vinegar, next 4 ingredients, ½ teaspoon salt, and ⅛ teaspoon pepper. Simmer 10 minutes or until liquid begins to thicken. Pour into a small bowl; discard bay leaf. Stir in nuts, oregano, and ⅛ teaspoon pepper. Cover; keep warm. Wipe pan with a paper towel.
2. Heat 1 tablespoon oil in pan over medium-high heat. Sprinkle pork chops with ¼ teaspoon salt and ¼ teaspoon pepper. Add pork chops to pan; cook 4 minutes on each side or until desired degree of doneness. Serve with chutney. **YIELD: 4 SERVINGS (SERVING SIZE: 1 CHOP AND 2 TABLESPOONS CHUTNEY).**

PER SERVING: CAL 277 (42% from fat); FAT 12.8g (sat 3.2g); PRO 24.9g; CARB 15.3g; FIB 0.6g; CHOL 65mg; IRON 1.5mg; SOD 492mg; CALC 45mg

PRUNE-STUFFED PORK TENDERLOIN

POINTS value: 4

PREP: 28 minutes ■ **COOK:** 40 minutes
■ **OTHER:** 20 minutes

We used garlic powder on the surface of the meat to give it a savory flavor without having to worry about burning fresh garlic in the browning process. Fresh garlic gives the sauce a more subtle flavor.

    1 cup prunes
    ½ cup apple juice
    1 tablespoon minced fresh parsley
    2 (1-pound) pork tenderloins
    1 teaspoon salt
    1 teaspoon dried Italian seasoning
    ½ teaspoon garlic powder
    ½ teaspoon freshly ground black pepper
    1 tablespoon olive oil
    1 cup thinly sliced onion, separated into rings
    1 cup chopped carrot
    3 garlic cloves, minced
    ⅔ cup fat-free, less-sodium chicken broth
    ¼ cup dry white wine
    1 large bay leaf

1. Combine prunes and apple juice in a saucepan. Bring to a simmer; remove from heat. Let stand 15 minutes.
2. Preheat oven to 400°.
3. Drain prunes, discarding juice. Combine prunes and parsley, and chop. Slice 1 pork tenderloin lengthwise, cutting to, but not through, other side. Open butterflied portions, laying pork flat. Place plastic wrap over pork; pound to ¼-inch thickness using a meat mallet or small heavy skillet. Repeat procedure with remaining tenderloin.
4. Combine salt and next 3 ingredients in a small bowl. Sprinkle half of herb mixture over tenderloins. Spread prune mixture evenly over tenderloins, leaving a ½-inch margin around outside edges. Roll up each tenderloin, jelly-roll fashion, starting with long side. Secure at 2-inch intervals with twine. Rub remaining herb mixture over tenderloins.
5. Heat oil in a large ovenproof skillet over medium-high heat. Brown pork on all sides (about 12 minutes). Remove pork from pan, and keep warm. Add onion and carrot to drippings in pan; sauté 4 minutes. Add minced garlic, and sauté 30 seconds. Stir in broth, wine, and bay leaf. Return pork and any accumulated juices to pan. Cover and bake at 400° for 20 minutes or until a thermometer registers 160°. Remove pork from pan, and let stand 5 minutes.
6. Discard bay leaf. Cut each tenderloin into 8 slices. Serve pork with sauce. YIELD: 8 SERVINGS (SERVING SIZE: 2 SLICES PORK AND 3 TABLESPOONS SAUCE).

PER SERVING: CAL 221 (23% from fat); FAT 5.7g (sat 1.6g); PRO 23.7g; CARB 19.1g; FIB 2.3g; CHOL 63mg; IRON 1.6mg; SOD 397mg; CALC 28mg

ROSEMARY-GARLIC PORK TENDERLOIN ✓

POINTS value: 3

pictured on page 132

PREP: 20 minutes ■ **COOK:** 23 minutes
■ **OTHER:** 2 hours and 15 minutes

Fragrant rosemary and garlic enhance a simple pork tenderloin. This herb paste also works well on chicken.

    ¼ cup minced fresh rosemary
    ¼ cup minced garlic (about 10 cloves)
    1 tablespoon olive oil
    2 teaspoons kosher salt
    1 teaspoon freshly ground black pepper
    2 (1-pound) pork tenderloins
    Cooking spray

1. Combine first 5 ingredients in a small bowl, mixing well to make a paste.
2. Make several 1-inch slits in pork, and stuff each slit with 1 teaspoon rosemary paste. Spread any remaining rosemary paste onto top and sides of pork. Cover and chill 2 hours.
3. Prepare grill.
4. Place pork on grill rack coated with cooking spray. Grill pork 23 minutes or until a thermometer registers 155°, turning once. Remove pork from grill; cover and let stand 15 minutes. YIELD: 8 SERVINGS (SERVING SIZE: 3 OUNCES).

Note: While pork stands, its internal temperature will reach 160°.

PER SERVING: CAL 154 (33% from fat); FAT 5.6g (sat 1.6g); PRO 22.8g; CARB 1.8g; FIB 0.3g; CHOL 63mg; IRON 1.4mg; SOD 516mg; CALC 17mg

SEARED PORK TENDERLOIN WITH DARK CHERRY RELISH

POINTS value: 4

PREP: 5 minutes ■ COOK: 22 minutes
■ OTHER: 5 minutes

This tart relish complements the spicy tenderloin with a mix of irresistible flavors. Also try the relish atop chicken or beef.

½ teaspoon chili powder
¼ teaspoon salt
¼ teaspoon coarsely ground black pepper
1 (1-pound) pork tenderloin
1 teaspoon canola oil
Cooking spray
1 (12-ounce) package frozen sweet cherries, thawed and finely chopped
3 tablespoons finely chopped red onion
1½ tablespoons sugar
2 teaspoons balsamic vinegar
1½ teaspoons grated fresh orange rind
⅛ teaspoon ground cloves
⅛ teaspoon crushed red pepper

1. Preheat oven to 425°.
2. Combine first 3 ingredients in a small bowl. Rub spice mixture evenly over pork.
3. Heat oil in a large nonstick skillet over medium-high heat. Add pork, and cook 6 minutes or until lightly browned, turning occasionally. Remove from pan, and place in an 11 x 7–inch baking dish coated with cooking spray. Bake at 425° for 15 minutes or until a thermometer registers 160° (slightly pink). Let stand 5 minutes before slicing.
4. While pork bakes, combine cherries and next 6 ingredients in a small bowl. Serve pork with relish. YIELD: 4 SERVINGS (SERVING SIZE: 3 OUNCES PORK AND ¼ CUP RELISH).

PER SERVING: CAL 220 (22% from fat); FAT 5.4g (sat 1.4g); PRO 23.8g; CARB 19.5g; FIB 2.1g; CHOL 63mg; IRON 1.5mg; SOD 201mg; CALC 22mg

LEEK AND PANCETTA CARBONARA

POINTS value: 6

PREP: 8 minutes ■ COOK: 13 minutes

Carbonara—the Italian word for "charcoal"—is a traditional Italian pasta dish, the origins of which are still disputed. One theory is that the dish was first made as a hearty meal for Italian charcoal workers.

1 (16-ounce) package uncooked thin spaghetti
6 ounces diced pancetta
3 cups sliced leek
2 garlic cloves, minced
½ teaspoon salt
½ teaspoon freshly ground black pepper
¼ teaspoon freshly ground nutmeg
2 large eggs
2 large egg whites
½ cup chopped fresh flat-leaf parsley
¼ cup (1 ounce) shaved fresh Parmesan cheese

1. Cook pasta according to package directions, omitting salt and fat. Drain, reserving 1 cup cooking liquid.
2. While pasta cooks, heat a large nonstick skillet over medium-high heat. Add pancetta; cook 7 minutes or until brown and crisp. Add leek, and cook 4 minutes or until soft. Add garlic; cook 1 minute or until lightly browned. Add cooked pasta, salt, pepper, and nutmeg to pan. Remove from heat, and keep warm.
3. Combine eggs and egg whites in a large bowl, stirring with a whisk until blended. Slowly add reserved hot cooking liquid, stirring with a whisk.
4. Place pasta mixture over medium-high heat. Add egg mixture; cook 1 minute or until slightly thick. Remove from heat; stir in parsley and cheese. Serve immediately. YIELD: 9 SERVINGS (SERVING SIZE: 1 CUP).

PER SERVING: CAL 291 (27% from fat); FAT 8.8g (sat 3.6g); PRO 12.2g; CARB 39.8g; FIB 2.8g; CHOL 62mg; IRON 2.8mg; SOD 511mg; CALC 64mg

Tea-Marinated Chicken with Cucumber-Mint
Gremolata, *page 100*

poultry

CHICKEN AND MUSHROOM ENCHILADA CASSEROLE

POINTS value: 5

PREP: 20 minutes ■ COOK: 49 minutes
■ OTHER: 5 minutes

This spicy main dish gets its heat from the fire-roasted salsa. If you'd like a tamer flavor, select a milder salsa.

- 2 cups 1% low-fat milk, divided
- ⅓ cup all-purpose flour
- ½ teaspoon ground cumin
- ¼ teaspoon salt
- 1 cup fire-roasted salsa verde (such as Zapata)
- 2 teaspoons canola oil
- 1 (8-ounce) package presliced mushrooms, chopped
- ¾ cup chopped red onion
- ½ teaspoon dried oregano
- 2 cups chopped rotisserie chicken
- 1 cup canned black beans, rinsed and drained
- 6 (6-inch) corn tortillas
- Cooking spray
- 1 cup (4 ounces) reduced-fat shredded sharp Cheddar cheese
- ½ cup fat-free sour cream

1. Preheat oven to 350°.
2. Combine ½ cup milk, flour, cumin, and salt in a saucepan; stir with a whisk. Stir in 1½ cups milk. Cook over medium heat 8 minutes or until thick, stirring constantly with whisk. Remove from heat; stir in salsa.
3. Heat oil in a large nonstick skillet over medium-high heat. Add mushrooms and onion; sauté 8 minutes or until onion is tender. Stir in oregano. Add mushroom mixture to milk mixture. Return pan to heat; add chicken and beans. Cook 2 minutes or until thoroughly heated, stirring constantly.
4. Stack tortillas, and cut into 4 wedges. Spread one-fourth of mushroom mixture (about 1 cup) in bottom of an 11 x 7–inch baking dish coated with cooking spray; top with 8 tortilla wedges. Spoon one-third of chicken mixture over tortilla wedges. Repeat layers twice with remaining mushroom mixture, tortilla wedges, and chicken mixture; top with remaining one-fourth of mushroom mixture. Sprinkle with cheese.
5. Bake, uncovered, at 350° for 30 minutes or until bubbly. Remove from oven, and let stand 5 minutes. Serve with sour cream. YIELD: 8 SERVINGS (SERVING SIZE: ⅛ OF CASSEROLE AND 1 TABLESPOON SOUR CREAM).

PER SERVING: CAL 252 (28% from fat); FAT 7.8g (sat 3.2g); PRO 21g; CARB 25.7g; FIB 3.2g; CHOL 47mg; IRON 1.8mg; SOD 400mg; CALC 244mg

ROTISSERIE TIPS

- When you're buying rotisserie chicken at the grocery store, pick it up at the end of your shopping trip so it will stay hot until you get home.
- Serve or refrigerate it within 2 hours (sooner in hot weather).
- Cut, shred, or chop the chicken and store it, uncovered, in a shallow container in the refrigerator to help it cool quickly. Cover the container when the chicken has cooled. The chicken will keep for 3 to 4 days in the refrigerator.

SPICY STIR-FRIED CHICKEN AND SPINACH

POINTS value: 5

PREP: 5 minutes ■ COOK: 13 minutes

Ponzu sauce, commonly used in Japanese cuisine, is a citrus-based sauce with a sweet, sour, and slightly salty taste. The spicy kick in this dish comes from the chili sauce, so adjust the amount of it to suit your taste.

- ¾ cup fat-free, less-sodium chicken broth
- 3 tablespoons ponzu sauce (such as Marukan)
- 1 tablespoon cornstarch
- 2 teaspoons chili sauce (such as Sriracha)
- 1 teaspoon dark sesame oil
- ¼ teaspoon freshly ground black pepper
- Cooking spray
- 2 garlic cloves, minced
- 1 (8-ounce) package presliced mushrooms
- 1 pound chicken breast tenders, cut into 1-inch pieces
- 1 (6-ounce) package fresh baby spinach
- ½ cup diagonally cut green onions (about 2 onions)
- 2 cups hot cooked Chinese noodles (such as KA-ME plain Chinese noodles)
- 1 tablespoon sesame seeds, toasted

1. Combine first 6 ingredients in a small bowl, stirring with a whisk. Set aside.
2. Heat a large nonstick skillet over medium-high heat; coat pan with cooking spray. Add garlic; sauté 30 seconds. Add mushrooms; sauté 4 minutes or until tender. Remove from pan, and set aside.
3. Coat pan with cooking spray; add chicken, and cook 4 to 5 minutes. Add reserved sauce mixture to pan; bring to a boil, and cook 1 minute. Reduce heat. Add spinach and green onions; cook 1 to 2 minutes or until

spinach wilts. Add reserved mushroom mixture and noodles; toss gently to combine. Sprinkle with sesame seeds. Serve immediately. YIELD: 4 SERVINGS (SERVING SIZE: 1½ CUPS).

PER SERVING: CAL 288 (10% from fat); FAT 3.1g (sat 0.2g); PRO 33.8g; CARB 31.6g; FIB 3.2g; CHOL 72mg; IRON 7.1mg; SOD 840mg; CALC 65mg

STORING AND HANDLING CHICKEN

Storing: Raw poultry can be stored in the refrigerator up to 2 days, and cooked poultry can be stored up to 3 days. Raw skinless, boneless chicken can marinate in the refrigerator up to 8 hours; raw chicken pieces with skin and bone can marinate up to a day. Freeze uncooked poultry up to 6 months and cooked poultry up to 3 months.

Handling: Wash your hands well with hot water and soap before and after handling poultry. Use hot water and soap to wash the cutting board and any utensils that come in contact with the raw meat. Also, be careful when rinsing raw poultry because you may splash water from the poultry onto a clean area.

SPICY OVEN-FRIED CHICKEN

POINTS value: 5

PREP: 10 minutes ■ COOK: 20 minutes
■ OTHER: 10 minutes

1 cup panko (Japanese breadcrumbs)
3 tablespoons salt-free fajita seasoning (such as Spice Islands)
2 tablespoons instant minced onion
¾ teaspoon salt, divided
2 large egg whites
2 teaspoons cornstarch
2 teaspoons fresh lemon juice
2¼ pounds chicken breast tenders
Cooking spray
½ cup light sour cream
3 tablespoons salsa

1. Preheat oven to 450°.
2. Combine first 3 ingredients and ½ teaspoon salt in a shallow dish. Combine egg whites, cornstarch, lemon juice, and remaining ¼ teaspoon salt in another shallow dish, stirring with a whisk until foamy.
3. Dip chicken tenders in egg white mixture; then dredge chicken in breadcrumb mixture, pressing firmly to coat. Place chicken on a wire rack, and let

stand 10 minutes. While chicken stands, place a large baking sheet in oven to heat.
4. Coat chicken well with cooking spray. Remove hot pan from oven; coat pan with cooking spray. Place chicken on pan in a single layer. Bake at 450° for 20 to 25 minutes or until chicken is done.
5. While chicken bakes, combine sour cream and salsa in a small bowl; stir well. Serve chicken with sauce. YIELD: 6 SERVINGS (SERVING SIZE: ABOUT 3 CHICKEN TENDERS AND ABOUT 2 TABLESPOONS SAUCE).

PER SERVING: CAL 238 (14% from fat); FAT 3.6g (sat 1.6g); PRO 41.9g; CARB 10.2g; FIB 0.6g; CHOL 110mg; IRON 1.1mg; SOD 463mg; CALC 39mg

CHORIZO-CHICKEN KEBABS

POINTS value: 5

PREP: 29 minutes ■ COOK: 8 minutes

Chorizo is a highly seasoned, coarsely ground pork sausage flavored with garlic, chili powder, and other spices. It is widely used in Mexican and Spanish cooking. We call for chicken chorizo here because it's lower in fat than traditional pork chorizo.

1 small red onion, peeled and cut in half crosswise
2 tablespoons pineapple juice
1 tablespoon olive oil
½ teaspoon salt
½ teaspoon dried oregano
1 pound skinless, boneless chicken breast, cut into 1-inch pieces
1 red bell pepper, cut into 1-inch pieces
1 green bell pepper, cut into 1-inch pieces
2 links chicken chorizo sausage (about 4½ ounces) or turkey kielbasa, cut into 16 pieces
Cooking spray

1. Separate layers of one half of onion; reserve remaining onion for another use. Cut layers into 24 (1-inch) pieces.
2. Combine pineapple juice and next 3 ingredients in a large bowl, stirring with a whisk. Add chicken, onion, and bell pepper to bowl; toss well to coat.
3. Prepare grill.
4. Thread chicken, onion, bell pepper, and sausage onto 4 (12-inch) metal skewers. Place kebabs on grill rack coated with cooking spray. Grill 4 to 5 minutes on each side or until chicken is done. YIELD: 4 SERVINGS (SERVING SIZE: 1 KEBAB).

PER SERVING: CAL 227 (25% from fat); FAT 6.4g (sat 1.5g); PRO 31.1g; CARB 9.7g; FIB 1.8g; CHOL 80mg; IRON 1.7mg; SOD 641mg; CALC 37mg

TACO STRIP STACKS

POINTS value: 7

PREP: 30 minutes ■ **COOK:** 8 minutes

Stirring in the tortilla strips gives the chicken mixture body and a great corn taste—providing a nice contrast to the crisp, cold lettuce and fresh veggies in this tostada-like entrée.

   4 (6-inch) corn tortillas, halved and cut crosswise into thin strips
   Cooking spray
   1½ pounds skinless, boneless chicken breast, cut into ¼-inch strips
   2½ tablespoons 40%-less-sodium taco seasoning
   ¼ cup water
   2 cups packed shredded iceberg lettuce
   ½ cup (2 ounces) reduced-fat shredded sharp Cheddar cheese
   2 cups chopped tomato (about 1 large)
   ½ cup sliced green onions
   ½ cup picante sauce
   ¼ cup light sour cream
   ¼ cup chopped fresh cilantro
   1 medium lime, quartered (optional)

1. Preheat oven to 425°.
2. Place tortilla strips in a single layer on a large foil-lined baking sheet. Bake at 425° for 4 minutes; stir, and bake an additional 4 minutes or until strips begin to turn golden. Transfer strips to a wire rack, and cool completely.
3. While tortilla strips bake, heat a large nonstick skillet over medium-high heat; coat pan with cooking spray. Coat chicken with taco seasoning, and add to pan; coat chicken with cooking spray. Cook chicken 5 minutes or until no longer pink, stirring often. Add ¼ cup water, stirring until blended. Add tortilla strips; toss gently, and spoon evenly into 4 shallow bowls. Top chicken mixture evenly with lettuce and next 6 ingredients in the order given. Serve with lime wedges, if desired. **YIELD: 4 SERVINGS (SERVING SIZE: 1 STACK).**

PER SERVING: CAL 359 (29% from fat); FAT 11.7g (sat 4g); PRO 46.1g; CARB 20.9g; FIB 3.3g; CHOL 115mg; IRON 2mg; SOD 701mg; CALC 207mg

TEA-MARINATED CHICKEN WITH CUCUMBER-MINT GREMOLATA ☑

POINTS value: 5

pictured on page 130

PREP: 9 minutes ■ **COOK:** 13 minutes
■ **OTHER:** 8 hours and 3 minutes

We also tested this recipe with Earl Grey tea bags and loved the flavor just as much. Serve with steamed yellow squash to round out the meal.

   4 (6-ounce) skinless, boneless chicken breast halves
   ¾ cup water
   3 lemon-flavored tea bags (such as Bigelow Lemon Lift)
   Ice cubes
   ¼ teaspoon salt
   ¼ teaspoon coarsely ground black pepper
   ¼ teaspoon paprika
   Cooking spray
   1 teaspoon extravirgin olive oil
   ¼ cup water
   Cucumber-Mint Gremolata
   4 lemon wedges

1. Place chicken breast halves between 2 sheets of plastic wrap, and pound to ½-inch thickness using a meat mallet or small heavy skillet; set aside.
2. Place ¾ cup water in a microwave-safe measuring cup, and microwave at HIGH 3 minutes or until boiling. Add tea bags, and steep 3 minutes. Remove tea bags, squeezing out excess liquid by pressing to the side of the measuring cup with the back of a spoon or fork. Discard tea bags, and add enough ice cubes to measure 1 cup. Pour tea mixture into a large zip-top plastic bag. Add chicken; seal bag, and marinate in refrigerator 8 hours, turning bag occasionally.
3. Remove chicken from bag, discarding tea. Pat chicken dry with paper towels; sprinkle evenly with salt, pepper, and paprika. Heat a large nonstick skillet over medium-high heat; coat pan with cooking spray. Add oil; tilt pan to coat bottom. Add chicken; cook 3 to 4 minutes on each side or until browned and done. Remove chicken to a serving platter; keep warm.
4. Add ¼ cup water to pan; bring to a boil over medium-high heat. Cook 2 minutes or until liquid is reduced to 2 tablespoons, scraping pan to loosen browned bits. Spoon drippings over chicken. Serve with Cucumber-Mint Gremolata and lemon wedges. **YIELD: 4 SERVINGS (SERVING SIZE: 1 CHICKEN BREAST HALF AND ¼ CUP GREMOLATA).**

PER SERVING: CAL 229 (22% from fat); FAT 5.7g (sat 1.1g); PRO 39.7g; CARB 2.4g; FIB 0.7g; CHOL 99mg; IRON 1.5mg; SOD 330mg; CALC 33mg

Cucumber-Mint Gremolata ✓

POINTS value: 1

- 1 medium cucumber, peeled, seeded, and finely chopped
- 2 teaspoons grated fresh lemon rind
- 2 teaspoons fresh lemon juice
- 2 teaspoons extravirgin olive oil
- ⅛ teaspoon salt
- ⅛ teaspoon crushed red pepper
- ¼ cup chopped fresh mint leaves

1. Combine first 6 ingredients in a small bowl. Stir in mint just before serving. YIELD: 1¼ CUPS.

PER ¼ CUP: CAL 24 (75% from fat); FAT 2g (sat 0.3g); PRO 0.3g; CARB 1.4g; FIB 0.5g; CHOL 0mg; IRON 0.2mg; SOD 59mg; CALC 10mg

HERBED CHICKEN STICKS

POINTS value: 7

PREP: 26 minutes ■ COOK: 20 minutes

Panko breadcrumbs, found in the Asian-foods section of your supermarket, provide the crunchy coating in this family favorite. Serve the chicken sticks solo, atop a main-dish salad, or tucked in a wrap.

- 1¾ cups panko (Japanese breadcrumbs)
- 2 tablespoons minced fresh parsley
- 1½ tablespoons minced fresh thyme
- 1½ tablespoons minced fresh rosemary
- ¾ cup fat-free buttermilk
- 1½ pounds skinless, boneless chicken breast, cut into ½-inch strips
- ¼ teaspoon salt
- ¼ teaspoon pepper
- 2 tablespoons butter, melted

1. Preheat oven to 425°.
2. Combine first 4 ingredients in a shallow bowl, stirring well. Place buttermilk in another shallow bowl.
3. Dip chicken strips in buttermilk, and dredge in panko mixture. Place breaded chicken on a baking sheet lined with parchment paper; sprinkle evenly with salt and pepper. Drizzle melted butter over chicken. Bake at 425° for 20 minutes or until lightly browned, turning after 10 minutes. YIELD: 4 SERVINGS (SERVING SIZE: ABOUT 5 CHICKEN TENDERS).

PER SERVING: CAL 350 (22% from fat); FAT 8.7g (sat 4.2g); PRO 44.3g; CARB 20.3g; FIB 1.8g; CHOL 114mg; IRON 2.2mg; SOD 407mg; CALC 86mg

CHICKEN WITH MUSHROOM CREAM SAUCE

POINTS value: 6

PREP: 2 minutes ■ COOK: 53 minutes

If you serve the creamy mushroom sauce over a single serving of ½ cup rice, the **POINTS** value will be 8.

- Cooking spray
- 4 (6-ounce) skinless, boneless chicken breast halves
- 1 teaspoon olive oil
- ½ cup chopped onion
- 1 (8-ounce) package presliced mushrooms
- 2 garlic cloves, minced
- 1 (14-ounce) can fat-free, less-sodium chicken broth
- 2½ tablespoons all-purpose flour
- ½ cup light sour cream
- 1 teaspoon fresh lemon juice
- ¾ teaspoon salt
- ¾ teaspoon dried rubbed sage
- ¼ teaspoon freshly ground black pepper
- 1 cup frozen green peas
- 2 cups hot cooked rice (optional)

1. Heat a large nonstick skillet over medium-high heat; coat pan with cooking spray. Add chicken, and sauté 5 minutes on each side or until browned. Remove chicken from pan; keep warm.
2. Heat oil in pan over medium-high heat. Add onion, and sauté 2 minutes. Add mushrooms and garlic, and sauté 5 minutes. Remove mushroom mixture from pan; keep warm.
3. Combine broth and flour in a small bowl, stirring well. Add broth mixture to pan, and bring to a boil over medium-high heat, stirring constantly. Return chicken and mushroom mixture to pan. Reduce heat to medium, and simmer 28 minutes or until chicken is done. Stir in sour cream and next 4 ingredients; cook 2 minutes. Add peas, and cook 30 seconds. Serve over rice, if desired. YIELD: 4 SERVINGS (SERVING SIZE: 1 CHICKEN BREAST HALF AND ⅓ CUP MUSHROOM SAUCE).

PER SERVING: CAL 314 (21% from fat); FAT 7.3g (sat 3g); PRO 46.1g; CARB 14.9g; FIB 2.7g; CHOL 110mg; IRON 2.4mg; SOD 889mg; CALC 71mg

SESAME CHICKEN STIR-FRY

POINTS value: 7

pictured on page 132

PREP: 13 minutes ■ **COOK:** 10 minutes

Prepare instant rice to keep this meal quick and easy. Adding a little chopped fresh cilantro gives the dish extra color and a boost of flavor.

- ⅓ cup fat-free, less-sodium chicken broth
- 2 tablespoons low-sodium soy sauce
- 1 tablespoon cornstarch
- 1 pound skinless, boneless chicken breast, cut into ¼-inch strips
- ¼ teaspoon salt
- 1 tablespoon peanut oil, divided
- 2 teaspoons dark sesame oil
- 1 pound asparagus, trimmed and cut into 2-inch pieces
- 1 cup matchstick-cut carrots
- ½ cup thinly sliced green onions
- 2 garlic cloves, minced
- 1½ tablespoons sesame seeds, toasted
- 2 cups hot cooked rice

1. Combine first 3 ingredients, stirring with a whisk; set aside.

2. Sprinkle chicken evenly with salt. Heat 1 teaspoon peanut oil and sesame oil in a large nonstick skillet over medium–high heat. Add chicken; cook 3 to 4 minutes or until done. Remove from pan; keep warm. Add 1 teaspoon peanut oil to pan. Add asparagus; cook 2 minutes. Add remaining 1 teaspoon peanut oil and carrots; cook 2 minutes or until browned. Stir in green onions and garlic; sauté 1 minute. Reduce heat to medium; return chicken to pan. Stir in broth mixture and sesame seeds; cook 1 minute or until thick. Serve immediately over rice. **YIELD: 4 SERVINGS (SERVING SIZE: 1¼ CUPS CHICKEN MIXTURE AND ½ CUP RICE).**

PER SERVING: CAL 365 (22% from fat); FAT 9g (sat 1.4g); PRO 31.4g; CARB 36.2g; FIB 2.8g; CHOL 66mg; IRON 8.7mg; SOD 595mg; CALC 52mg

GINGERED SWEET-AND-SOUR CHICKEN BREASTS

POINTS value: 6

PREP: 14 minutes ■ **COOK:** 12 minutes
■ **OTHER:** 30 minutes

This dish is so quick to prepare that you can have it ready in less time than it takes to get takeout.

- 3 garlic cloves, minced
- 1 tablespoon minced peeled fresh ginger
- 1 tablespoon low-sodium soy sauce
- 2 teaspoons dark sesame oil
- ¼ cup dry sherry, divided
- 4 (6-ounce) skinless, boneless chicken breast halves
- ½ cup sweet-and-sour duck sauce (such as Dai Day)
- Cooking spray

1. Combine first 4 ingredients and 2 tablespoons sherry in a medium bowl, stirring with a whisk. Add chicken to marinade, turning to coat. Cover and marinate at room temperature 30 minutes.

2. Combine remaining 2 tablespoons sherry and duck sauce in a small bowl. Heat a large nonstick skillet over medium–high heat; coat pan with cooking spray. Remove chicken from marinade, discarding marinade. Add chicken to pan, and coat with cooking spray; cook 4 minutes on each side. Reduce heat to low, and add duck sauce mixture. Cover and cook 4 minutes or until sauce is thoroughly heated. Serve immediately. **YIELD: 4 SERVINGS (SERVING SIZE: 1 CHICKEN BREAST HALF AND 2 TABLESPOONS SAUCE).**

Note: You can substitute a mixture of 1 tablespoon cider vinegar and 3 tablespoons water for the sherry, if desired.

PER SERVING: CAL 275 (14% from fat); FAT 4.4g (sat 0.9g); PRO 39.8g; CARB 15.2g; FIB 0.1g; CHOL 99mg; IRON 1.5mg; SOD 380mg; CALC 24mg

PREPARING FRESH GINGER

1. Use a vegetable peeler or paring knife to remove the tough skin and reveal the yellowish flesh.

2. Cut the peeled ginger into slices; then stack the slices, and cut into strips. Line up the strips, and cut crosswise into small pieces to mince.

GRILLED CHICKEN WITH AVOCADO SALSA ☑

POINTS value: 6

pictured on page 131

PREP: 17 minutes ■ COOK: 12 minutes

1 avocado, peeled and chopped
1 cup grape tomatoes, halved
½ cup chopped cucumber
½ cup chopped fresh cilantro
¼ cup sliced radishes
¼ cup chopped red onion
2 garlic cloves, minced
¼ teaspoon grated fresh lime rind
2 tablespoons fresh lime juice
1 teaspoon olive oil
½ teaspoon ground cumin
¼ teaspoon chili powder
½ teaspoon salt, divided
½ teaspoon freshly ground black pepper, divided
4 (6-ounce) skinless, boneless chicken breast halves
Cooking spray

1. Prepare grill.
2. Combine first 12 ingredients, ¼ teaspoon salt, and ¼ teaspoon pepper in a medium bowl; stir gently to combine. Cover and chill.
3. Sprinkle chicken with ¼ teaspoon salt and ¼ teaspoon pepper. Place chicken on grill rack coated with cooking spray; grill 6 minutes on each side or until done. Serve chicken with salsa. YIELD: 4 SERVINGS (SERVING SIZE: 1 CHICKEN BREAST HALF AND ABOUT ½ CUP SALSA).

PER SERVING: CAL 298 (34% from fat); FAT 11.1g (sat 2g); PRO 41.1g; CARB 8.2g; FIB 3.7g; CHOL 99mg; IRON 2.1mg; SOD 419mg; CALC 43mg

HAWAIIAN CHICKEN ☑

POINTS value: 6

PREP: 10 minutes ■ COOK: 15 minutes

2 cups water
1 cup fresh cilantro leaves
1½ tablespoons canola oil
Cooking spray
1½ teaspoons minced jalapeño pepper
1½ cups finely chopped fresh pineapple
1 tablespoon fresh lime juice
½ teaspoon salt, divided
4 (6-ounce) skinless, boneless chicken breast halves

1. Bring 2 cups water to a boil in a large nonstick skillet. Add cilantro; cook 15 seconds. Drain and plunge cilantro leaves into ice water; drain, and squeeze dry. Finely chop cilantro leaves; place in a small bowl. Add oil, stirring with a whisk.
2. Heat a small skillet over medium heat; coat pan with cooking spray. Add jalapeño, and cook 1 minute or until soft. Add pineapple; cook 4 minutes or until lightly browned. Remove from heat; stir in lime juice, 1 tablespoon cilantro oil, and ¼ teaspoon salt.
3. Preheat grill.
4. Sprinkle chicken with remaining ¼ teaspoon salt; brush evenly with remaining cilantro oil. Place chicken on grill rack coated with cooking spray; grill 3 to 4 minutes on each side or until done. Serve chicken with salsa. YIELD: 4 SERVINGS (SERVING SIZE: 1 CHICKEN BREAST HALF AND ¼ CUP PINEAPPLE SALSA).

PER SERVING: CAL 264 (26% from fat); FAT 7.5g (sat 0.9g); PRO 39.7g; CARB 7.9g; FIB 1g; CHOL 99mg; IRON 1.5mg; SOD 404mg; CALC 30mg

OVEN-BARBECUED CHICKEN

POINTS value: 5

PREP: 17 minutes ■ COOK: 40 minutes

With this dish, you get the flavor of barbecue without having to fire up the grill.

6 (8-ounce) bone-in chicken breast halves, skinned
Cooking spray
½ cup finely chopped onion
1 cup barbecue sauce
2 tablespoons honey Dijon mustard
2 tablespoons tomato paste

1. Preheat oven to 400°.
2. Place chicken in a 13 x 9–inch baking dish coated with cooking spray. Coat chicken with cooking spray. Bake, uncovered, at 400° for 20 minutes.
3. While chicken bakes, heat a small nonstick skillet over medium-low heat; coat pan with cooking spray. Add onion, and cook 5 minutes or until almost tender, stirring constantly. Place onion in a blender, and process until almost smooth, scraping down sides often. Add barbecue sauce, mustard, and tomato paste to blender; pulse 2 to 3 times until blended.
4. Spoon sauce over chicken. Bake, uncovered, an additional 20 minutes or until chicken is done. YIELD: 6 SERVINGS (SERVING SIZE: 1 CHICKEN BREAST HALF).

PER SERVING: CAL 243 (13% from fat); FAT 3.6g (sat 0.7g); PRO 34.6g; CARB 15.2g; FIB 1g; CHOL 86mg; IRON 1.4mg; SOD 701mg; CALC 26mg

Brussels sprouts resemble tiny cabbages because they are, in fact, members of the cabbage family. They're at their peak in the late fall and early winter. In the fall, you're more likely to find Brussels sprouts on the stalk, which is usually a sign of freshness and yields better flavor. There's really no difference in taste between the small and large sprouts. Store them in the refrigerator in a paper bag up to 3 days; if they're refrigerated for longer, they'll develop an unpleasantly strong flavor.

LEMON-ROASTED CHICKEN WITH BRUSSELS SPROUTS AND BACON

POINTS value: 6

PREP: 9 minutes ▪ **COOK:** 42 minutes

The flavorful Brussels sprouts share the plate equally with the chicken. After tasting this recipe, the sprouts may move higher up on your list of favorite vegetables.

- 4 (8-ounce) bone-in chicken breast halves
- 1 pound Brussels sprouts, trimmed and halved
- 1 tablespoon olive oil
- 1 teaspoon dried thyme
- ½ teaspoon salt
- ½ teaspoon black pepper
- 4 thin lemon slices
- 1 cup fat-free, less-sodium chicken broth
- ½ teaspoon grated fresh lemon rind
- 2 tablespoons fresh lemon juice
- 2 tablespoons minced shallots
- 1 tablespoon butter
- 3 center-cut bacon slices, cooked and crumbled

1. Preheat oven to 450°.
2. Combine first 3 ingredients in a large bowl, tossing to coat. Place chicken, breast sides up, in a large roasting pan. Arrange Brussels sprouts around chicken. Sprinkle thyme, salt, and pepper under skin of chicken and on Brussels sprouts. Place 1 lemon slice under skin of each chicken breast.
3. Bake at 450° for 15 minutes; stir gently. Reduce oven temperature to 375°; bake an additional 25 minutes or until a thermometer inserted into center of chicken registers 165°. Transfer chicken and Brussels sprouts to a serving platter; discard skin. Cover; keep warm.
4. Place pan over 2 burners over medium–high heat. Combine broth and next 3 ingredients in a small bowl;

add to pan. Cook 2 minutes, scraping pan to loosen browned bits. Remove pan from heat; add butter. Stir until butter melts; drizzle evenly over chicken and Brussels sprouts. Sprinkle with bacon. YIELD: 4 SERVINGS (SERVING SIZE: 1 CHICKEN BREAST HALF AND ⅔ CUP BRUSSELS SPROUTS).

PER SERVING: CAL 295 (31% from fat); FAT 10.1g (sat 3.4g); PRO 40g; CARB 11.7g; FIB 4.3g; CHOL 98mg; IRON 3mg; SOD 671mg; CALC 69mg

COQ AU VIN

POINTS value: 7

PREP: 20 minutes ▪ **COOK:** 1 hour and 40 minutes

To make peeling pearl onions easy, cook them in boiling water to cover 5 minutes. Drain and cut off the root ends with a paring knife. Holding each onion by the pointed top, gently squeeze to force the onion out of the peel through the cut end. Serve the chicken and chunky, rich-tasting sauce over hot cooked noodles. A ½-cup serving of noodles has a **POINTS** value of 2.

- 2 center-cut bacon slices
- 2 (8-ounce) bone-in chicken breast halves, skinned
- 2 chicken thighs (about ½ pound), skinned
- 2 chicken drumsticks (about ½ pound), skinned
- ½ teaspoon salt, divided
- ½ teaspoon pepper, divided
- 1 teaspoon butter
- 2 cups (1-inch-long) pieces carrot (about 2 large)
- 2 cups pearl onions, peeled
- 1½ cups small mushrooms
- 2 garlic cloves, minced
- 1½ cups fat-free, less-sodium chicken broth
- ¼ cup all-purpose flour
- 2 cups dry red wine
- 2 teaspoons fresh thyme
- 2 large bay leaves
- 1 tablespoon chopped fresh flat-leaf parsley

1. Cook bacon in a 6-quart Dutch oven over medium heat until crisp; drain, reserving drippings in pan. Remove pan from heat. Crumble bacon, and set aside.
2. While bacon cooks, sprinkle chicken with ¼ teaspoon salt and ¼ teaspoon pepper. When bacon is done, brown chicken pieces in pan drippings over medium-high heat 5 minutes on each side. Remove chicken; keep warm.
3. Add butter to pan drippings, and melt over medium heat. Add carrot and next 3 ingredients to pan. Cook

3 minutes, stirring constantly. Gradually add chicken broth to flour, stirring with a whisk until blended; stir into vegetable mixture. Stir in remaining ¼ teaspoon salt, remaining ¼ teaspoon pepper, wine, thyme, and bay leaves. Bring to a boil; cover, reduce heat, and simmer 1 hour, stirring occasionally. Uncover; simmer 15 minutes or until sauce is thick and slightly reduced. Discard bay leaves. Sprinkle evenly with parsley and crumbled bacon. YIELD: 4 SERVINGS (SERVING SIZE: 1 CHICKEN BREAST HALF OR 1 DRUMSTICK AND 1 THIGH AND 1 CUP SAUCE).

PER SERVING: CAL 334 (16% from fat); FAT 5.9g (sat 2g); PRO 39.8g; CARB 30g; FIB 2.4g; CHOL 109mg; IRON 3.1mg; SOD 761mg; CALC 79mg

BAKED CHICKEN AND RISOTTO CASSEROLE

POINTS value: 8

PREP: 9 minutes ■ COOK: 43 minutes
■ OTHER: 5 minutes

This recipe has the goodness of a traditional Italian risotto without all the stirring, since it bakes in the oven.

  4 (8-ounce) bone-in chicken breast halves, skinned
  ½ teaspoon salt
  ½ teaspoon freshly ground black pepper
  1 tablespoon olive oil
  2 cups minced onion (about 2 large)
  ½ cup dry white wine
  1 (14-ounce) can fat-free, less-sodium chicken broth
  1 bay leaf
  1 cup uncooked Arborio rice
  ¼ cup (1 ounce) grated fresh Parmesan cheese
  Chopped fresh Italian parsley (optional)

1. Preheat oven to 350°.
2. Sprinkle chicken with salt and pepper. Heat oil in an ovenproof Dutch oven over medium-high heat. Add chicken; cook 3 to 4 minutes on each side or until browned. Remove chicken, reserving pan drippings.
3. Add onion; cook 4 minutes. Add wine, scraping pan to loosen browned bits. Add broth and bay leaf; bring to a boil. Stir in rice, and arrange chicken, rib sides down, in pan. Cover and bake at 350° for 30 minutes or until chicken is done. Remove from oven and let stand, covered, 5 minutes. Discard bay leaf. Sprinkle with cheese and, if desired, parsley. YIELD: 4 SERVINGS (SERVING SIZE: 1 CHICKEN BREAST HALF AND 1 CUP RICE).

PER SERVING: CAL 425 (15% from fat); FAT 7.2g (sat 1.9g); PRO 42.4g; CARB 46.7g; FIB 3.4g; CHOL 89mg; IRON 1.6mg; SOD 763mg; CALC 101mg

CHICKEN VINDALOO ☑.

POINTS value: 7

PREP: 20 minutes ■ COOK: 52 minutes
■ OTHER: 30 minutes

Vindaloo is a curry dish that is usually very spicy. Our recipe is packed with flavor, not heat, from a variety of spices. One of those is garam masala, an Indian spice blend of black pepper, cinnamon, cloves, coriander, cumin, and cardamom that can be found in large supermarkets or specialty stores.

  1 tablespoon olive oil
  2 cups thinly sliced onion (about 1 large)
  2 garlic cloves
2½ tablespoons white vinegar
  2 teaspoons minced peeled fresh ginger
  1 teaspoon ground cumin
  1 teaspoon ground turmeric
  1 teaspoon garam masala
  ½ teaspoon salt
  ½ teaspoon ground coriander
  ½ teaspoon ground cinnamon
  ½ teaspoon ground red pepper
1½ pounds skinless, boneless chicken thighs, cut into bite-sized pieces
  Cooking spray
  1 (14.5-ounce) can diced tomatoes, undrained
  1 cup fat-free, less-sodium chicken broth
  1 (5.5-ounce) extralarge bag boil-in-bag brown rice

1. Heat oil in a large skillet over medium-high heat. Add onion; sauté 6 minutes or until onion begins to brown. Combine onion, garlic, and next 9 ingredients in a food processor; process until blended.
2. Combine chicken and onion mixture in a large zip-top plastic bag, seal and marinate in refrigerator 30 minutes.
3. Heat pan over medium-high heat; coat pan with cooking spray. Add chicken and marinade; cook 5 minutes. Add tomatoes and broth; bring to a boil. Cover, reduce heat, and simmer 20 minutes. Uncover and simmer 15 minutes, or until chicken is done and sauce thickens.
4. While chicken mixture cooks, prepare rice according to package directions. Spoon rice into bowls, and top with chicken mixture. YIELD: 6 SERVINGS (SERVING SIZE: ABOUT ¾ CUP CHICKEN MIXTURE AND ½ CUP RICE).

PER SERVING: CAL 333 (32% from fat); FAT 11.8g (sat 2.9g); PRO 24.3g; CARB 31.3g; FIB 4g; CHOL 74mg; IRON 2.3mg; SOD 459mg; CALC 49mg

MOJITO CHICKEN THIGHS ☑.

POINTS value: 7

PREP: 10 minutes ▪ **COOK:** 14 minutes ▪ **OTHER:** 1 hour

Fresh mint and lime juice give a mojito cocktail its distinctive flavor. Here, they make the base of a great marinade.

⅓ cup chopped fresh mint
1½ teaspoons grated fresh lime rind
¼ cup fresh lime juice
2 teaspoons olive oil
¼ teaspoon salt
¼ teaspoon freshly ground black pepper
2 garlic cloves, minced
8 (3-ounce) skinless, boneless chicken thighs
Cooking spray

1. Combine first 7 ingredients in a large zip-top plastic bag; reserve 2 tablespoons marinade. Add chicken to bag; seal bag, and toss well to coat chicken. Marinate in refrigerator 1 hour.
2. Prepare grill.
3. Remove chicken from bag, discarding marinade. Place chicken on grill rack coated with cooking spray; cover and grill 7 to 8 minutes on each side or until chicken is done. Spoon reserved marinade evenly over grilled chicken before serving. YIELD: 4 SERVINGS (SERVING SIZE: 2 CHICKEN THIGHS AND 1½ TEASPOONS MARINADE).

PER SERVING: CAL 274 (50% from fat); FAT 15.1g (sat 3.9g); PRO 30.7g; CARB 2.3g; FIB 0.4g; CHOL 112mg; IRON 1.7mg; SOD 250mg; CALC 26mg

LEMON-BASIL GRILLED CHICKEN THIGHS ☑.

POINTS value: 7

PREP: 8 minutes ▪ **COOK:** 8 minutes
▪ **OTHER:** 30 minutes

12 (3-ounce) skinless, boneless chicken thighs
½ cup fresh basil leaves, torn
4 garlic cloves, chopped
1 teaspoon grated fresh lemon rind
¼ cup fresh lemon juice
1 tablespoon olive oil
1 teaspoon kosher salt
½ teaspoon freshly ground black pepper
Cooking spray

1. Combine first 8 ingredients in a large zip-top plastic bag; seal. Marinate in refrigerator 30 minutes or up to 8 hours, turning bag occasionally.

2. Prepare grill.
3. Remove chicken from marinade, discarding marinade. Place chicken on grill rack coated with cooking spray; grill 4 to 5 minutes on each side or until done.
YIELD: 6 SERVINGS (SERVING SIZE: 2 CHICKEN THIGHS).

PER SERVING: CAL 272 (50% from fat); FAT 15.1g (sat 3.9g); PRO 30.7g; CARB 1.9g; FIB 0.3g; CHOL 112mg; IRON 1.8mg; SOD 424mg; CALC 25mg

CHICKEN ITALIANO

POINTS value: 8

PREP: 16 minutes ▪ **COOK:** 56 minutes

2 teaspoons dried Italian seasoning, divided
1 teaspoon salt
1 teaspoon garlic powder
½ teaspoon black pepper
2 pounds chicken thighs, skinned
1 tablespoon olive oil
1 cup vertically sliced onion
½ cup green bell pepper strips
3 garlic cloves, minced
½ cup water
1 (28-ounce) can crushed tomatoes, undrained
2 bay leaves
2½ cups hot cooked spaghetti (about 4½ ounces uncooked pasta)
5 tablespoons grated fresh Parmesan cheese

1. Combine 1 teaspoon Italian seasoning and next 3 ingredients; sprinkle over both sides of chicken.
2. Heat oil in a large nonstick skillet over medium-high heat, and add chicken. Cook chicken 3 minutes on each side or until browned, and remove chicken from pan. Add onion, bell pepper, and garlic; sauté 2 minutes or until lightly browned. Add ½ cup water, scraping pan to loosen browned bits. Add tomatoes, remaining 1 teaspoon Italian seasoning, chicken, and bay leaves to pan; bring to a boil. Cover; reduce heat, and simmer 40 minutes. Uncover and simmer 5 minutes or until chicken is very tender. Discard bay leaves.
3. Using a slotted spoon, remove chicken to a large bowl. Remove meat from bones, and shred chicken. Return shredded chicken to pan, stirring to combine. Serve over spaghetti. Sprinkle each serving evenly with Parmesan cheese. YIELD: 5 SERVINGS (SERVING SIZE: ABOUT 1 CUP CHICKEN MIXTURE, ½ CUP SPAGHETTI, AND 1 TABLE-SPOON PARMESAN CHEESE).

PER SERVING: CAL 382 (32% from fat); FAT 13.5g (sat 3.8g); PRO 29.5g; CARB 34.2g; FIB 4.5g; CHOL 82mg; IRON 4.2mg; SOD 863mg; CALC 133mg

CAJUN CHICKEN AND OKRA ☑.

POINTS value: 7

pictured on page 133

PREP: 8 minutes ■ COOK: 54 minutes

If you can't find drumsticks already skinned, have your butcher skin them, or use a paper towel to pull off the skin with ease.

Cooking spray
8 chicken drumsticks (about 2½ pounds), skinned
1 green bell pepper, diced
1 celery stalk, sliced
½ cup chopped onion
1 cup frozen cut okra, thawed
1 (14.5-ounce) can Cajun-style stewed tomatoes, undrained and chopped
½ teaspoon dried thyme
1 teaspoon hot pepper sauce (such as Tabasco)
2 cups hot cooked white or brown rice
⅛ teaspoon salt
2 tablespoons chopped fresh parsley (optional)

1. Heat a large nonstick skillet over medium-high heat; coat pan with cooking spray. Add chicken, and cook 8 minutes or until browned on all sides, turning occasionally. Remove chicken from pan; set aside.
2. Coat pan with cooking spray. Add bell pepper, celery, and onion; lightly coat vegetables with cooking spray. Cook 2 minutes, stirring frequently.
3. Stir in okra, tomatoes, and thyme. Place chicken on top of vegetable mixture; sprinkle evenly with hot pepper sauce. Bring mixture to a boil; cover, reduce heat, and simmer 35 to 40 minutes or until chicken is done.
4. Place cooked rice on a serving platter. Using a slotted spoon, remove chicken and arrange on top of rice. Bring sauce in pan to a boil over medium-high heat. Cook 2 to 3 minutes or until sauce is slightly thick and measures about 2 cups. Stir in salt; spoon mixture evenly over chicken. Sprinkle with parsley, if desired.
YIELD: 4 SERVINGS (SERVING SIZE: 2 DRUMSTICKS, ½ CUP SAUCE, AND ½ CUP RICE).

PER SERVING: CAL 368 (14% from fat); FAT 5.9g (sat 1.5g); PRO 37.3g; CARB 40.3g; FIB 4.3g; CHOL 122mg; IRON 3.9g; SOD 607mg; CALC 95mg

SLOW-COOKER SPICY CHICKEN CACCIATORE

POINTS value: 5

PREP: 14 minutes ■ COOK: 6 hours and 36 minutes
■ OTHER: 10 minutes

Broil the yellow bell peppers until lightly browned to add a smoky flavor to this dish. If you're short on time, skip that step.

2 yellow bell peppers, seeded and each cut lengthwise into 4 quarters
2 tablespoons olive oil
2 cups vertically sliced sweet onion
4 garlic cloves, minced
2 teaspoons dried Italian seasoning, divided
¾ teaspoon salt, divided
¾ teaspoon crushed red pepper
4 (8-ounce) bone-in chicken breasts halves, skinned
8 chicken thighs (about 2 pounds), skinned
2 (14.5-ounce) cans no-salt-added diced tomatoes, undrained
1 (14.5-ounce) can Italian-style stewed tomatoes, undrained
1 (6-ounce) can tomato paste
1 tablespoon brown sugar
⅓ cup chopped fresh parsley
4 cups water
2 cups instant polenta

1. Preheat broiler.
2. Place bell pepper quarters, skin sides up, on a foil-lined baking sheet; flatten with palm of hand. Broil 6 minutes or until skins are blackened. Place peppers in a zip-top plastic bag; seal. Let stand 10 minutes or until skins loosen. Peel and discard skins; chop.
3. Place oil in a 6-quart slow cooker. Add onion, garlic, 1½ teaspoons Italian seasoning, ¼ teaspoon salt, and crushed red pepper. Stir to combine. Layer chicken over onion mixture; sprinkle with chopped bell pepper. Combine diced tomatoes, stewed tomatoes, and tomato paste in a medium bowl; pour over chicken. Sprinkle with brown sugar. Cover and cook on LOW for 6 hours and 30 minutes. Stir in parsley, remaining ½ teaspoon Italian seasoning, and ½ teaspoon salt.
4. To prepare polenta, bring 4 cups water to a boil in a saucepan; stir in polenta. Reduce heat, and cook until thick (about 3 minutes), stirring frequently. Serve cacciatore over polenta. YIELD: 13 SERVINGS (SERVING SIZE: 1 CUP CACCIATORE AND ½ CUP POLENTA).

PER SERVING: CAL 266 (21% from fat); FAT 6.1g (sat 1.4g); PRO 22g; CARB 24.7g; FIB 5g; CHOL 56mg; IRON 1.5mg; SOD 296mg; CALC 40mg

PORCINI CHICKEN FRICASSEE

POINTS value: 6

PREP: 13 minutes ■ **COOK:** 1 hour and 34 minutes
■ **OTHER:** 15 minutes

Dried porcini mushrooms give a rich, meaty texture to the sauce that coats the chicken. The sauce is also excellent served over mashed potatoes.

1 (14-ounce) can fat-free, less-sodium chicken broth
1 cup (1 ounce) dried porcini mushrooms
¾ cup water
¼ cup all-purpose flour
2 tablespoons tomato paste
1½ tablespoons olive oil
4 chicken thighs (about 1 pound), skinned
4 chicken drumsticks (about 1 pound), skinned
2 (8-ounce) bone-in chicken breast halves, skinned
1 cup finely chopped red onion
2 (8-ounce) packages presliced button mushrooms
3 tablespoons chopped fresh thyme
½ teaspoon salt
½ teaspoon freshly ground black pepper
3 tablespoons fresh lemon juice

1. Bring chicken broth and porcini mushrooms to a boil in a small saucepan; remove from heat, cover, and let stand 15 minutes. Using a slotted spoon, remove mushrooms from broth, and set aside. Carefully pour broth into a 2-cup glass measuring cup, leaving sediment in pan. Add ¾ cup water to broth; add flour, stirring with a whisk until smooth. Stir in tomato paste.

2. Heat oil in a large skillet over medium-high heat. Add chicken, and cook 5 minutes on each side or until golden. Remove chicken from pan. Stir onion into drippings. Cover and reduce heat to low; cook 4 to 5 minutes or until onion is tender, stirring often. Stir in broth mixture, porcini mushrooms, button mushrooms, and next 3 ingredients.

3. Return chicken and any accumulated juices to pan. Bring to a boil; cover, reduce heat, and simmer 45 minutes or until chicken is tender, stirring occasionally. Uncover and simmer 15 minutes or until sauce is slightly reduced, stirring often. Stir in lemon juice. YIELD: 6 SERVINGS (SERVING SIZE: 1 CHICKEN BREAST HALF OR 1 DRUMSTICK AND 1 THIGH AND ⅔ CUP SAUCE).

PER SERVING: CAL 297 (33% from fat); FAT 10.9g (sat 2.5g); PRO 34.9g; CARB 13.9g; FIB 3.1g; CHOL 93mg; IRON 3.1mg; SOD 486mg; CALC 29mg

CHICKEN SAUSAGE AND APPLE SKILLET

POINTS value: 4

PREP: 14 minutes ■ **COOK:** 17 minutes

Serve this hearty winter meal with refrigerated mashed sweet potatoes.

Cooking spray
6 (3-ounce) chicken and apple sausages (such as Al Fresco)
1 small onion, thinly sliced
3 McIntosh apples, each cut into 12 wedges
¼ cup apple juice
¼ cup fat-free, less-sodium chicken broth
1½ teaspoons chopped fresh thyme

1. Heat a large nonstick skillet over medium heat; coat pan with cooking spray. Add sausages; cook 7 minutes or until done. Remove from pan. Slice each link into 4 diagonal slices; keep warm.

2. Heat pan over medium-high heat. Add onion; sauté 5 minutes or until lightly browned. Add apples; sauté 2 minutes. Add sausage and remaining ingredients; simmer 2 minutes or until liquid evaporates. YIELD: 7 SERVINGS (SERVING SIZE: 1 CUP).

PER SERVING: CAL 185 (51% from fat); FAT 10.4g (sat 3g); PRO 12.4g; CARB 11.9g; FIB 2.5g; CHOL 69mg; IRON 0.2mg; SOD 639mg; CALC 7mg

HERBED APRICOT-GLAZED CORNISH HENS

POINTS value: 6

PREP: 14 minutes ■ **COOK:** 27 minutes

This is an excellent dish to serve to special guests. Pair it with Couscous with Dried Apricots, Cinnamon, and Toasted Nuts on page 153.

> 2 (1½-pound) Cornish hens, halved lengthwise and skinned
> 2 tablespoons minced fresh rosemary, divided
> ½ teaspoon salt
> ¼ teaspoon freshly ground black pepper
> Cooking spray
> ½ cup apricot preserves
> ¼ cup Dijon mustard
> 2 tablespoons fresh lemon juice

1. Preheat oven to 400°.
2. Pat hens dry with paper towels, and sprinkle undersides evenly with 1 tablespoon rosemary, salt, and pepper. Arrange hens on a foil-lined broiler pan coated with cooking spray. Bake at 400° for 15 minutes.
3. While hens bake, heat preserves in a medium saucepan over medium heat 2 minutes, stirring until melted. Add mustard and lemon juice; simmer 1 minute, stirring until thoroughly heated. Stir in remaining 1 tablespoon rosemary.
4. Remove hens from oven; brush with glaze. Bake an additional 12 minutes or until done. **YIELD: 4 SERVINGS** **(SERVING SIZE: ½ HEN).**

Note: You can substitute 4 (8-ounce) bone-in, skinned chicken breast halves for the hens. Just bake the chicken breasts an additional 15 minutes after brushing them with glaze.

PER SERVING: CAL 263 (18% from fat); FAT 5.4g (sat 1.4g); PRO 32.2g; CARB 19.9g; FIB 0.2g; CHOL 146mg; IRON 1.2mg; SOD 615mg; CALC 22mg

CORNISH HENS

Cornish hens are miniature 4- to 6-week-old chickens with short legs and a broad, muscular breast. They weigh from 1¼ to 1½ pounds each—enough meat to feed one or two people. They are available frozen at most supermarkets (sometimes fresh, too). Refrigerate the hens as soon as you get home, and use them within 2 days. If the hens are packaged tightly in cellophane and you're not planning to use them within a few hours, loosen the packaging or remove it and loosely wrap the hens in wax paper.

TURKEY ROLL-UPS WITH APPLE AND SAGE STUFFING

POINTS value: 7

PREP: 25 minutes ■ **COOK:** 47 minutes

This dish will remind you of Thanksgiving Day, with all your favorite flavors rolled up inside turkey cutlets.

> 4 teaspoons butter, divided
> ½ cup diced peeled Granny Smith apple
> ⅓ cup diced celery
> ⅓ cup minced shallots
> 1½ cups crumbled cornbread
> ¼ cup chopped pecans, toasted
> 1¼ teaspoons dried rubbed sage
> ½ teaspoon pepper, divided
> ¼ teaspoon salt, divided
> 2½ cups fat-free, less-sodium chicken broth, divided
> 10 (3-ounce) turkey breast cutlets
> 2 teaspoons olive oil
> 1 tablespoon all-purpose flour
> ⅓ cup dry white wine

1. Melt 1 teaspoon butter in a large skillet over medium-high heat. Add apple, celery, and shallots; cook 3 to 4 minutes. Remove from heat. Add cornbread, pecans, sage, ¼ teaspoon pepper, and ⅛ teaspoon salt; stir well. Stir in ½ cup broth. Set aside.
2. Place turkey between 2 sheets of plastic wrap, and pound to ¼-inch thickness using a meat mallet or small heavy skillet. Spread 2 tablespoons stuffing mixture down center of each cutlet, leaving a ½-inch border. Roll up each turkey cutlet, jelly-roll fashion, starting with a short side. Secure with wooden picks. Heat oil in pan; place roll-ups, seam sides down, in pan, and cook 6 minutes. Turn, and cook 5 minutes. Remove roll-ups from pan; keep warm.
3. Melt remaining 1 tablespoon butter in pan. Add flour, and cook 1 minute, stirring constantly with a whisk. Stir in wine, and cook 30 seconds. Stir in remaining 2 cups broth, ¼ teaspoon pepper, and ⅛ teaspoon salt; cook 8 minutes or until mixture thickens, stirring occasionally with a whisk. Gently return roll-ups to gravy; cover and simmer 20 minutes, turning roll-ups after 10 minutes. **YIELD: 5 SERVINGS (SERVING SIZE: 2 ROLL-UPS).**

PER SERVING: CAL 342 (29% from fat); FAT 11.2g (sat 2.9g); PRO 45.4g; CARB 15.5g; FIB 1.4g; CHOL 77mg; IRON 2.9mg; SOD 693mg; CALC 25mg

GRILLED TURKEY CUTLETS WITH BASIL-MINT-TOMATO RELISH ☑

POINTS value: 4

PREP: 19 minutes ■ **COOK:** 4 minutes ■ **OTHER:** 2 hours

Take advantage of summer's bounty with the fresh-from-the-garden taste of this relish.

- 1 teaspoon grated fresh lemon rind
- 2 tablespoons fresh lemon juice
- 2 tablespoons chopped fresh basil
- 1 tablespoon chopped fresh mint
- 2 garlic cloves, minced
- 1 teaspoon olive oil
- 8 (3-ounce) turkey breast cutlets
- ¼ teaspoon salt
- Cooking spray
- Basil-Mint-Tomato Relish

1. Combine first 6 ingredients in a large zip-top plastic bag; add turkey. Seal bag, and shake well to coat. Marinate in refrigerator 2 hours, turning bag occasionally.
2. Prepare grill.
3. Remove turkey from marinade, discarding marinade. Sprinkle salt evenly over turkey. Place turkey on grill rack coated with cooking spray; grill 2 to 3 minutes on each side or until no longer pink. Serve with Basil-Mint-Tomato Relish. **YIELD: 4 SERVINGS (SERVING SIZE: 2 CUTLETS AND ½ CUP RELISH).**

PER SERVING: CAL 221 (13% from fat); FAT 3.2g (sat 0.3g); PRO 43g; CARB 5g; FIB 1.2g; CHOL 68mg; IRON 2.6mg; SOD 373mg; CALC 20mg

Basil-Mint-Tomato Relish ☑
POINTS value: 0

- 2 cups grape tomatoes, halved
- 2 tablespoons chopped fresh basil
- 1 tablespoon chopped fresh mint
- ½ teaspoon grated fresh lemon rind
- 1 tablespoon fresh lemon juice
- 1 teaspoon olive oil
- 1 small garlic clove, minced
- ⅛ teaspoon salt

1. Combine all ingredients in a bowl. **YIELD: 2 CUPS.**

PER ½ CUP: CAL 26 (45% from fat); FAT 1.3g (sat 0.2g); PRO 0.8g; CARB 3.7g; FIB 1g; CHOL 0mg; IRON 0.3mg; SOD 77mg; CALC 12mg

TURKEY AND GREENS NOODLE BOWL

POINTS value: 5

PREP: 5 minutes ■ **COOK:** 27 minutes

Serve this warm and spicy one-dish meal when you need to knock the chill off a blustery winter night.

- 3½ cups fat-free, less-sodium chicken broth
- ½ (12-ounce) package whole wheat blend wide noodles (such as Ronzoni Healthy Harvest)
- 1 (16.4-ounce) package hot turkey Italian sausages, casings removed
- 1 red onion, halved and thinly sliced
- 1 (14.5-ounce) can no-salt-added diced tomatoes, undrained
- ½ teaspoon freshly ground black pepper
- 1 (16-ounce) bag washed and trimmed kale
- 1 (15-ounce) can no-salt-added cannellini beans, rinsed and drained

1. Bring broth to a boil in a large saucepan; add noodles. Cover and simmer 6 minutes or until tender. Do not drain.
2. While noodles simmer, cook sausages in a large Dutch oven over medium–high heat 10 minutes or until browned; stir to crumble. Add onion; cook 4 minutes.
3. Add tomatoes and pepper to turkey mixture; bring to a boil. Add half of kale; cover and simmer 1 minute or until kale wilts. Repeat procedure with remaining kale. Add noodles, broth, and beans to turkey mixture; cover and simmer 5 minutes. **YIELD: 8 SERVINGS (SERVING SIZE: 1½ CUPS).**

PER SERVING: CAL 239 (27% from fat); FAT 7.1g (sat 0.1g); PRO 17.3g; CARB 30.4g; FIB 5.7g; CHOL 35mg; IRON 3.3mg; SOD 710mg; CALC 98mg

Fresh Orange and Spring Greens Salad, *page 112*

salads

BERRIES AND MELON SALAD WITH POMEGRANATE-GINGER SPLASH

POINTS value: 1

PREP: 15 minutes

> 3 cups cubed seeded watermelon
> 2 cups quartered strawberries
> 1 cup blueberries
> ⅓ cup blueberry-pomegranate juice
> 3 tablespoons "measures-like-sugar" calorie-free sweetener (such as Splenda)
> 1½ tablespoons fresh lime juice
> 1½ teaspoons grated peeled fresh ginger
> ¾ teaspoon vanilla extract

1. Combine first 3 ingredients in a large bowl; toss gently. Set aside.
2. Combine blueberry-pomegranate juice and next 4 ingredients, stirring with a whisk.
3. Spoon fruit evenly into 5 dishes; drizzle about 1 tablespoon juice mixture over fruit. YIELD: 5 SERVINGS (SERVING SIZE: ABOUT 1¼ CUPS FRUIT AND ABOUT 1 TABLESPOON JUICE MIXTURE).

PER SERVING: CAL 78 (5% from fat); FAT 0.4g (sat 0g); PRO 1.3g; CARB 19.1g; FIB 2.4g; CHOL 0mg; IRON 0.6mg; SOD 3mg; CALC 21mg

WATERMELON AND FETA SALAD

POINTS value: 3

PREP: 10 minutes

> 4 cups arugula, roughly chopped
> ½ cup (2 ounces) crumbled feta cheese
> ¼ cup thinly sliced sweet onion
> 1 tablespoon fresh lime juice
> 1 teaspoon honey
> ½ teaspoon honey Dijon mustard
> ¼ teaspoon salt
> ¼ teaspoon freshly ground black pepper
> 4 teaspoons olive oil
> 4 cups chopped seeded watermelon

1. Combine first 3 ingredients in a large bowl. Set aside.
2. Combine lime juice and next 4 ingredients in a small bowl, stirring with a whisk. Gradually add oil, stirring with a whisk.
3. Pour vinaigrette over arugula mixture; toss. Add watermelon, and toss gently. YIELD: 4 SERVINGS (SERVING SIZE: 1½ CUPS).

PER SERVING: CAL 140 (52% from fat); FAT 8.1g (sat 2.8g); PRO 3.6g; CARB 15.5g; FIB 1.1g; CHOL 13mg; IRON 0.8mg; SOD 315mg; CALC 115mg

---

HOW TO SECTION AN ORANGE

1. Peel the orange with a paring knife, and remove the bitter white pith.

2. Holding the orange over a bowl to catch the juices, slice between membranes and on both sides of each segment of the orange. Lift the segments out with the knife blade.

FRESH ORANGE AND SPRING GREENS SALAD

POINTS value: 1

pictured on page 134

PREP: 15 minutes ■ COOK: 5 minutes

To toast almonds, cook them in a small skillet over medium heat for about 5 minutes. Be sure to stir constantly to prevent burning.

> 4 large navel oranges
> ¼ cup cider vinegar
> 2 tablespoons "measures-like-sugar" calorie-free sweetener (such as Splenda)
> 1 tablespoon canola oil
> ¼ teaspoon crushed red pepper
> ⅛ teaspoon salt
> ½ cup halved and thinly sliced red onion
> 1 (5-ounce) package spring greens
> ¼ cup slivered almonds, toasted

1. Grate 2 teaspoons rind from 1 orange. Place rind in a large bowl. Peel and section oranges over a medium bowl, collecting juice. Drain orange sections, reserving sections and ¼ cup orange juice; save remaining juice for another use. Add reserved juice, vinegar, and next 4 ingredients to rind, stirring well.
2. Add onion and greens to dressing; toss well. Add reserved orange sections, and toss gently. Sprinkle with almonds. Serve immediately. YIELD: 8 SERVINGS (SERVING SIZE: 1 CUP SALAD AND ½ TABLESPOON ALMONDS).

PER SERVING: CAL 81 (40% from fat); FAT 3.6g (sat 0.3g); PRO 1.8g; CARB 11.7g; FIB 2.5g; CHOL 0mg; IRON 0.5mg; SOD 42mg; CALC 52mg

FRESH HERB INSALATA

POINTS value: 2

PREP: 9 minutes

- 1 (7-ounce) bag butter lettuce and radicchio mix (such as Fresh Express Riviera blend)
- ½ cup fresh basil leaves
- ½ cup fresh mint leaves
- ½ cup fresh flat-leaf parsley leaves
- 2 tablespoons fresh lemon juice
- 2 tablespoons extravirgin olive oil
- 1 tablespoon honey
- 1 tablespoon minced shallots
- ¼ teaspoon salt
- ¼ to ½ teaspoon freshly ground black pepper

1. Combine first 4 ingredients in a large bowl.
2. Combine lemon juice and next 5 ingredients, stirring well with a whisk. Pour over salad greens; toss well. Serve immediately. YIELD: 4 SERVINGS (SERVING SIZE: 2 CUPS).

PER SERVING: CAL 99 (65% from fat); FAT 7.2g (sat 1g); PRO 1.3g; CARB 8.4g; FIB 1.3g; CHOL 0mg; IRON 1.3mg; SOD 158mg; CALC 42mg

CAESAR ROMAINE WITH BLACK BREAD CROUTONS

POINTS value: 1

PREP: 6 minutes ■ COOK: 10 minutes

Make the dressing up to a week in advance, and then refrigerate. Toast and cool the croutons ahead, too.

- 2 (0.8-ounce) slices pumpernickel or dark rye bread, cut into ½-inch cubes
- 1 (10-ounce) package torn hearts of romaine lettuce
- ¼ cup finely chopped red onion
- ⅓ cup fat-free buttermilk
- 2 tablespoons fat-free sour cream
- 1½ teaspoons anchovy paste
- 1 garlic clove, minced
- ¼ teaspoon dried oregano
- ¼ teaspoon coarsely ground black pepper

1. Preheat oven to 350°.
2. Arrange bread cubes in a single layer on a baking sheet. Bake at 350° for 10 minutes. Remove from oven, and cool completely.
3. While bread cubes bake, combine lettuce and onion in a large bowl. Set aside.
4. Combine buttermilk and next 4 ingredients in a medium bowl, stirring with a whisk until blended.

5. Add dressing and croutons to lettuce mixture; toss gently to coat. Sprinkle each serving with pepper, and serve immediately. YIELD: 6 SERVINGS (SERVING SIZE: 1 CUP).

PER SERVING: CAL 43 (8% from fat); FAT 0.4g (sat 0.1g); PRO 2.4g; CARB 7.8g; FIB 1.7g; CHOL 2mg; IRON 0.9mg; SOD 290mg; CALC 58mg

GREEK SPINACH SALAD

POINTS value: 4

PREP: 15 minutes ■ OTHER: 10 minutes

- ¼ cup boiling water
- 2 tablespoons chopped sun-dried tomatoes, packed without oil
- 2 cups sliced cucumber (about 1 large)
- 2 cups grape tomatoes
- ½ cup fresh mint leaves
- ½ cup vertically sliced red onion
- 1 (6-ounce) package fresh baby spinach
- ¾ cup low-fat buttermilk
- ½ cup light mayonnaise
- ⅓ cup (1½ ounces) crumbled feta cheese
- 2 tablespoons minced green onions
- 1 tablespoon chopped pitted kalamata olives
- 1 tablespoon red wine vinegar
- 1 teaspoon Dijon mustard
- ¾ teaspoon dried oregano
- ½ teaspoon cracked black pepper
- ¼ teaspoon garlic powder

1. Combine ¼ cup boiling water and sun-dried tomatoes in a small bowl; let stand 10 minutes.
2. While sun-dried tomatoes soak, combine cucumber and next 4 ingredients in a large bowl; toss well.
3. Combine buttermilk and next 9 ingredients in a small bowl; stir well. Drain sun-dried tomatoes; stir into buttermilk mixture. Serve salad with dressing. YIELD: 5 SERVINGS (SERVING SIZE: 2 CUPS SALAD AND 3 TABLE-SPOONS DRESSING).

PER SERVING: CAL 164 (62% from fat); FAT 11.3g (sat 3.4g); PRO 4.9g; CARB 11.5g; FIB 2.6g; CHOL 18mg; IRON 1.8mg; SOD 455mg; CALC 156mg

KALAMATA OLIVES

Olives are one of the classic ingredients of Greek cuisine. Kalamata olives take their name from a city in the southern Peloponnese and are the most flavorful olives from that region. These black, firm olives are almond-shaped with a pointed tip. Authentic kalamata olives are cured in brine that contains high-quality red wine vinegar.

SUN-DRIED TOMATO AND GOAT CHEESE SALAD

POINTS value: 2

PREP: 10 minutes

Look for mâche, or lamb's lettuce, in most whole-foods markets and some large supermarkets. If you can't find it, substitute baby spinach or arugula.

- 4 cups mâche
- 2 cups chopped trimmed baby watercress leaves or large watercress
- 1 cup chopped yellow tomato
- ½ cup thinly sliced red onion
- ¼ cup (2 ounces) goat cheese, crumbled
- 2 tablespoons chopped drained oil-packed sun-dried tomato halves
- 1 tablespoon oil from sun-dried tomatoes
- 1 tablespoon red wine vinegar
- 1 teaspoon honey
- ½ teaspoon Dijon mustard
- ¼ teaspoon salt
- ¼ teaspoon freshly ground black pepper

1. Combine mâche and watercress in a large bowl. Add tomato and next 3 ingredients; toss gently to mix.
2. Combine sun-dried tomato oil and next 3 ingredients in a small bowl, stirring with a whisk until blended. Stir in salt and pepper. Drizzle dressing over salad; toss gently to mix. YIELD: 4 SERVINGS (SERVING SIZE: 1¾ CUPS).

PER SERVING: CAL 98 (63% from fat); FAT 6.9g (sat 2.4g); PRO 4.5g; CARB 5.9g; FIB 1.4g; CHOL 7mg; IRON 1.4mg; SOD 256mg; CALC 79mg

CRUNCHY COLESLAW WITH SPRING PEAS

POINTS value: 1

PREP: 9 minutes

Using frozen peas saves time and lets you prepare this recipe year-round. Opt for blanched early spring peas when available.

- 4 cups shredded coleslaw mix
- ½ cup frozen green peas, thawed
- ½ cup chopped yellow bell pepper
- ½ cup matchstick-cut carrots
- ¼ cup finely chopped onion
- 3 tablespoons cider vinegar
- 2 tablespoons sugar
- 1½ teaspoons canola oil
- ¼ teaspoon salt

1. Place all ingredients in a large bowl; toss gently to coat. Serve immediately. YIELD: 8 SERVINGS (SERVING SIZE: ABOUT ⅔ CUP).

PER SERVING: CAL 43 (19% from fat); FAT 0.9g (sat 0.1g); PRO 1g; CARB 7.8g; FIB 1.5g; CHOL 0mg; IRON 0.2mg; SOD 91mg; CALC 7mg

FAST ASIAN SLAW

POINTS value: 0

pictured on page 137

PREP: 7 minutes

Top with shrimp, pan-seared tofu, or cooked chicken for a satisfying main dish. Or serve this quick slaw on the side with your favorite stir-fry. Find preshredded slaw in the produce department of your supermarket.

- 3 cups angel hair coleslaw
- 1 cup finely shredded bok choy
- ½ cup thinly sliced green onions
- ⅓ cup chopped fresh cilantro
- ⅓ cup chopped fresh mint
- 2 tablespoons rice vinegar
- 1½ tablespoons low-sodium soy sauce
- 1 teaspoon sesame oil
- ⅛ teaspoon salt
- ⅛ teaspoon freshly ground black pepper

1. Combine first 5 ingredients in a large bowl; toss well. Combine vinegar, soy sauce, and sesame oil; pour over slaw, and toss to coat. Sprinkle with salt and pepper, tossing gently. YIELD: 4 SERVINGS (SERVING SIZE: 1 CUP).

PER SERVING: CAL 36 (30% from fat); FAT 1.2g (sat 0.2g); PRO 1.3g; CARB 4.7g; FIB 1.9g; CHOL 0mg; IRON 0.5mg; SOD 328mg; CALC 35mg

SWEET LEMON-JÍCAMA SLAW

POINTS value: 1

PREP: 10 minutes

This crunchy, refreshing, citrusy slaw features jícama, a Mexican root vegetable with a texture similar to a water chestnut.

- 2 cups matchstick-cut peeled jícama
- ¼ cup thinly sliced red onion
- 2 jalapeño peppers, seeded and finely chopped
- 1 teaspoon grated fresh lemon rind
- 3 tablespoons fresh lemon juice
- 2 tablespoons sugar
- 2 tablespoons chopped fresh cilantro
- 1 teaspoon canola oil

1. Combine all ingredients in a medium bowl, and toss well. YIELD: 5 SERVINGS (SERVING SIZE: ½ CUP).

PER SERVING: CAL 52 (17% from fat); FAT 1g (sat 0.1g); PRO 0.5g; CARB 11g; FIB 2.7g; CHOL 0mg; IRON 0.4mg; SOD 3mg; CALC 9mg

ABOUT JÍCAMA

Jícama (HEE-ka-ma) is a staple in Latin America, Central America, and Mexico. It resembles a turnip or a large radish. It has white flesh and tan, brown, or gray thin skin that should be peeled before eating jícama raw. When cooked, jícama tends to take on the flavors of the ingredients it's combined with. Look for jícama in the produce section of large supermarkets and in Mexican markets. Select roots that have thin skins (a thick skin means the jícama is old). You can store jícama up to 1 week in a plastic bag in the refrigerator.

BEET SALAD WITH GREEN BEANS

POINTS value: 2

PREP: 13 minutes ■ COOK: 24 minutes
■ OTHER: 15 minutes

⅓ cup red wine vinegar
2 tablespoons olive oil
1 tablespoon minced shallots
1 teaspoon sugar
1 teaspoon Dijon mustard
½ teaspoon salt
¼ teaspoon freshly ground black pepper
1 (12-ounce) package trimmed fresh green beans
1 pound fresh beets, peeled and cut into ½-inch pieces
2 tablespoons chopped walnuts, toasted
2 tablespoons crumbled goat cheese

1. Combine first 7 ingredients in a small bowl, stirring with a whisk. Set aside.
2. Place green beans in a vegetable steamer. Steam, covered, 11 minutes or until tender. Drain, and place in a large bowl. Pour half of dressing over beans; chill.
3. Place beets in steamer. Steam, covered, 13 minutes or until tender. Drain well, and place in a medium bowl. Pour remaining dressing over beets; chill.
4. Combine beets and green beans; toss gently. Top with walnuts and goat cheese. YIELD: 8 SERVINGS (SERVING SIZE: ½ CUP).

PER SERVING: CAL 90 (57% from fat); FAT 5.7g (sat 1.3g); PRO 2.7g; CARB 7.9g; FIB 2.6g; CHOL 3mg; IRON 1mg; SOD 212mg; CALC 35mg

GREEN BEAN, ROASTED BEET, AND FETA SALAD

POINTS value: 1

PREP: 26 minutes ■ COOK: 58 minutes
■ OTHER: 20 minutes

To get a jump start on this recipe, prepare the beets and green beans up to a day in advance.

5 medium beets (about 2 pounds), trimmed, peeled, and cut into ½-inch wedges
Cooking spray
5 teaspoons olive oil, divided
1¼ pounds green beans, trimmed
2 tablespoons thawed orange juice concentrate
1 tablespoon white wine vinegar
⅛ teaspoon salt
⅛ teaspoon pepper
1 head Bibb lettuce, separated into leaves
¼ cup sliced red onion
¼ cup (1 ounce) crumbled feta cheese

1. Preheat oven to 400°.
2. Place beets on a large rimmed baking sheet coated with cooking spray; drizzle with 2 teaspoons oil, and toss well. Bake at 400° for 50 minutes or until beets are tender and lightly browned, stirring once. Cool beets 20 minutes or until they reach room temperature.
3. Cook beans in boiling water 3 to 5 minutes or until crisp-tender. Drain; rinse with cold water. Drain.
4. Combine orange juice concentrate, remaining 1 tablespoon oil, vinegar, salt, and pepper in a small bowl; stir well with a whisk.
5. Place lettuce on a large platter; top with green beans, beets, and onion slices. Drizzle with dressing, and sprinkle with feta cheese. YIELD: 8 SERVINGS (SERVING SIZE: 1 CUP LETTUCE, ABOUT ¾ CUP BEETS, ⅓ CUP BEANS, AND ½ TABLE-SPOON CHEESE).

PER SERVING: CAL 90 (40% from fat); FAT 4g (sat 1.1g); PRO 3.1g; CARB 12.2g; FIB 3.9g; CHOL 4mg; IRON 1.5mg; SOD 134mg; CALC 66mg

HANDLING BEETS

When handling and preparing beets, wear disposable latex gloves to prevent your fingers from getting stained. If you prefer not to use gloves, remove beet-juice stains by rubbing your hands with the cut side of a raw potato half.

CUCUMBER SALAD WITH FETA CHEESE

POINTS value: 1

PREP: 18 minutes ■ **OTHER:** 3 hours

Jalapeño pepper and feta cheese contribute a little heat and extra tang to a traditional marinated cucumber salad.

  ½ cup cider vinegar
  2 tablespoons water
  1 tablespoon sugar
  1 tablespoon canola oil
  ¼ teaspoon salt
  ¼ teaspoon freshly ground black pepper
  4 cups thinly sliced peeled cucumber
  ½ cup vertically sliced red onion
  1 jalapeño pepper, seeded and chopped
  ¼ cup (1 ounce) crumbled feta cheese

1. Combine first 6 ingredients in a medium bowl, stirring with a whisk until blended. Add cucumber, onion, and jalapeño; toss to coat. Cover and chill at least 3 hours. Sprinkle evenly with cheese. YIELD: 6 SERVINGS (SERVING SIZE: ABOUT ¾ CUP CUCUMBER MIXTURE AND 2 TEASPOONS CHEESE).

PER SERVING: CAL 65 (53% from fat); FAT 3.8g (sat 1.1g); PRO 1.6g; CARB 5.5g; FIB 0.9g; CHOL 6mg; IRON 0.3mg; SOD 170mg; CALC 48mg

TEX-MEX SALAD

POINTS value: 2

PREP: 6 minutes

With ¼ cup of light ranch dressing drizzled over the top, this hearty salad has extra creaminess and a **POINTS** value of only 3.

  2 tablespoons fresh lime juice
  1 teaspoon honey Dijon mustard
  ½ teaspoon ground cumin
  ¼ teaspoon salt
  ¼ teaspoon freshly ground black pepper
Dash of chili powder
  2½ tablespoons canola oil
  6 cups chopped romaine lettuce
  1 cup multicolored cherry tomatoes, quartered
  ⅓ cup no-salt-added black beans, rinsed and drained
  ¼ cup (1 ounce) reduced-fat shredded sharp Cheddar cheese
  ⅓ cup crushed baked blue tortilla chips (about 9; such as Guiltless Gourmet)

1. Combine first 6 ingredients in a small bowl. Add oil; stir with a whisk.
2. Combine lettuce and next 3 ingredients in a large bowl; toss gently. Drizzle with vinaigrette; toss to coat. Divide salad among 6 plates; sprinkle each serving with tortilla chips. Serve immediately. YIELD: 6 SERVINGS (SERVING SIZE: ABOUT 1½ CUPS).

PER SERVING: CAL 108 (65% from fat); FAT 7.8g (sat 1.3g); PRO 3.2g; CARB 7.5g; FIB 2.4g; CHOL 4mg; IRON 0.9mg; SOD 135mg; CALC 70mg

BULGUR AND PINE NUT SALAD

POINTS value: 2

PREP: 5 minutes ■ **COOK:** 18 minutes
■ **OTHER:** 10 minutes

Bulgur, a popular grain in Middle Eastern cuisine, is big on nutrition. In fact, it has fewer calories and less fat than brown rice, with more than twice the fiber.

  2 cups water
  1 cup uncooked bulgur
  ½ teaspoon salt, divided
  ¼ cup fresh lemon juice
  1 tablespoon extravirgin olive oil
  ½ teaspoon Dijon mustard
  ½ teaspoon freshly ground black pepper
  ⅓ cup chopped fresh mint
  ⅓ cup golden raisins
  ⅓ cup dried cranberries
  2 tablespoons pine nuts, toasted

1. Combine 2 cups water, bulgur, and ¼ teaspoon salt in a medium saucepan. Bring to a boil; cover, reduce heat, and simmer 12 to 15 minutes or until tender. Remove from heat, drain off excess liquid, and cool.
2. While bulgur cooks, combine remaining ¼ teaspoon salt, lemon juice, and next 3 ingredients in a small bowl, stirring well with a whisk. Set aside.
3. Combine cooled bulgur, mint, and next 3 ingredients. Drizzle vinaigrette over top; toss gently to mix. YIELD: 7 SERVINGS (SERVING SIZE: ½ CUP).

PER SERVING: CAL 145 (25% from fat); FAT 4.1g (sat 0.5g); PRO 3.1g; CARB 26.3g; FIB 4.5g; CHOL 0mg; IRON 0.9mg; SOD 179mg; CALC 15mg

BULGUR SALAD WITH TOMATOES, CAPERS, AND FRESH HERBS ☑.

POINTS value: 2

PREP: 9 minutes ■ **COOK:** 5 minutes ■ **OTHER:** 5 minutes

- ¾ cup water
- ¾ cup bulgur wheat with soy cereal (such as Hodgson Mill)
- 1½ cups chopped seeded tomato (about 2 medium)
- ⅓ cup chopped fresh parsley
- 2 tablespoons chopped fresh basil
- 2 tablespoons capers
- 2 tablespoons cider vinegar
- 2 tablespoons fresh lemon juice
- 1 tablespoon chopped fresh oregano
- 1 tablespoon extravirgin olive oil
- 1 garlic clove, minced
- ¼ teaspoon salt

1. Bring ¾ cup water to a boil in a medium saucepan. Add bulgur; cover, reduce heat, and simmer 4 minutes or until liquid is absorbed. Remove from heat, and place cooked bulgur in a single layer on a jelly-roll pan; let stand at room temperature until cool.
2. While bulgur cools, combine tomato and next 9 ingredients in a medium bowl. Add bulgur, and toss until blended. YIELD: 6 SERVINGS (SERVING SIZE: ABOUT ½ CUP).

PER SERVING: CAL 92 (29% from fat); FAT 3g (sat 0.4g); PRO 5.7g; CARB 13.9g; FIB 2.3g; CHOL 0mg; IRON 1.3mg; SOD 186mg; CALC 36mg

LENTIL AND GARDEN VEGETABLE SALAD ☑.

POINTS value: 3

PREP: 15 minutes ■ **COOK:** 36 minutes

Dried lentils don't require prior soaking, unlike other dried beans. Just wash and drain them well before cooking. To shorten the assembly of the salad, cook the lentils ahead.

- 1 cup uncooked lentils
- 2 tablespoons olive oil, divided
- 1 cup finely chopped onion
- 2 garlic cloves, minced
- 1 cup chopped celery
- 1 cup chopped seeded peeled cucumber
- 1 cup grape tomatoes, halved
- ¼ cup balsamic vinegar
- ¼ cup water
- ½ teaspoon salt
- ½ teaspoon freshly ground black pepper

1. Combine lentils and water to cover in a medium saucepan. Bring to a boil; cover, reduce heat, and simmer 25 minutes or just until tender. Drain and rinse with cold water; drain well, and place in a medium bowl.
2. Heat 1 tablespoon oil in a medium skillet over medium heat. Add onion and garlic, and sauté 8 minutes or until tender. Add onion mixture, remaining 1 tablespoon oil, celery, and remaining ingredients to lentils; toss well. Serve immediately, or cover and chill until ready to serve. YIELD: 6 SERVINGS (SERVING SIZE: 1 CUP).

PER SERVING: CAL 177 (25% from fat); FAT 5g (sat 0.7g); PRO 9.3g; CARB 25.1g; FIB 8.6g; CHOL 0mg; IRON 3.4mg; SOD 217mg; CALC 43mg

LENTIL NUTRITION

Lentils are the smallest of the legumes, a family of edible seeds from pods that also includes dried peas, chickpeas, and beans. Lentils contain iron, protein, and virtually no fat. One cup of cooked lentils provides 90% of the recommended daily allowance of folic acid, an important nutrient for women of childbearing age that helps protect against birth defects.

SPICY VEGETABLE SALAD WITH PASTA

POINTS value: 2

pictured on page 135

PREP: 16 minutes ■ **COOK:** 13 minutes ■ **OTHER:** 15 minutes

For milder flavor, substitute regular pitted green olives for the jalapeño-stuffed olives.

- 4 ounces uncooked multigrain rotini
- 1 cup grape tomatoes, halved
- 1 cup diced green bell pepper
- 12 queen-sized jalapeño-stuffed green olives, sliced
- ¼ cup finely chopped green onions
- 2 tablespoons chopped fresh cilantro
- ½ teaspoon grated fresh lemon rind
- 2 tablespoons fresh lemon juice
- 2 teaspoons extravirgin olive oil

1. Cook pasta according to package directions, omitting salt and fat. Drain; rinse with cold water. Drain.
2. While pasta cooks, combine tomatoes and next 7 ingredients in a medium bowl. Add pasta; toss. Let stand 15 minutes. YIELD: 6 SERVINGS (SERVING SIZE: ABOUT ¾ CUP).

PER SERVING: CAL 110 (28% from fat); FAT 3.4g (sat 0.3g); PRO 3g; CARB 18g; FIB 1.5g; CHOL 0mg; IRON 0.8mg; SOD 255mg; CALC 12mg

GARDEN VEGETABLE SHRIMP SALAD ☑.

POINTS value: 4

PREP: 12 minutes ■ **COOK:** 10 minutes

Long, thin enoki mushrooms have small white caps and grow in clusters. Frequently used in Japanese, Korean, and Chinese cuisines, they can be found in the produce section of most supermarkets.

- 1 **cup green beans, trimmed**
- 4 **cups torn romaine lettuce**
- 1 **cup cherry tomatoes, halved**
- ½ **cup matchstick-cut carrots**
- ½ **cup enoki mushrooms**
- ½ **pound medium shrimp, peeled and deveined**
- ½ **teaspoon garlic powder**

Cooking spray

Quick and Easy Balsamic Vinaigrette

1. Cook beans in boiling water to cover 5 minutes or until crisp-tender. Drain, and rinse with cold water. Drain.
2. Combine green beans, lettuce, and next 3 ingredients in a large bowl. Set aside.
3. Sprinkle shrimp with garlic powder. Heat a large nonstick skillet over medium-high heat; coat pan with cooking spray. Add shrimp; cook 3 to 4 minutes or until done. Chill, if desired.
4. Arrange lettuce mixture evenly on 2 plates. Top each with half of shrimp and 2 tablespoons Quick and Easy Balsamic Vinaigrette. **YIELD: 2 SERVINGS (SERVING SIZE: ABOUT 3 CUPS).**

PER SERVING: CAL 239 (23% from fat); FAT 6g (sat 0.9g); PRO 27.1g; CARB 19.5g; FIB 6.1g; CHOL 172mg; IRON 4.9mg; SOD 413mg; CALC 142mg

Quick and Easy Balsamic Vinaigrette ☑.

POINTS value: 1

- 2 **tablespoons balsamic vinegar**
- 1 **tablespoon fresh lemon juice**
- 1½ **teaspoons olive oil**
- 1 **teaspoon Dijon mustard**
- ¼ **teaspoon finely minced garlic**
- ⅛ **teaspoon salt**
- ⅛ **teaspoon freshly ground black pepper**

1. Combine all ingredients in a small bowl, stirring with a whisk. **YIELD: ¼ CUP.**

PER TABLESPOON: CAL 25 (61% from fat); FAT 1.7g (sat 0.2g); PRO 0.1g; CARB 2.1g; FIB 0g; CHOL 0mg; IRON 0.1mg; SOD 105mg; CALC 3mg

TUNA, BEAN, AND TOMATO SALAD ☑.

POINTS value: 4

PREP: 13 minutes

To prevent the salad from looking mushy after it's tossed together, drain the tuna and then use a fork to break it into large chunks.

- ½ **teaspoon grated fresh lemon rind**
- 3 **tablespoons fresh lemon juice**
- 2 **tablespoons capers, drained**
- 1½ **tablespoons extravirgin olive oil**
- ¼ **teaspoon freshly ground black pepper**
- 3 **(3-ounce) cans albacore tuna in water, drained and flaked into large chunks**
- 1 **(15-ounce) can cannellini beans, rinsed and drained**
- 1 **cup cherry tomatoes, halved**
- ⅓ **cup chopped red onion**
- ¼ **cup chopped pitted kalamata olives**
- 3 **tablespoons chopped fresh basil**
- 4 **cups trimmed arugula**

1. Combine first 5 ingredients in a large bowl, stirring with a whisk.
2. Add tuna and next 5 ingredients to bowl; toss gently to combine. Serve over arugula. **YIELD: 4 SERVINGS (SERVING SIZE: ABOUT 1 CUP TUNA MIXTURE AND 1 CUP ARUGULA).**

PER SERVING: CAL 208 (38% from fat); FAT 8.8g (sat 1.1g); PRO 18.8g; CARB 14g; FIB 3.7g; CHOL 26mg; IRON 1.7mg; SOD 619mg; CALC 67mg

STEAK SALAD WITH BEETS AND BLUE CHEESE

POINTS value: 6

pictured on page 136

PREP: 10 minutes ■ **COOK:** 25 minutes
■ **OTHER:** 25 minutes

- ½ **pound beets (about 2 medium), trimmed**

Cooking spray

- 8 **ounces flank steak**
- ½ **teaspoon garlic powder**
- ¼ **teaspoon salt**
- ¼ **teaspoon crushed red pepper**
- 4 **cups chopped romaine lettuce**
- ½ **cup thinly sliced red onion**
- 2 **plum tomatoes, cut into wedges**
- 2 **tablespoons crumbled blue cheese**
- ¼ **cup fat-free balsamic vinaigrette (such as Maple Grove Farms)**

1. Preheat oven to 450°.

2. Wash beets thoroughly, leaving skins on. Place beets on a foil-lined baking sheet. Spray beets with cooking spray. Bake at 450° for 25 minutes or until tender. Cool, peel, and thinly slice beets.

3. While beets bake, sprinkle steak with garlic powder, salt, and pepper. Prepare grill. Place steak on grill rack coated with cooking spray. Grill 6 to 8 minutes on each side or until desired degree of doneness. Let steak stand 5 minutes; cut diagonally across grain into thin slices.

4. Arrange lettuce on plates. Top with beets, onion, tomato, and blue cheese. Arrange steak evenly over lettuce mixture; drizzle each serving evenly with vinaigrette. YIELD: 2 SERVINGS (SERVING SIZE: 2 CUPS SALAD MIXTURE, 3 OUNCES STEAK, AND 2 TABLESPOONS VINAIGRETTE).

PER SERVING: CAL 319 (31% from fat); FAT 11g (sat 4.9g); PRO 29.3g; CARB 26.5g; FIB 6.9g; CHOL 49mg; IRON 3.8mg; SOD 955mg; CALC 129mg

EIGHT-SPICE CHICKEN SALAD

POINTS value: 4

PREP: 24 minutes ■ COOK: 13 minutes
■ OTHER: 4 minutes

Five-spice powder is a traditional ingredient in Chinese cooking that represents five distinct flavor profiles: sweet, sour, bitter, savory, and salty. We added coriander, brown sugar, and salt along with the five-spice powder for more sweet and salty flavor.

- 2 teaspoons five-spice powder
- 1 teaspoon ground coriander
- 1 teaspoon brown sugar
- ¾ teaspoon garlic salt
- ½ teaspoon instant minced onion
- ¼ teaspoon freshly ground black pepper
- 4 (6-ounce) skinless, boneless chicken breast halves
- 1 tablespoon canola oil
- 6 tablespoons low-fat sesame ginger dressing (such as Newman's Own)
- 2 tablespoons fresh lime juice
- 6 cups shredded romaine lettuce (about 2 hearts of romaine)
- 1 cup packaged cabbage-and-carrot coleslaw
- 1 cup julienne-cut snow peas

1. Combine first 6 ingredients in a shallow dish. Dredge chicken in spice mixture.

2. Heat oil in a large nonstick skillet over medium-high heat. Add chicken, and cook 6 minutes on each side or until done. Cool. Shred chicken with 2 forks to measure 5 cups.

3. Combine dressing and lime juice in a large bowl, stirring with a whisk. Add lettuce, coleslaw, peas, and chicken; toss gently. YIELD: 6 SERVINGS (SERVING SIZE: ABOUT 1¾ CUPS).

PER SERVING: CAL 193 (22% from fat); FAT 4.8g (sat 0.6g); PRO 27.9g; CARB 8.4g; FIB 2.4g; CHOL 66mg; IRON 2.2mg; SOD 398mg; CALC 51mg

CHICKEN SALAD WITH HONEY VINAIGRETTE

POINTS value: 7

PREP: 14 minutes ■ COOK: 4 minutes

- 6 cups torn romaine lettuce
- 3 cups shredded cooked chicken breast
- 2 cups grape tomatoes, halved
- ½ cup (2 ounces) reduced-fat shredded sharp Cheddar cheese
- ½ cup diced red onion
- ⅓ cup honey
- 2 tablespoons olive oil
- 2 tablespoons rice wine vinegar
- 4 teaspoons Dijon mustard
- ½ teaspoon salt
- ½ teaspoon freshly ground black pepper
- 6 tablespoons coarsely chopped pecans, toasted

1. Combine first 5 ingredients in a large bowl; toss gently.

2. Combine honey and next 5 ingredients in a small bowl, stirring with a whisk.

3. Divide salad mixture evenly among 6 plates; drizzle with dressing, and sprinkle with pecans. YIELD: 6 SERVINGS (SERVING SIZE: ABOUT 1½ CUPS SALAD, ABOUT 1½ TABLESPOONS DRESSING, AND 1 TABLESPOON PECANS).

PER SERVING: CAL 326 (43% from fat); FAT 15.5g (sat 3.5g); PRO 26.2g; CARB 22.7g; FIB 2.8g; CHOL 67mg; IRON 1.8mg; SOD 336mg; CALC 116mg

HONEY, A SUPERFOOD

One of man's oldest medicines, honey has medicinal properties that come from a range of compounds, including antioxidants and oligosaccharides. Adding honey to your diet raises the number of antioxidants in your body, which helps protect against heart disease and cancer. The oligosaccharides increase the good bacteria in your intestines and help reduce blood pressure and cholesterol. Remember that antioxidant abilities can vary depending on the bees' nectar sources and how the honey is processed, but, in general, the darker the honey, the more antioxidants it contains.

THAI NOODLE CHICKEN SALAD

POINTS value: 6

PREP: 15 minutes ■ COOK: 5 minutes
■ OTHER: 15 minutes

Look for rice stick noodles in the Asian-foods section of most supermarkets or in Asian-food stores. Or substitute 4 to 5 cups of cooked thin spaghetti.

- 1 pound skinless, boneless chicken breast halves
- 1 bay leaf
- 1 (6-ounce) package uncooked rice stick noodles
- 1 large red bell pepper, cut into 3-inch strips (about 1 cup)
- 1 small cucumber, peeled, quartered horizontally, and thinly sliced (about 1 cup)
- 4 green onions, thinly sliced (about 1 cup)
- ¼ cup chopped fresh basil
- ¼ cup chopped fresh cilantro
- ¼ cup chopped fresh mint
- ⅓ cup rice vinegar
- ¼ cup fresh lime juice
- 3 tablespoons canola oil
- 1½ teaspoons salt
- 1 teaspoon sugar
- ½ teaspoon freshly ground black pepper
- 5 cups torn romaine lettuce
- 3 tablespoons chopped dry-roasted peanuts

1. Place chicken and bay leaf in a medium saucepan; fill pan with water to cover chicken. Bring to a boil; boil 1 minute. Remove from heat; cover and let stand 15 minutes or until chicken is fully cooked. Remove chicken from liquid, and cool; shred into small pieces.
2. While chicken stands, place rice stick noodles in a large bowl; cover with hot water, and let stand 15 minutes or until softened. Drain rice stick noodles; return to bowl. Add chicken, bell pepper, and next 5 ingredients; toss to combine.
3. Combine vinegar and next 5 ingredients in a small bowl; stir well with a whisk. Pour over noodle mixture, and toss well to combine. Cover and chill until ready to serve.
4. Prior to serving, stir in lettuce; toss well. Divide salad evenly among 6 plates. Sprinkle each serving with 1½ teaspoons chopped peanuts. YIELD: 6 SERVINGS (SERVING SIZE: ABOUT 2 CUPS SALAD AND 1½ TEASPOONS PEANUTS).

PER SERVING: CAL 303 (31% from fat); FAT 10.5g (sat 1.1g); PRO 21.7g; CARB 32.3g; FIB 3.5g; CHOL 44mg; IRON 1.7mg; SOD 644mg; CALC 53mg

RICE STICK NOODLES

Popular in Asian cuisine, rice stick noodles are made from rice flour. They are more tender and elastic than wheat pastas, so they have a unique texture. As they cook, these white noodles become translucent and assume the flavors of the ingredients they are cooked with.

ITALIAN COBB SALAD

POINTS value: 5

PREP: 8 minutes ■ COOK: 4 minutes

Using prosciutto instead of ham puts an Italian spin on the traditional version of this famous salad.

- Olive oil–flavored cooking spray
- 4 ounces thinly sliced prosciutto, chopped
- 1 (10-ounce) package Italian-blend salad greens
- 2 cups chopped cooked chicken
- 1 cup (4 ounces) shredded part-skim mozzarella cheese
- 2 hard-cooked large eggs, sliced
- ½ cup fat-free balsamic vinaigrette (such as Maple Grove Farms)

1. Heat a large nonstick skillet over medium-high heat; coat pan with cooking spray. Add prosciutto; sauté 4 minutes or until browned.
2. Arrange salad greens on 6 plates. Top evenly with chicken, cheese, egg, and prosciutto. Drizzle evenly with vinaigrette. YIELD: 6 SERVINGS (SERVING SIZE: ABOUT 1⅔ CUPS).

PER SERVING: CAL 231 (42% from fat); FAT 10.7g (sat 4.5g); PRO 25.5g; CARB 6.7g; FIB 0.7g; CHOL 133mg; IRON 1.4mg; SOD 717mg; CALC 167mg

sandwiches

Catfish Sandwiches with Tartar Sauce, *page 122*

CATFISH SANDWICHES WITH TARTAR SAUCE

POINTS value: 6

pictured on page 138

PREP: 14 minutes ■ **COOK:** 10 minutes

- ½ cup fat-free mayonnaise
- 1 tablespoon sweet pickle relish
- ½ teaspoon garlic powder
- 1½ teaspoons fresh lemon juice
- 1 teaspoon Worcestershire sauce
- ⅓ cup yellow cornmeal
- 2 teaspoons salt-free Cajun seasoning
- ¼ teaspoon salt
- 4 (6-ounce) catfish fillets, cut in half
- 2 teaspoons canola oil
- Cooking spray
- 4 (1.4-ounce) light wheat hamburger buns, toasted
- 4 green leaf lettuce leaves
- 4 (¼-inch-thick) slices tomato
- 4 lemon wedges

1. Combine first 5 ingredients in a small dish; set aside.
2. Combine cornmeal, Cajun seasoning, and salt in a shallow dish. Dredge fillet halves in cornmeal mixture, shaking off excess.
3. Heat a large nonstick skillet over medium–high heat. Add oil, swirling to coat. Add fish; cook 5 minutes. Coat fish with cooking spray, turn, and cook 5 minutes or until fish flakes easily when tested with a fork.
4. Spread 1 tablespoon mayonnaise mixture on each bun half. Top each bottom half with 1 lettuce leaf, 1 tomato slice, 2 fillet halves, and top half of bun. Serve with lemon wedges. YIELD: 4 SERVINGS (SERVING SIZE: 1 SANDWICH AND 1 LEMON WEDGE).

PER SERVING: CAL 316 (26% from fat); FAT 9.2g (sat 1.6g); PRO 33g; CARB 33.3g; FIB 5.6g; CHOL 102mg; IRON 2.6mg; SOD 733mg; CALC 100mg

CRAB SALAD SANDWICHES WITH ARUGULA, BACON, AND TOMATO

POINTS value: 5

PREP: 13 minutes ■ **COOK:** 22 minutes

Prepare the crab salad ahead of time. Cover and chill it until you're ready to assemble these dressed-up BLTs.

- 2 (6-ounce) cans crabmeat (such as Bumble Bee Fancy Lump), drained
- ¼ cup finely chopped celery
- ¼ cup finely chopped onion
- ⅓ cup low-fat mayonnaise
- ½ teaspoon grated fresh lemon rind
- 2 teaspoons fresh lemon juice
- ½ teaspoon dried dill
- ¼ teaspoon freshly ground black pepper
- 4 center-cut bacon slices
- 8 slices whole wheat bread, toasted
- 1 cup loosely packed arugula or baby spinach
- 8 (¼-inch-thick) slices tomato

1. Combine first 8 ingredients in a medium bowl. Set aside.
2. Cook bacon in a large skillet over medium heat until crisp. Drain on paper towels, and cut in half.
3. Top each of 4 bread slices with about ⅓ cup crab salad, ¼ cup arugula, 2 tomato slices, 2 bacon slice halves, and a remaining bread slice. Serve immediately. YIELD: 4 SERVINGS (SERVING SIZE: 1 SANDWICH).

PER SERVING: CAL 234 (35% from fat); FAT 9.1g (sat 0.9g); PRO 19.3g; CARB 24.1g; FIB 6.9g; CHOL 60mg; IRON 2.2mg; SOD 893mg; CALC 123mg

CANNED CRABMEAT

Choose canned crabmeat, found in the refrigerated section of large supermarkets or seafood markets, when you want a less-expensive but still high-quality substitute for fresh. You can find an even less-expensive option on the grocery aisle in a can or shelf-stable pouch. Although generally lower in quality than refrigerated canned versions, it's convenient, available year-round, and can be stored for longer periods of time.

OYSTER PO' BOYS

POINTS value: 7

PREP: 10 minutes ▪ **COOK:** 12 minutes
▪ **OTHER:** 10 minutes

Re-create this New Orleans classic at home, only with less fat and fewer calories.

- ¼ cup light mayonnaise
- 2 tablespoons minced green onions
- 2½ teaspoons salt-free Cajun seasoning, divided
- 2 teaspoons fresh lemon juice, divided
- 1 teaspoon cornstarch
- 1 large egg white
- ½ cup dry breadcrumbs
- 1 (12-ounce) container shucked oysters, drained
- Cooking spray
- 4 (3.3-ounce) wheat sub rolls (such as Cobblestone Mill)
- 1 cup shredded iceberg lettuce

1. Preheat oven to 450°.
2. Combine mayonnaise, green onions, ½ teaspoon Cajun seasoning, and 1 teaspoon lemon juice in a medium bowl. Chill until ready to use.
3. Combine remaining 1 teaspoon lemon juice, cornstarch, and egg white, stirring with a whisk. Combine breadcrumbs and remaining 2 teaspoons Cajun seasoning in a shallow dish. Dip oysters in egg white mixture. Dredge in breadcrumb mixture, pressing firmly to coat. Place oysters on a wire rack over wax paper, and let stand 10 minutes. Place a jelly-roll pan in oven while oysters stand.
4. Coat oysters well with cooking spray. Remove hot pan from oven; coat pan with cooking spray. Place oysters on pan in a single layer. Bake at 450° for 12 minutes, turning once.
5. Halve sub rolls horizontally. Hollow out top and bottom halves of rolls, leaving a ¼-inch border. Reserve torn bread for another use. Spread mayonnaise mixture evenly on each roll half. Top bottom half of each roll with ¼ cup lettuce, one-fourth of oysters, and top half of roll. YIELD: 4 SERVINGS (SERVING SIZE: 1 SANDWICH).

PER SERVING: CAL 353 (24% from fat); FAT 9.5g (sat 1.9g); PRO 15.7g; CARB 52.7g; FIB 4.4g; CHOL 42mg; IRON 7.7mg; SOD 764mg; CALC 147mg

CRANBERRY CHICKEN SANDWICHES

POINTS value: 7

PREP: 14 minutes ▪ **COOK:** 5 minutes

We used only the breast meat from a deli rotisserie chicken for these sandwiches. Use the leftover dark meat to prepare Italian Cobb Salad on page 120 or Pad Thai Chicken Noodle Soup on page 161.

- ½ cup (4 ounces) tub-style light cream cheese
- ¼ cup cranberry chutney (such as Crosse & Blackwell)
- 2 tablespoons chopped pecans or walnuts, toasted
- 8 (0.8-ounce) slices light wheat bread, toasted
- 2 cups shredded cooked chicken breast (about 9 ounces)
- 4 Bibb lettuce leaves

1. Combine first 3 ingredients in a small bowl; stir well.
2. Spread cream cheese mixture evenly on each bread slice. Top each of 4 bread slices evenly with chicken and lettuce leaves. Top with remaining bread slices, coated sides down. YIELD: 4 SERVINGS (SERVING SIZE: 1 SANDWICH).

PER SERVING: CAL 348 (26% from fat); FAT 10g (sat 4g); PRO 30.4g, CARB 32.9g; FIB 2.8g; CHOL 73mg; IRON 2.7mg; SOD 392mg; CALC 83mg

GRILLED CHICKEN CAESAR PANINI

POINTS value: 7

PREP: 4 minutes ▪ **COOK:** 8 minutes

- ¼ cup light Caesar dressing
- 8 (0.5-ounce) slices Italian bread
- 4 slices reduced-fat provolone cheese (such as Alpine Lace)
- 2 cups shredded cooked chicken breast
- 1 cup baby arugula or baby spinach
- Olive oil–flavored cooking spray

1. Preheat panini grill.
2. Spread ½ tablespoon dressing evenly on each bread slice. Top each of 4 bread slices with 1 slice cheese, ½ cup chicken, ¼ cup arugula, and a remaining bread slice. Coat sandwiches with cooking spray, place on panini grill, and cook 4 to 5 minutes or until golden brown. YIELD: 4 SERVINGS (SERVING SIZE: 1 SANDWICH).
Note: If you don't have a panini grill, place sandwiches in a large nonstick skillet over medium heat. Place a piece of foil over sandwiches; top with a heavy skillet. Cook 2 to 3 minutes on each side or until golden and cheese melts.

PER SERVING: CAL 289 (35% from fat); FAT 11.2g (sat 3.6g); PRO 29.8g; CARB 16.9g; FIB 0.9g; CHOL 75mg; IRON 1.7mg; SOD 546mg; CALC 191mg

SESAME-GINGER CHICKEN SANDWICHES WITH PEANUT SAUCE

POINTS value: 7

PREP: 10 minutes ■ **COOK:** 13 minutes

If your chicken breasts are a little thick on one end, pound the breasts with the heel of your hand to even out the thickness before cooking.

>   2 tablespoons creamy peanut butter
>   1 tablespoon low-sodium soy sauce
>   1 tablespoon cider vinegar
>   1 garlic clove, minced
>   1½ teaspoons ground ginger, divided
>   4 (6-ounce) skinless, boneless chicken breast halves
>   4 teaspoons sesame seeds
>   ½ teaspoon salt
>   Cooking spray
>   4 (1.4-ounce) light wheat hamburger buns, toasted
>   1 small cucumber, peeled and sliced (about ¾ cup)
>   1 cup alfalfa sprouts

1. Combine first 4 ingredients in a small bowl. Add ½ teaspoon ginger, stirring with a whisk until well blended. Set aside.

2. Sprinkle both sides of chicken evenly with remaining 1 teaspoon ginger, sesame seeds, and salt. Heat a large nonstick skillet over medium-high heat; coat pan with cooking spray. Add chicken, and cook 6 minutes on each side or until chicken is done.

3. Place 1 chicken breast half on bottom half of each bun; top each with about 2 teaspoons peanut sauce, one-fourth of cucumber slices, ¼ cup alfalfa sprouts, and top half of bun. YIELD: 4 SERVINGS (SERVING SIZE: 1 SANDWICH).

PER SERVING: CAL 333 (24% from fat); FAT 8.7g (sat 1.5g); PRO 46.6g; CARB 24.1g; FIB 5.3g; CHOL 99mg; IRON 3.5mg; SOD 766mg; CALC 96mg

CHICKEN AND STUFFING BURGERS

POINTS value: 6

PREP: 8 minutes ■ **COOK:** 9 minutes
■ **OTHER:** 10 minutes

The stuffing makes the burgers moist and reminds you of a Thanksgiving meal-on-the-go.

>   1 cup sage and onion–seasoned stuffing mix (such as Pepperidge Farm), crushed
>   ¼ cup fat-free, less-sodium chicken broth
>   1 pound lean ground chicken
>   ½ cup chopped green onions
>   3 tablespoons fresh thyme
>   1 large egg, lightly beaten
>   1 large egg yolk
>   ¼ teaspoon salt
>   ¼ teaspoon freshly ground black pepper
>   1 tablespoon canola oil
>   Apricot chutney or prepared mustard (optional)
>   4 (1.4-ounce) light wheat hamburger buns, toasted
>   4 (¼-inch-thick) slices tomato
>   4 small green leaf lettuce leaves

1. Combine stuffing mix and broth in a large bowl; let stand 10 minutes.

2. Add chicken and next 6 ingredients; combine gently with hands just until blended. Divide mixture into 4 equal portions, shaping each into a ½-inch-thick patty.

3. Heat oil in a large nonstick skillet over medium-high heat. Add patties, and cook 4 minutes or until lightly browned. Turn patties, and cook 3 minutes or until done.

4. Spread chutney or mustard on bottom half of each bun, if desired. Top each with 1 patty, 1 tomato slice, 1 lettuce leaf, and top half of bun. YIELD: 4 SERVINGS (SERVING SIZE: 1 BURGER).

PER SERVING: CAL 295 (24% from fat); FAT 7.8g (sat 1.1g); PRO 32.8g; CARB 31.8g; FIB 6.2g; CHOL 170mg; IRON 3mg; SOD 633mg; CALC 95mg

JAPANESE SOY-GLAZED TURKEY BURGERS

POINTS value: 8

PREP: 3 minutes ▪ **COOK:** 13 minutes

The secret to moist, tender turkey burgers is to toss the ingredients lightly with your fingers or a fork just until blended.

   1 teaspoon sesame oil
Cooking spray
  ¾ cup frozen chopped onion, thawed
   2 tablespoons low-sodium soy sauce, divided
   2 tablespoons dry sherry, divided
 1¼ pounds ground turkey
  ½ cup panko (Japanese breadcrumbs)
   1 large egg white, lightly beaten
 1½ tablespoons sugar
   1 tablespoon hot water
   4 (1.4-ounce) light wheat hamburger buns, toasted
   4 (¼-inch-thick) slices tomato
   4 small green leaf lettuce leaves

1. Heat oil in a large nonstick skillet coated with cooking spray over medium-high heat. Add onion; sauté 2 minutes. Add 1 tablespoon soy sauce and 1 tablespoon sherry; sauté 30 seconds. Transfer onion mixture to a large bowl. Wipe pan with a paper towel.

2. Add turkey, panko, and egg white to onion mixture; combine gently with hands just until blended. Divide mixture into 4 equal portions, shaping each into a 4-inch-wide patty.

3. Heat pan over medium-high heat; coat pan with cooking spray. Place patties in pan, and cook 4 minutes on each side or until done.

4. While patties cook, combine sugar and 1 tablespoon hot water in a small bowl, stirring well. Add remaining 1 tablespoon soy sauce and remaining 1 tablespoon sherry; pour over patties in pan. Cook 30 seconds, turning once to coat burgers.

5. Top bottom half of each bun with 1 patty; spoon any remaining glaze in pan over each. Top each with 1 tomato slice, 1 lettuce leaf, and top half of bun. **YIELD: 4 SERVINGS (SERVING SIZE: 1 BURGER).**

PER SERVING: CAL 366 (35% from fat); FAT 14.2g (sat 3.4g); PRO 31.8g; CARB 34.2g; FIB 5.1g; CHOL 112mg; IRON 3.4mg; SOD 646mg; CALC 72mg

GREEK TURKEY BURGERS

POINTS value: 7

PREP: 13 minutes ▪ **COOK:** 8 minutes

Pepperoncini peppers add a bit of spiciness, and the feta cheese contributes richness to these burgers.

   1 pound ground turkey breast
   1 large egg white, beaten
  ½ cup (2 ounces) crumbled reduced-fat feta cheese
  ¼ cup dry breadcrumbs
  ¼ cup chopped seeded pepperoncini pepper
  ½ teaspoon dried oregano
  ¼ teaspoon salt
  ¼ teaspoon freshly ground black pepper
   4 teaspoons prepared mustard
   4 (1.4-ounce) light wheat hamburger buns, toasted
   4 (⅛-inch-thick) slices red onion
   4 (¼-inch-thick) slices tomato
   4 green leaf lettuce leaves

1. Place first 8 ingredients in a large bowl, and combine gently with hands just until blended. Divide turkey mixture into 4 equal portions, shaping each into a ½-inch-thick patty.

2. Heat a large nonstick skillet over medium heat. Place patties in pan, and cook 4 to 5 minutes on each side or until done.

3. Spread 1 teaspoon mustard on bottom half of each bun; top each with 1 patty, 1 onion slice, 1 tomato slice, 1 lettuce leaf, and top half of bun. **YIELD: 4 SERVINGS (SERVING SIZE: 1 BURGER).**

PER SERVING: CAL 316 (35% from fat); FAT 12.3g (sat 3.9g); PRO 32.7g; CARB 28.7g; FIB 5.3g; CHOL 76mg; IRON 3.2mg; SOD 745mg; CALC 144mg

THAI TURKEY BURGERS

POINTS value: 6

PREP: 10 minutes ▪ **COOK:** 8 minutes

For these gourmet-style burgers, look for your favorite chili dipping sauce in the Asian-foods section of the supermarket. Or use sweet chili and pineapple sauce.

- ¼ cup fat-free mayonnaise
- 1½ teaspoons grated peeled fresh ginger
- ¼ teaspoon grated fresh lime rind
- 1 teaspoon fresh lime juice
- 1 teaspoon low-sodium soy sauce
- 1 pound ground turkey breast
- ¼ cup sweet chili sauce (such as Blue Dragon)
- 1½ tablespoons chopped fresh mint
- ¼ teaspoon salt
- Cooking spray
- 4 (1.4-ounce) light wheat hamburger buns
- 12 spinach leaves
- 12 slices English cucumber
- 8 slices red bell pepper

1. Prepare grill.
2. Combine first 5 ingredients in a small bowl; set aside.
3. Combine turkey and next 3 ingredients in a small bowl. Divide mixture into 4 equal portions, shaping each into a ½-inch-thick patty.
4. Place patties on grill rack coated with cooking spray. Grill 4 to 5 minutes on each side or until done.
5. Spread 1 tablespoon mayonnaise mixture on bottom half of each bun; top each with 3 spinach leaves, 1 patty, 3 cucumber slices, 2 red bell pepper slices, and top half of bun. **YIELD: 4 SERVINGS (SERVING SIZE: 1 BURGER).**

PER SERVING: CAL 292 (30% from fat); FAT 9.7g (sat 2.6g); PRO 28.5g; CARB 32.5g; FIB 5.4g; CHOL 72mg; IRON 3.5mg; SOD 844mg; CALC 116mg

SWEET CHILI SAUCE

This Thai sauce is sweet and mildly spicy. The reddish sauce, which has both chopped chilies and whole chili seeds, works well over chicken or seafood, as a dipping sauce for spring rolls, or mixed with ground meat for burgers or meat loaf. Once opened, the sauce lasts up to a year when stored in the refrigerator.

STEAK AND FETA HOAGIES

POINTS value: 7

pictured on page 134

PREP: 10 minutes ▪ **COOK:** 7 minutes
▪ **OTHER:** 3 minutes

Use the discarded bread from the hoagie rolls to make fresh breadcrumbs for Salmon Mini Loaves with Homemade Tartar Sauce on page 70.

- 4 (3-ounce) whole wheat hoagie rolls
- 12 ounces boneless lean sirloin steak
- 1 teaspoon chili powder
- ½ teaspoon coarsely ground black pepper
- Cooking spray
- 3 cups mixed baby greens
- ½ cup (2 ounces) crumbled reduced-fat feta cheese
- ½ cup thinly sliced red bell pepper
- ¼ cup thinly sliced red onion
- ¼ cup fat-free red wine vinaigrette

1. Preheat oven to 350°.
2. Halve hoagie rolls horizontally. Hollow out top and bottom halves of rolls, leaving a ½-inch border. Reserve torn bread for another use. Place rolls on a baking sheet, cut sides down, and bake at 350° for 5 minutes or until toasted. Remove from oven, and set aside.
3. While rolls toast, sprinkle both sides of steak with chili powder and black pepper. Heat a large nonstick skillet over medium-high heat; coat pan with cooking spray. Add steak, and cook 2 to 3 minutes on each side or until desired degree of doneness. Remove pan from heat, and let steak stand in pan 3 minutes.
4. While steak stands, combine greens and next 4 ingredients in a medium bowl, tossing to mix. Set aside.
5. Cut steak diagonally against grain. Top bottom half of each roll evenly with steak slices; drizzle any remaining juices from pan over each. Top each with one-fourth of salad mixture and top half of roll. **YIELD: 4 SERVINGS (SERVING SIZE: 1 SANDWICH).**

PER SERVING: CAL 346 (26% from fat); FAT 9.9g (sat 3.6g); PRO 27.9g; CARB 38.5g; FIB 6.6g; CHOL 55mg; IRON 3.8mg; SOD 794mg; CALC 139mg

GRILLED CAPRESE SANDWICHES

POINTS value: 6

PREP: 17 minutes ■ **COOK:** 12 minutes

A fresh caprese salad is a staple in Italy. Combine similar ingredients and apply a little heat to create these delicious sandwiches.

- ½ teaspoon Italian seasoning
- ¼ teaspoon freshly ground black pepper
- ½ cup finely chopped fresh basil
- 8 slices whole wheat bread (such as Arnold)
- 8 (¼-inch-thick) slices tomato
- 8 ounces fresh mozzarella cheese, cut into 8 slices
- Olive oil–flavored cooking spray

1. Combine Italian seasoning and pepper in a small bowl. Add basil, and toss well. Top each of 4 bread slices with 2 tomato slices and 2 cheese slices. Sprinkle evenly with basil mixture, and top with remaining bread slices.
2. Coat 1 side of each sandwich with cooking spray. Place 2 sandwiches, coated sides down, in a large non-stick skillet over medium-low heat. Cook 3 minutes. Coat sandwiches with cooking spray, turn, and cook 3 minutes or until bread is golden. Repeat procedure with remaining sandwiches. **YIELD: 4 SERVINGS (SERVING SIZE: 1 SANDWICH).**

PER SERVING: CAL 300 (43% from fat); FAT 14.4g (sat 7.2g); PRO 23.2g; CARB 22.1g; FIB 6.7g; CHOL 31mg; IRON 1.9mg; SOD 561mg; CALC 506mg

MOZZARELLA EN CAROZZA

POINTS value: 6

PREP: 7 minutes ■ **COOK:** 8 minutes

Literally translated, this sandwich means "mozzarella in a carriage." It is traditionally fried until the cheese oozes out of its bread (or "carriage"). Our healthier version uses low-fat dairy products and minimal oil to yield similar mouthwatering results.

- 8 (0.9-ounce) slices white wheat bread (such as Nature's Own)
- 6 (0.8-ounce) slices part-skim mozzarella cheese, torn in half
- 1 cup egg substitute
- ¼ cup 1% low-fat milk
- 2 teaspoons minced fresh sage
- ¼ teaspoon salt
- ¼ cup grated fresh Parmesan cheese
- 2 teaspoons olive oil, divided
- ½ cup tomato-basil pasta sauce (such as Classico)

1. Top each of 4 bread slices with 1½ slices cheese and 1 bread slice.
2. Combine egg substitute and next 3 ingredients, stirring with a whisk. Dip each sandwich in egg mixture, allowing excess to drip off. Sprinkle each side of sandwiches with ½ tablespoon Parmesan cheese.
3. Heat 1 teaspoon oil in a large nonstick skillet over medium-high heat. Add 2 sandwiches to pan; cook 2 minutes on each side or until golden. Repeat procedure with remaining oil and sandwiches.
4. Heat pasta sauce in a small microwave-safe bowl at HIGH 30 seconds or until thoroughly heated. Serve sandwiches with pasta sauce. **YIELD: 4 SERVINGS (SERVING SIZE: 1 SANDWICH AND 2 TABLESPOONS SAUCE).**

PER SERVING: CAL 296 (40% from fat); FAT 13g (sat 6.1g); PRO 22.9g; CARB 27g; FIB 5.6g; CHOL 23mg; IRON 4.2mg; SOD 869mg; CALC 620mg

PORTOBELLO MUSHROOM AND ROASTED PEPPER SANDWICHES

POINTS value: 7

PREP: 10 minutes ■ **COOK:** 6 minutes

Portobello mushrooms have a wonderful meaty flavor. Look for portobellos that are smooth skinned and firm. Coupled with sweet bell peppers and creamy goat cheese, they make satisfying sandwiches.

> 4 large portobello mushroom caps
> 1 tablespoon olive oil
> 1 tablespoon finely minced garlic
> ½ teaspoon freshly ground black pepper, divided
> ¼ teaspoon salt
> Cooking spray
> 2 tablespoons light mayonnaise
> 8 (1.3-ounce) slices sourdough bread (such as Cobblestone Mill), toasted
> 1 cup packed baby arugula
> 1 cup bottled roasted red bell peppers, drained
> ½ cup (2 ounces) crumbled goat cheese

1. Preheat broiler.
2. Rub both sides of mushroom caps with oil, garlic, ¼ teaspoon pepper, and salt. Place mushroom caps on a baking sheet coated with cooking spray. Broil 3 minutes on each side or until tender. Cut mushrooms into thin slices.
3. Spread ½ tablespoon mayonnaise on each of 4 bread slices. Top each with one-fourth of mushroom slices, ¼ cup arugula, ¼ cup bell peppers, and 2 tablespoons cheese. Sprinkle evenly with remaining ¼ teaspoon pepper. Top with remaining bread slices. **YIELD: 4 SERVINGS (SERVING SIZE: 1 SANDWICH).**

PER SERVING: CAL 315 (34% from fat); FAT 11.8g (sat 3.8g); PRO 12.2g; CARB 41.2g; FIB 3.9g; CHOL 14mg; IRON 3.8mg; SOD 773mg; CALC 125mg

MUSHROOM AND SWISS PANINI

POINTS value: 6

pictured on page 137

PREP: 6 minutes ■ **COOK:** 10 minutes

Crusty grilled bread surrounds melted cheese and mushrooms, making this grown-up grilled cheese irresistible.

> Olive oil–flavored cooking spray
> 2 tablespoons minced shallots
> 1 (8-ounce) package sliced baby portobello mushrooms
> 1 garlic clove, minced
> 1 teaspoon minced fresh thyme
> ¼ teaspoon salt
> ¼ teaspoon freshly ground black pepper
> ¼ cup low-fat mayonnaise
> 8 (0.9-ounce) slices Italian bread (such as Chicago Italian Bread loaf)
> 8 (0.75-ounce) slices reduced-fat Swiss cheese (such as Jarlsburg Lite)

1. Heat a large nonstick skillet over medium-high heat; coat pan with cooking spray. Add shallots; cook 1 minute or until tender. Add mushrooms; cook 5 minutes, stirring occasionally. Add garlic and next 3 ingredients; cook 1 minute, stirring occasionally. Remove pan from heat.
2. Preheat panini grill.
3. Spread ½ tablespoon mayonnaise on each bread slice; top 4 bread slices with 1 slice cheese, cutting cheese to fit, if needed. Top each with one-fourth of mushroom mixture, 1 cheese slice, and 1 bread slice. Coat sandwiches with cooking spray. Place sandwiches on panini grill, and cook 3 to 4 minutes or until golden and cheese melts. **YIELD: 4 SERVINGS (SERVING SIZE: 1 SANDWICH).**

Note: If you don't have a panini grill, place sandwiches in a large nonstick skillet over medium heat. Place a piece of foil over sandwiches; top with a heavy skillet. Cook 2 to 3 minutes on each side or until golden and cheese melts.

PER SERVING: CAL 300 (30% from fat); FAT 10g (sat 4.3g); PRO 21.3g; CARB 31.6g; FIB 2.3g; CHOL 23mg; IRON 2mg; SOD 656mg; CALC 504mg

Steak Diane, *page 91*

Tea-Marinated Chicken with
Cucumber-Mint Gremolata, *page 100*

Grilled Chicken
with Avocado Salsa,
page 103

Moroccan Lamb with
Tomato Chutney, *page 92*

Sesame Chicken Stir-Fry,
page 102

Rosemary-Garlic Pork Tenderloin,
page 95

Cajun Chicken and Okra,
page 107

Fresh Orange and Spring Greens Salad, *page 112*

Steak and Feta Hoagies, *page 126*

Spicy Vegetable Salad with Pasta,
page 117

Steak Salad with Beets
and Blue Cheese, *page 118*

Fast Asian Slaw,
page 114

Mushroom and Swiss Panini,
page 128

Catfish Sandwiches with Tartar Sauce, *page 122*

Taco Pepper Rice, *page 154*

Lemony Broccoli, *page 147*

Braised Brussels Sprouts with Cranberries and Bacon, *page 148*

Greek Egg and Lemon Soup,
page 158

Roasted Onion and Apple Salad with Apple-Bacon Vinaigrette, *page 172*

Butternut Squash Soup, *page 157*

Pad Thai Chicken Noodle Soup, *page 161*

side dishes

Moroccan-Style Carrots with Mustard Seeds and Orange, *page 149*

MARINATED ASPARAGUS

POINTS value: 2

PREP: 7 minutes ■ **COOK:** 11 minutes ■ **OTHER:** 8 hours

This is a fantastic make-ahead dish that only gets better the longer it marinates.

- 8 cups water
- 1½ pounds asparagus, trimmed
- ¼ cup olive oil
- ¼ cup white wine vinegar
- 1 (2-ounce) jar diced pimiento, undrained
- 3 tablespoons chopped fresh parsley
- 3 tablespoons finely chopped green onions
- 3 garlic cloves, minced
- 1 teaspoon sugar
- 1 teaspoon Italian seasoning
- ¼ teaspoon salt
- ¼ teaspoon freshly ground black pepper

1. Bring 8 cups water to a boil in a Dutch oven; add asparagus, and cook 3 to 4 minutes or until crisp-tender. Remove asparagus with a slotted spoon. Plunge into ice water; drain. Pat asparagus dry with paper towels. Place in a zip-top plastic bag.
2. Combine oil and next 9 ingredients in a small bowl, stirring with a whisk. Pour marinade over asparagus in bag. Seal bag, and refrigerate 8 hours.
3. Transfer asparagus to a serving dish; drizzle marinade over asparagus. YIELD: 6 SERVINGS (SERVING SIZE: ABOUT 10 SPEARS).

PER SERVING: CAL 102 (84% from fat); FAT 9.5g (sat 1.4g); PRO 1.7g; CARB 4.6g; FIB 1.7g; CHOL 0mg; IRON 1.7mg; SOD 102mg; CALC 27mg

SAUTÉED GREEN BEANS WITH BACON

POINTS value: 1

PREP: 7 minutes ■ **COOK:** 14 minutes

To make this dish ahead, cook the green beans in boiling water and then plunge them into an ice-water bath to stop the cooking process and preserve color. Refrigerate the beans until you're ready to complete the recipe.

- 2 pounds green beans, trimmed
- 4 bacon slices, chopped
- 1 cup chopped onion
- ½ cup chopped green bell pepper
- ½ teaspoon salt
- ½ teaspoon freshly ground black pepper

1. Cook green beans in boiling water 12 minutes or until tender. Drain.
2. While green beans cook, place bacon in a large non-stick skillet, and cook over medium heat 7 minutes or until crisp. Remove bacon from pan, reserving 1 tablespoon drippings in pan; set bacon aside.
3. Add onion and bell pepper to drippings in pan; sauté 4 minutes or until tender. Stir in green beans, salt, and pepper; sauté 2 to 3 minutes or until thoroughly heated. Stir in bacon. YIELD: 6 SERVINGS (SERVING SIZE: ⅔ CUP).

PER SERVING: CAL 97 (38% from fat); FAT 4.1g (sat 1.5g); PRO 4.4g; CARB 12.7g; FIB 5.2g; CHOL 7mg; IRON 1.6mg; SOD 307mg; CALC 58mg

EDAMAME AND NEW POTATOES WITH ROSEMARY ☑

POINTS value: 3

PREP: 5 minutes ■ **COOK:** 13 minutes

Edamame, or green soybeans, are an excellent source of fiber. Substitute ¾ teaspoon fresh rosemary for the dried, if you prefer.

- 5 small red potatoes (about 12 ounces), quartered
- 1½ cups frozen shelled edamame (green soybeans)
- 2 tablespoons chopped fresh parsley
- 1 tablespoon extravirgin olive oil
- 1 teaspoon grated fresh lemon rind
- ¼ teaspoon salt
- ¼ teaspoon dried rosemary, chopped

1. Steam potato and edamame, covered, 13 minutes or until tender.
2. Transfer potato and edamame to a medium bowl; add parsley and remaining ingredients. Toss gently to combine. YIELD: 4 SERVINGS (SERVING SIZE: ¾ CUP).

PER SERVING: CAL 163 (37% from fat); FAT 6.7g (sat 0.9g); PRO 8g; CARB 19.6g; FIB 4.6g; CHOL 0mg; IRON 2.1mg; SOD 157mg; CALC 49mg

SOYBEAN NUTRITION

Edamame, also known as green soybeans, have been used as a major source of protein in Asia for more than three thousand years. A half cup provides about 18 grams of protein, which is comparable to a 3-ounce serving of chicken or beef. But unlike many other protein sources, soybeans are low in calories and don't contain saturated fat.

SWEET-AND-SOUR BEETS

POINTS value: 2

PREP: 7 minutes ■ **COOK:** 38 minutes

These beets may be chilled and served cold or offered hot. They are a great accompaniment to sandwiches and a wonderful contrast to melted-cheese dishes.

> 1 **pound beets, trimmed, peeled, and cut into wedges**
> **Cooking spray**
> ⅔ **cup water**
> ⅓ **cup cider vinegar**
> ¼ **cup sugar**
> 2 **teaspoons cornstarch**
> ¼ **teaspoon salt**
> ⅛ **teaspoon ground cloves**
> 1 **teaspoon butter**
> 2 **tablespoons chopped fresh dill**

1. Preheat oven to 425°.
2. Place beets on a large rimmed baking sheet coated with cooking spray. Bake at 425° for 30 minutes or until browned and tender.
3. While beets bake, combine water and next 5 ingredients in a saucepan over medium heat; stir well with a whisk. Bring mixture to a boil. Reduce heat, and simmer, uncovered, 5 minutes, stirring occasionally.
4. Add beets to pan; simmer until thoroughly heated. Stir in butter. Sprinkle with dill. YIELD: 4 SERVINGS (SERVING SIZE: ½ CUP).

PER SERVING: CAL 99 (10% from fat); FAT 1.1g (sat 0.6g); PRO 1.3g; CARB 21.2g; FIB 2.2g; CHOL 3mg; IRON 0.7mg; SOD 217mg; CALC 16mg

ROASTED BALSAMIC BEETS, CARROTS, AND RED ONION

POINTS value: 1

PREP: 12 minutes ■ **COOK:** 25 minutes

Don't be tempted to stir the vegetables too soon. They must remain undisturbed in the intense heat to caramelize.

> 3 **beets, peeled**
> 2 **carrots, peeled**
> 1 **red bell pepper, seeded and cut into 1-inch pieces**
> 1 **onion, peeled and cut into ½-inch wedges**
> 2 **teaspoons canola oil**
> 1 **teaspoon sugar**
> 1 **teaspoon balsamic vinegar**
> ¼ **teaspoon salt**

1. Preheat oven to 425°.
2. Pat beets dry with paper towels, and cut beets into ½-inch wedges. Cut carrots into 2-inch pieces, cutting larger pieces in half.
3. Combine beets, carrots, and next 4 ingredients in a large roasting pan; arrange vegetables in a single layer in pan.
4. Bake at 425° for 15 minutes; stir gently. Bake an additional 10 minutes or just until vegetables are tender. Remove from oven, and sprinkle with vinegar and salt; stir gently. YIELD: 6 SERVINGS (SERVING SIZE: ½ CUP).

PER SERVING: CAL 56 (29% from fat); FAT 1.8g (sat 0.2g); PRO 1.3g; CARB 9.6g; FIB 2.4g; CHOL 0mg; IRON 0.5mg; SOD 146mg; CALC 19mg

LEMONY BROCCOLI

POINTS value: 1

pictured on page 139

PREP: 4 minutes ■ **COOK:** 5 minutes

Serve this broccoli dish with roasted meats or seafood. The lemon sauce can also be used to brighten the flavor of steamed asparagus, green beans, or Brussels sprouts.

> 1 **tablespoon butter**
> ½ **teaspoon grated fresh lemon rind**
> 1 **tablespoon fresh lemon juice**
> 1 **teaspoon olive oil**
> 4 **cups broccoli florets**
> 2 **tablespoons water**
> ¼ **teaspoon salt**
> ¼ **teaspoon freshly ground black pepper**

1. Place first 4 ingredients in a small microwave-safe bowl; cover and microwave at HIGH 45 seconds. Stir to blend.
2. Place broccoli in a large microwave-safe bowl. Add 2 tablespoons water, and cover with wax paper. Microwave at HIGH 4 minutes or until crisp-tender. Drain well; place broccoli in a serving bowl. Drizzle lemon mixture over broccoli; toss gently to coat. Sprinkle with salt and pepper. YIELD: 4 SERVINGS (SERVING SIZE: ABOUT 1 CUP).

PER SERVING: CAL 56 (69% from fat); FAT 4.3g (sat 2g); PRO 2.2g; CARB 4.2g; FIB 2.1g; CHOL 8mg; IRON 0.6mg; SOD 187mg; CALC 36mg

SAUTÉED BOK CHOY WITH GINGER AND GARLIC ☑

POINTS value: 1

PREP: 15 minutes ■ **COOK:** 5 minutes

Bok choy has a milder flavor than other dark leafy greens. It is also low in calories and is a good source of calcium.

> 2 teaspoons canola oil
> 2 garlic cloves, minced
> 1 tablespoon minced peeled fresh ginger
> 1 pound bok choy, trimmed and sliced
> ½ teaspoon salt
> ¼ teaspoon freshly ground black pepper
> 2 to 3 teaspoons fresh lemon juice

1. Heat oil in a large nonstick skillet over medium-high heat. Add garlic and ginger; sauté 1 minute. Add bok choy, salt, and pepper; sauté 3 minutes or until bok choy wilts. Remove from heat, add lemon juice, and toss gently to coat. Serve immediately. **YIELD: 4 SERVINGS (SERVING SIZE: ABOUT ¾ CUP).**

PER SERVING: CAL 38 (62% from fat); FAT 2.6g (sat 0.3g); PRO 1.7g; CARB 3.5g; FIB 1.1g; CHOL 0mg; IRON 0.9mg; SOD 360mg; CALC 110mg

MAPLE-GLAZED BRUSSELS SPROUTS WITH WALNUTS AND SHALLOTS

POINTS value: 2

PREP: 9 minutes ■ **COOK:** 22 minutes

Roasting brings out the natural sugars in Brussels sprouts. We enhanced the sweet flavor by tossing the sprouts with maple syrup.

> 1¼ pounds Brussels sprouts, trimmed and halved lengthwise
> 1 tablespoon olive oil
> ¼ teaspoon salt
> ¼ teaspoon freshly ground black pepper
> 1 tablespoon butter
> 2 shallots, thinly sliced (about ¾ cup)
> 2½ tablespoons maple syrup
> 2 tablespoons chopped walnuts, toasted

1. Preheat oven to 425°.
2. Combine Brussels sprouts and oil in a bowl; toss to coat. Arrange Brussels sprouts in a single layer on a baking sheet. Bake at 425° for 22 minutes or until browned and tender, stirring once. Transfer Brussels sprouts to a large bowl; sprinkle evenly with salt and pepper.

3. While Brussels sprouts bake, melt butter in a large nonstick skillet over medium-high heat. Add shallots; sauté 5 minutes or until golden brown, stirring frequently. Remove from heat; add syrup. Pour syrup mixture over Brussels sprouts; toss to coat. Sprinkle with walnuts. **YIELD: 6 SERVINGS (SERVING SIZE: ½ CUP).**

PER SERVING: CAL 126 (44% from fat); FAT 6.1g (sat 1.7g); PRO 3.8g; CARB 17g; FIB 3.6g; CHOL 5mg; IRON 1.6mg; SOD 136mg; CALC 52mg

MAPLE SYRUP

Maple syrup comes in different grades, and its color ranges from light golden to dark brown. The lighter the syrup, the milder the flavor. Use lighter varieties over pancakes or when baking cakes and cookies. Darker versions also work well over pancakes and when baking, but they are best used in baking when you want to add intense maple flavor. Whichever maple syrup you buy, make sure it's labeled "pure maple syrup."

BRAISED BRUSSELS SPROUTS WITH CRANBERRIES AND BACON

POINTS value: 4

pictured on page 140

PREP: 4 minutes ■ **COOK:** 17 minutes

Brussels sprouts may become your favorite vegetable after one bite of this dish! Salty bacon and sweet cranberries helped these sprouts earn our Test Kitchens' highest rating.

> 2 bacon slices
> 1 pound Brussels sprouts, trimmed and halved lengthwise
> ½ cup water
> ¼ cup sweetened dried cranberries
> ¼ teaspoon salt
> ¼ teaspoon freshly ground black pepper

1. Cook bacon in a large nonstick skillet over medium heat until crisp. Remove bacon from pan; crumble.
2. Add Brussels sprouts to drippings in pan, and sauté 4 minutes or until lightly browned. Stir in ½ cup water and next 3 ingredients. Cover; simmer 5 minutes or until sprouts are tender. Uncover and cook 2 minutes or until liquid evaporates; sprinkle with crumbled bacon. **YIELD: 4 SERVINGS (SERVING SIZE: ¾ CUP).**

PER SERVING: CAL 179 (59% from fat); FAT 11.8g (sat 4.3g); PRO 4.8g; CARB 15.6g; FIB 4.3g; CHOL 14mg; IRON 1.5mg; SOD 277mg; CALC 44mg

SPICY ASIAN CABBAGE

POINTS value: 1

PREP: 12 minutes ■ **COOK:** 6 minutes

This quick and easy side dish works well with any Asian-style meat, such as Korean Beef on page 89.

    2 teaspoons dark sesame oil
    Cooking spray
    4 cups shredded green cabbage
    1 cup thinly sliced red bell pepper
    1 cup thinly sliced green onions
    ½ cup matchstick-cut carrots
    2 teaspoons grated peeled fresh ginger
    3 tablespoons hot jalapeño jelly
    2 tablespoons low-sodium soy sauce

1. Heat oil in a large nonstick skillet coated with cooking spray over medium–high heat. Add cabbage and next 4 ingredients; sauté 4 minutes or until vegetables are crisp-tender. Add jelly and soy sauce; cook 1 minute or until jelly melts. Stir to coat. YIELD: 5 SERVINGS (SERVING SIZE: ½ CUP).

PER SERVING: CAL 76 (24% from fat); FAT 2g (sat 0.3g); PRO 1.4g; CARB 13.6g; FIB 2.9g; CHOL 0mg; IRON 0.7mg; SOD 284mg; CALC 43mg

RICHLY BROWNED CABBAGE, ONION, AND PEPPERS

POINTS value: 1

PREP: 10 minutes ■ **COOK:** 11 minutes

The trick to getting the most flavor from cabbage? Stir it only every 3 minutes or so while cooking, allowing the cabbage to develop to a golden brown color and take on a rich flavor.

    2 teaspoons canola oil
    4 cups coarsely chopped green cabbage
    1 cup chopped onion (1 medium)
    ½ cup chopped green bell pepper
    1 garlic clove, minced
    ¾ teaspoon sugar, divided
    ⅛ teaspoon crushed red pepper
    ½ teaspoon salt

1. Heat oil in a Dutch oven over medium-high heat. Add cabbage, next 3 ingredients, ½ teaspoon sugar, and crushed red pepper; cook 10 minutes or until

golden brown, stirring occasionally. Remove from heat; add remaining ¼ teaspoon sugar and salt. YIELD: 3 SERVINGS (SERVING SIZE: 1 CUP).

PER SERVING: CAL 89 (33% from fat); FAT 3.3g (sat 0.3g); PRO 2.4g; CARB 14.4g; FIB 4.3g; CHOL 0mg; IRON 0.8mg; SOD 418mg; CALC 64mg

MOROCCAN-STYLE CARROTS WITH MUSTARD SEEDS AND ORANGE

POINTS value: 2

pictured on page 145

PREP: 6 minutes ■ **COOK:** 11 minutes

Mustard seeds contain plentiful amounts of phytonutrients, which may help prevent cancer. The spicy, pungent seeds may be used whole or ground into a powder. For the best flavor, use within 1 year of purchase.

    1 (16-ounce) package diagonally cut carrots
    1 tablespoon canola oil
    1 teaspoon mustard seeds
    1 teaspoon cumin seeds
    ½ cup finely chopped onion
    1 garlic clove, minced
    1 teaspoon brown sugar
    ¼ teaspoon salt
    ⅛ teaspoon ground red pepper
    2 tablespoons minced fresh cilantro
    2 tablespoons orange juice

1. Steam carrots, covered, 7 minutes or until tender.
2. While carrots cook, heat oil in a large nonstick skillet over medium heat. Add mustard and cumin seeds; sauté 2 minutes or until mustard seeds begin to pop.
3. Add onion and garlic; sauté 1 minute. Add carrots, brown sugar, salt, and red pepper; sauté 3 minutes. Transfer carrot mixture to a bowl. Add cilantro and orange juice; toss to combine. YIELD: 4 SERVINGS (SERVING SIZE: 1 CUP).

PER SERVING: CAL 99 (38% from fat); FAT 4.2g (sat 0.3g); PRO 1.7g; CARB 15.1g; FIB 3.8g; CHOL 0mg; IRON 0.9mg; SOD 228mg; CALC 54mg

MAPLE-ROASTED CARROTS AND PARSNIPS

POINTS value: 3

PREP: 16 minutes ■ **COOK:** 45 minutes

For the best browning, spread the carrots and parsnips in a single layer and stir only once during roasting.

- 1 pound carrots, cut into 1¼-inch sticks (about 3 cups)
- 1 pound parsnips, cut into 1¼-inch sticks (about 3 cups)
- 2 tablespoons maple syrup
- 1½ tablespoons olive oil
- ¼ teaspoon salt
- ¼ teaspoon freshly ground black pepper
- 1 tablespoon balsamic vinegar

1. Preheat oven to 425°.
2. Combine first 6 ingredients in a large bowl; toss to coat. Arrange vegetable mixture in a single layer on a foil-lined jelly-roll pan. Bake at 425° for 45 minutes or until browned and crisp, turning once. Drizzle with vinegar, and serve immediately. **YIELD: 5 SERVINGS (SERVING SIZE: ⅔ CUP).**

PER SERVING: CAL 165 (26% from fat); FAT 4.7g (sat 0.6g); PRO 2g; CARB 31g; FIB 4.4g; CHOL 0mg; IRON 0.9mg; SOD 191mg; CALC 69mg

CARAMELIZED BABY ONIONS

POINTS value: 2

PREP: 7 minutes ■ **COOK:** 25 minutes

These tiny onions are prized for their tenderness and sweetness.

- 2 (10-ounce) packages fresh pearl onions
- ¾ cup water, divided
- 1 tablespoon light brown sugar
- 2 teaspoons butter
- ½ teaspoon salt
- ¼ teaspoon black pepper

1. Place onions in a large saucepan with water to cover. Bring to a boil, and cook, uncovered, 5 minutes. Drain, and plunge into ice water just until cool enough to handle. Cut root ends from onions. Holding onions by the tops, gently squeeze onions from skins through cut ends.
2. Combine peeled onions and ½ cup water in a large nonstick skillet. Bring to a boil over medium–high heat; cook 10 minutes or until all liquid evaporates, stirring often. Reduce heat to medium; add remaining ¼ cup water, sugar, and remaining ingredients. Cook 7 minutes or until onions are tender and glazed, stirring often. **YIELD: 3 SERVINGS (SERVING SIZE: ½ CUP).**

PER SERVING: CAL 106 (21% from fat); FAT 2.5g (sat 1.6g); PRO 0.1g; CARB 17.8g; FIB 2.2g; CHOL 7mg; IRON 0.1mg; SOD 435mg; CALC 5mg

CAULIFLOWER GRATIN

POINTS value: 2

PREP: 9 minutes ■ **COOK:** 35 minutes

Pureeing part of the cauliflower makes this dish creamier without adding any calories or fat.

- 1 head cauliflower (about 1½ pounds)
- ½ cup (2 ounces) shredded fresh Parmesan cheese, divided
- ¼ cup fat-free sour cream
- 2 tablespoons fat-free half-and-half
- ½ teaspoon seasoned salt
- ¼ teaspoon pepper
- Cooking spray
- ¼ cup Italian-seasoned breadcrumbs
- 1 teaspoon butter, melted

1. Preheat oven to 400°.
2. Cut cauliflower lengthwise into quarters, removing outer leaves and stalk; break into florets. Steam, covered, in a Dutch oven 8 minutes or until tender.
3. Place 2 cups cauliflower, ¼ cup cheese, and next 4 ingredients in a food processor; process until smooth. Place remaining cauliflower in a bowl, and stir in pureed cauliflower mixture. Spoon into a 1½-quart baking dish coated with cooking spray. Combine remaining ¼ cup cheese, breadcrumbs, and butter in a small bowl, tossing well with a fork. Sprinkle crumb mixture over cauliflower mixture.
4. Bake at 400° for 25 minutes or until golden and bubbly. **YIELD: 4 SERVINGS (SERVING SIZE: ¼ OF GRATIN).**

PER SERVING: CAL 115 (36% from fat); FAT 4.6g (sat 2.5g); PRO 7.1g; CARB 12.1g; FIB 1.9g; CHOL 13mg; IRON 0.8mg; SOD 484mg; CALC 166mg

SHERRY-CREAMED MUSHROOMS

POINTS value: 1

PREP: 10 minutes ■ **COOK:** 15 minutes

If you can't find small mushrooms, just cut larger ones in half. Serve these mushrooms as a side dish or over cooked pasta, rice, chicken, or beef.

Cooking spray
- ½ cup finely chopped onion
- 1 garlic clove, minced
- 1 pound small mushrooms
- ¼ cup dry sherry
- 1 teaspoon olive oil
- ¼ teaspoon salt
- ¼ cup light sour cream
- ⅛ teaspoon freshly ground black pepper
- 2 tablespoons chopped fresh parsley

1. Heat a large nonstick skillet over medium-high heat; coat pan with cooking spray. Add chopped onion, and sauté 2 minutes or until onion begins to brown. Add garlic, and sauté 15 seconds or until lightly browned. Add mushrooms and next 3 ingredients. Cover, reduce heat to medium, and cook 8 minutes or until tender. Uncover and cook 4 minutes or until liquid thickens. Remove from heat, and stir in sour cream and pepper. Sprinkle with chopped parsley. **YIELD: 5 SERVINGS (SERVING SIZE: ½ CUP).**

PER SERVING: CAL 56 (43% from fat); FAT 2.7g (sat 1.1g); PRO 3.4g; CARB 5.4g; FIB 1.3g; CHOL 5mg; IRON 0.6mg; SOD 130mg; CALC 23mg

IRISH MASHED POTATOES AND CABBAGE

POINTS value: 2

PREP: 19 minutes ■ **COOK:** 31 minutes

This Irish vegetable combination, called *colcannon*, makes a fine accompaniment to Chicken and Stuffing Burgers on page 124 or any roasted meat.

- 2 cups angel hair slaw
- Cooking spray
- 1 cup thinly sliced green onions
- 6 cups cubed peeled Yukon gold potato (2 pounds)
- 1 cup fat-free buttermilk
- ½ teaspoon salt
- ½ teaspoon freshly ground black pepper
- 3 tablespoons butter, melted and divided

1. Steam angel hair slaw in a large saucepan or Dutch oven 8 minutes or until tender; place in a serving bowl.
2. Wipe pan dry with a paper towel; coat pan with cooking spray. Place over medium heat; add onions, and sauté 3 minutes or until tender. Add onions to cabbage.
3. Place potato in pan; add water to cover. Bring to a boil; cover, reduce heat, and simmer 15 minutes or until tender. Drain potato, and return to pan; add buttermilk, salt, and pepper, mashing until smooth. Stir in cabbage mixture and 2 tablespoons butter; return potato mixture to serving bowl. Drizzle remaining 1 tablespoon butter over potatoes, and serve immediately. **YIELD: 8 SERVINGS (SERVING SIZE: ¾ CUP).**

PER SERVING: CAL 137 (29% from fat); FAT 4.4g (sat 2.7g); PRO 3.3g; CARB 21.5g; FIB 3.6g; CHOL 12mg; IRON 0.8mg; SOD 223mg; CALC 59mg

POTATOES WITH ROSEMARY AND PANCETTA

POINTS value: 1

PREP: 9 minutes ■ **COOK:** 29 minutes

Arrange the potatoes over the bottom of the pan to help them brown and crisp. Then cover the pan to ensure they cook completely.

- 1 ounce thinly sliced pancetta, coarsely chopped
- 1 (20-ounce) package refrigerated sliced potatoes (such as Simply Potatoes)
- ½ cup sliced onion
- 2 garlic cloves, minced
- 1½ teaspoons chopped fresh rosemary
- ½ teaspoon salt
- ½ teaspoon freshly ground black pepper
- 1 teaspoon olive oil

1. Cook pancetta in a large nonstick skillet over medium-high heat 6 minutes or until crisp. Drain pancetta on a paper towel; set aside.
2. Combine potatoes and next 5 ingredients in a large bowl; toss gently to combine.
3. Add oil to pan, and heat over medium-high heat. Add potato mixture; cover and cook 23 minutes or until tender and browned, turning once. Sprinkle with pancetta, and serve immediately. **YIELD 6 SERVINGS (SERVING SIZE: ABOUT ½ CUP POTATOES AND 1 TEASPOON PANCETTA).**

PER SERVING: CAL 88 (24% from fat); FAT 2.3g (sat 0.8g); PRO 3.2g; CARB 13g; FIB 2.6g; CHOL 3mg; IRON 0.8mg; SOD 374mg; CALC 5mg

- Russet (or baking) potatoes are long tubers with numerous eyes. These high-starch, low-moisture potatoes are dry and fluffy when cooked.

- Red potatoes are low-starch, high-moisture potatoes with a dense, waxy flesh that lets them hold their shape well when cooked. They have the thinnest skins of any potato, so they're usually cooked with their skins on.

- Bright orange sweet potatoes aren't really potatoes—they're members of the morning glory family.

- Yukon Gold potatoes are moist, with yellow, buttery flesh. They hold their shape well when cooked.

SCALLOPED POTATO AND FENNEL GRATIN

POINTS value: 3

PREP: 15 minutes ■ **COOK:** 39 minutes

This creamy side dish earned our Test Kitchens' highest rating. Sliced fennel adds a welcome hint of spice, but you may substitute leeks, if desired.

   3 cups thinly sliced peeled baking potato (about 1 pound)
   2 cups thinly sliced fennel bulb (about 1 medium bulb)
   2 cups 1% low-fat milk, divided
  ¾ teaspoon salt, divided
  ¼ teaspoon freshly ground black pepper
Cooking spray
  ¼ cup light sour cream
   1 tablespoon all-purpose flour
  ½ cup reduced-fat shredded Cheddar cheese
  ¼ cup (1 ounce) grated fresh Parmesan cheese, divided
   1 teaspoon Dijon mustard

1. Preheat oven to 400°.
2. Combine potato, fennel, 1½ cups milk, ½ teaspoon salt, and pepper in a large deep skillet over medium-high heat. Bring mixture to a boil. Cover, reduce heat, and simmer 5 minutes.
3. Transfer potato and fennel with a slotted spoon to an 11 x 7–inch baking dish coated with cooking spray; set aside. Bring cooking liquid in pan to a simmer over medium heat.
4. Combine sour cream, remaining ½ cup milk, flour, and remaining ¼ teaspoon salt in a small bowl; stir well.

Add mixture to pan. Cook over medium heat 2 minutes or until slightly thick; stir with a whisk. Stir in Cheddar cheese, 2 tablespoons Parmesan cheese, and mustard.
5. Pour mixture over potato and fennel. Sprinkle with remaining 2 tablespoons Parmesan cheese. Cover with foil, and bake at 400° for 25 minutes or until potato is tender.
6. Preheat broiler.
7. Remove foil and broil, 4 inches from heat, 5 to 6 minutes or until golden brown. YIELD: 6 SERVINGS (SERVING SIZE: 1 CUP).

PER SERVING: CAL 166 (30% from fat); FAT 5.5g (sat 3.4g); PRO 8.7g; CARB 21.4g; FIB 1.9g; CHOL 17mg; IRON 1.2mg; SOD 486mg; CALC 239mg

APPLE-GLAZED SWEET POTATO SLICES

POINTS value: 2

PREP: 5 minutes ■ **COOK:** 13 minutes

The apple juice concentrate and natural sugars in the sweet potatoes may cause the potato slices to char before they are done. We remedy this by microwaving the potatoes first to jump-start the cooking process and reduce the amount of grill time.

   3 tablespoons thawed apple juice concentrate, undiluted
   2 teaspoons brown sugar
   2 teaspoons canola oil
   1 teaspoon chopped fresh thyme
   1 teaspoon hot sauce (such as Tabasco)
  ⅛ teaspoon freshly ground black pepper
   3 small sweet potatoes, peeled and each cut lengthwise into 4 slices
Butter-flavored cooking spray
  ¼ teaspoon salt

1. Prepare grill.
2. Combine first 6 ingredients in a small bowl; set aside.
3. Arrange potato slices in a single layer on a large microwave-safe dish. Microwave at HIGH 5 minutes or just until tender. Cool slightly.
4. Coat one side of potato slices with cooking spray. Place slices, coated sides down, on grill rack coated with cooking spray. Grill, covered, 5 minutes. Brush slices with apple juice mixture; turn, and grill, covered, 3 minutes. Brush with apple juice mixture; remove from grill, and sprinkle with salt. Serve immediately. YIELD: 6 SERVINGS (SERVING SIZE: 2 SLICES).

PER SERVING: CAL 108 (13% from fat); FAT 1.6g (sat 0.2g); PRO 1.4g; CARB 22.5g; FIB 2.6g; CHOL 0mg; IRON 0.7mg; SOD 169mg; CALC 30mg

MAPLE-GLAZED ACORN SQUASH

POINTS value: 3

PREP: 4 minutes ■ **COOK:** 55 minutes

To keep an acorn squash from moving when halved, cut a small slice out of one side so that it lays flat on the cutting board.

- 3 tablespoons sugar-free maple-flavored syrup (such as Cary's)
- 1 tablespoon butter, melted
- ½ teaspoon ground cardamom
- 1 tablespoon golden raisins
- 1 acorn squash (about 1 pound)
- 1 cup water

1. Preheat oven to 350°.
2. Combine first 3 ingredients in a small bowl, stirring with a whisk. Stir in raisins; set aside.
3. Cut squash in half lengthwise, discarding seeds. Place squash halves, cut sides down, in a baking dish; add 1 cup water to dish. Bake at 350° for 45 minutes or until squash is tender when pierced with a fork. Remove squash from dish; discard water. Pierce squash pulp several times with a fork. Return squash to dish, skin sides down. Brush pierced pulp with syrup mixture. Bake at 350° for 10 minutes or until glaze is warm and bubbly. YIELD: 2 SERVINGS (SERVING SIZE: ½ SQUASH).

PER SERVING: CAL 170 (31% from fat); FAT 5.9g (sat 3.7g); PRO 2.1g; CARB 32.4g; FIB 3.8g; CHOL 15mg; IRON 1.8mg; SOD 84mg; CALC 81mg

COUSCOUS WITH DRIED APRICOTS, CINNAMON, AND TOASTED NUTS

POINTS value: 2

PREP: 11 minutes ■ **COOK:** 2 minutes ■ **OTHER:** 5 minutes

Couscous is often mistakenly called a grain; it's actually a granular pasta.

- 1½ cups fat-free, less-sodium chicken broth
- 1 tablespoon olive oil
- 1 teaspoon grated fresh lemon rind
- ½ teaspoon ground cinnamon
- 1 (7.6-ounce) package wheat couscous (such as Near East)
- ⅔ cup sliced green onions
- ½ cup chopped dried apricots
- 3 tablespoons chopped fresh mint or parsley
- 3 tablespoons sliced almonds, toasted
- 1 tablespoon fresh lemon juice

1. Combine first 4 ingredients in a medium saucepan, and bring to a boil. Stir in couscous. Remove from heat; cover and let stand 5 minutes or until liquid is absorbed. Fluff with a fork.
2. Transfer couscous to a bowl; stir in green onions and remaining ingredients. YIELD: 10 SERVINGS (SERVING SIZE: ½ CUP).

PER SERVING: CAL 122 (21% from fat); FAT 2.9g (sat 0.3g); PRO 3.9g; CARB 21.1g; FIB 2.2g; CHOL 0mg; IRON 0.6mg; SOD 89mg; CALC 17mg

PASTA WITH FRESH TOMATOES, HERBS, AND LEMON

POINTS value: 2

PREP: 9 minutes ■ **COOK:** 12 minutes ■ **OTHER:** 30 seconds

Add 3 cups shredded cooked chicken breast to make this pasta a main dish. The **POINTS** value will be 5.

- 6 ounces uncooked spaghetti
- 2 cups grape tomatoes, halved
- ¼ cup thinly sliced fresh basil
- 2 teaspoons olive oil
- 1 teaspoon chopped fresh thyme
- 1 teaspoon chopped fresh rosemary
- ¼ teaspoon grated fresh lemon rind
- ¼ teaspoon salt
- ¼ teaspoon freshly ground black pepper

1. Cook pasta according to package directions, omitting salt and fat. Drain, reserving 2 tablespoons cooking liquid.
2. While pasta cooks, combine tomatoes and next 7 ingredients in a large bowl. Add reserved cooking liquid and cooked pasta. Let stand 30 seconds; toss well. Serve immediately. YIELD: 6 SERVINGS (SERVING SIZE: ⅔ CUP).

PER SERVING: CAL 129 (15% from fat); FAT 2.1g (sat 0.3g); PRO 4.2g; CARB 23.3g; FIB 1.6g; CHOL 0mg; IRON 1.2mg; SOD 103mg; CALC 15mg

BROWN RICE AND ONION PILAF

POINTS value: 3

PREP: 5 minutes ■ COOK: 10 minutes

For a sweet caramelized flavor, make sure to cook the onion until it becomes a rich brown color.

    1 (5.3-ounce) package boil-in-bag brown rice
Cooking spray
    1 cup chopped Vidalia or other sweet onion
 1½ cups spinach, coarsely chopped
  ¼ cup pine nuts, toasted
    4 sun-dried tomato halves, chopped
  ¼ teaspoon salt
  ⅛ teaspoon freshly ground black pepper

1. Cook rice according to package directions, omitting salt and fat.
2. While rice cooks, heat a medium nonstick skillet over medium-high heat; coat pan with cooking spray. Add onion, and cook 5 to 6 minutes or until browned, stirring frequently. Remove from heat. Stir in cooked rice, spinach, and remaining ingredients; toss gently until spinach wilts. YIELD: 6 SERVINGS (SERVING SIZE: ½ CUP).

PER SERVING: CAL 141 (24% from fat); FAT 3.7g (sat 0.7g); PRO 3.2g; CARB 23.6g; FIB 2.5g; CHOL 0mg; IRON 1mg; SOD 112mg; CALC 27mg

GREEN CHILE RICE

POINTS value: 4

PREP: 5 minutes ■ COOK: 12 minutes
■ OTHER: 30 minutes

Try this rice with Mexican entrées, or serve it with roasted meats. Substitute spicier chiles, such as poblanos, if you want added heat.

    2 small Anaheim chiles
Cooking spray
    1 cup water
    1 cup 1% low-fat milk
    2 tablespoons butter
  ½ teaspoon salt
  ¼ teaspoon dried oregano
    2 cups instant rice
  ½ cup (2 ounces) crumbled queso fresco

1. Preheat broiler.
2. Cut chiles in half lengthwise; discard seeds and membranes. Place chile halves, skin sides up, on a broiler pan coated with cooking spray; flatten with

hand. Broil 6 minutes or until skins are blackened. Place chiles in a zip-top plastic bag; seal. Let stand 15 minutes. Peel and finely chop chiles. Set aside, and keep warm.
3. Combine 1 cup water and next 4 ingredients in a medium saucepan over medium heat; bring to a boil, stirring occasionally. Remove from heat; stir in rice. Cover and let stand 15 minutes or until liquid is absorbed; fluff rice with a fork. Stir in chiles and cheese. YIELD: 6 SERVINGS (SERVING SIZE: ½ CUP).

PER SERVING: CAL 205 (25% from fat); FAT 5.6g (sat 3.2g); PRO 5.5g; CARB 32.9g; FIB 1.1g; CHOL 15mg; IRON 2.4mg; SOD 263mg; CALC 93mg

TACO PEPPER RICE ☑

POINTS value: 4

pictured on page 139
PREP: 5 minutes ■ COOK: 11 minutes

Pair this rice dish with Artichoke Quesadillas on page 78 for an authentic Mexican meal.

  ½ cup water
  ⅛ teaspoon ground turmeric
  ½ cup instant brown rice
Cooking spray
  ¾ cup diced onion
  ¾ cup diced red bell pepper
    2 tablespoons 40%-less-sodium taco seasoning (such as Old El Paso)
    2 teaspoons extravirgin olive oil

1. Combine ½ cup water and turmeric in a small saucepan; bring to a boil. Add rice; return to a boil. Cover, reduce heat, and simmer 5 minutes. Remove from heat, and let stand 5 minutes or until water is absorbed.
2. While rice stands, heat a large nonstick skillet over medium-high heat; coat pan with cooking spray. Add onion and bell pepper; sauté 4 to 5 minutes or until lightly browned and tender. Add rice, taco seasoning, and oil to onion mixture; toss well. YIELD: 3 SERVINGS (SERVING SIZE: ½ CUP).

PER SERVING: CAL 186 (40% from fat); FAT 8.2g (sat 0.7g); PRO 3.3g; CARB 31g; FIB 3.4g; CHOL 0mg; IRON 0.8mg; SOD 334mg; CALC 23mg

soups & stews

Pad Thai Chicken Noodle Soup, *page 161*

COOL AND CREAMY TROPICAL FRUIT SOUP

POINTS value: 2

PREP: 7 minutes

This beautifully colored soup is full of fresh taste. With a **POINTS** value of 2, it makes a great snack or a refreshing summer dessert.

> 2 cups strawberries
> 12 ounces unsweetened pineapple juice
> 1 ripe mango, peeled and seeded
> ½ cup fat-free half and half
> 2 tablespoons sugar
> 1 teaspoon grated peeled fresh ginger
> ⅛ teaspoon crushed red pepper

1. Place all ingredients in a blender; process until smooth. Serve immediately or chilled. YIELD: 4 SERVINGS (SERVING SIZE: ABOUT 1 CUP).

PER SERVING: CAL 147 (3% from fat); FAT 0.5g (sat 0.1g); PRO 1.1g; CARB 34.6g; FIB 2.6g; CHOL 0mg; IRON 0.6mg; SOD 34mg; CALC 48mg

GINGERED CARROT SOUP

POINTS value: 3

PREP: 12 minutes ▪ **COOK:** 48 minutes
▪ **OTHER:** 5 minutes

Fresh ginger adds peppery flavor to this nutritious soup. Top the soup with 1 tablespoon of plain fat-free yogurt, if you'd like, to add some creaminess. The **POINTS** value remains the same.

> 1 tablespoon canola oil
> 1 pound carrots, peeled and cut into 1-inch slices
> 1 cup chopped onion (1 medium)
> 1½ tablespoons minced peeled fresh ginger
> 3 tablespoons all-purpose flour
> 4 cups fat-free, less-sodium chicken broth
> 1 teaspoon grated fresh orange rind
> 1 cup fresh orange juice
> 1 teaspoon sugar
> ½ teaspoon pepper
> ¼ teaspoon salt
> ¼ cup plain fat-free yogurt (optional)

1. Heat oil in a large saucepan over medium heat. Add carrot, onion, and ginger; cook, covered, 5 minutes, stirring occasionally. Add flour; cook 2 minutes, stirring occasionally.

2. Add broth and next 5 ingredients; bring to a boil. Cover, reduce heat, and simmer 35 minutes or until carrot is tender. Cool slightly.

3. Place one-third of carrot mixture in a blender, and process 1 minute or until very smooth. Pour pureed mixture into a large bowl. Repeat procedure with remaining two-thirds of carrot mixture. Ladle soup into bowls, and top with yogurt, if desired. YIELD: 4 SERVINGS (SERVING SIZE: 1½ CUPS).

PER SERVING: CAL 160 (23% from fat); FAT 4g (sat 0.3g); PRO 5.5g; CARB 27.1g; FIB 4g; CHOL 0mg; IRON 0.8mg; SOD 790mg; CALC 52mg

LEEK AND POTATO SOUP

POINTS value: 4

PREP: 18 minutes ▪ **COOK:** 48 minutes

Serve this soup warm on a winter day or chilled on a summer evening.

> 1 tablespoon olive oil
> 3 cups chopped leeks (white and pale green parts only; about 2 leeks)
> 2 tablespoons all-purpose flour
> 6 small red potatoes, peeled and cut into ¾-inch pieces (about 3 cups)
> 6 cups fat-free, less-sodium chicken broth
> ¼ teaspoon freshly ground black pepper
> 1⅓ cups light sour cream, divided
> 3 teaspoons fresh lemon juice
> 2 tablespoons minced fresh chives

1. Heat oil in a Dutch oven over medium-high heat. Add leek; cook, covered, 5 minutes or until tender, stirring occasionally. Stir in flour; cook 2 minutes, stirring constantly. Add potato, broth, and pepper. Bring to a boil; cover, reduce heat, and simmer 30 minutes or until potato is very tender, stirring occasionally.

2. Place one-third of leek mixture in a blender; process until smooth. Pour pureed mixture into pan. Repeat procedure with remaining two-thirds of leek mixture. Stir in 1 cup sour cream; cook 2 minutes over medium heat or until thoroughly heated. Stir in lemon juice. Ladle soup into bowls, and top with remaining sour cream and chives. YIELD: 6 SERVINGS (SERVING SIZE: 1⅓ CUPS SOUP, ABOUT 1 TABLESPOON SOUR CREAM, AND 1 TEASPOON CHIVES).

PER SERVING: CAL 204 (40% from fat); FAT 9g (sat 4.4g); PRO 7.1g; CARB 25.4g; FIB 2.1g; CHOL 21mg; IRON 1.7mg; SOD 605mg; CALC 89mg

1. Use a sharp kitchen knife to cut 1 inch from the top and bottom of the squash; discard.

2. Use a serrated peeler to peel away the thick skin until you reach the squash's orange flesh.

3. Cut the squash in half lengthwise. With a spoon or melon baller, scoop out the seeds and membranes; discard. Then cut the squash according to the recipe's directions.

BUTTERNUT SQUASH SOUP

POINTS value: 2

pictured on page 143

PREP: 20 minutes ■ **COOK:** 59 minutes

With butternut squash as its base, this soup is creamy and healthy.

    2 teaspoons olive oil, divided
    7 cups cubed seeded peeled butternut squash (2 pounds)
    2 cups chopped peeled Braeburn apple
    1½ cups chopped sweet onion (1 medium)
    3 cups fat-free, less-sodium chicken broth
    1 cup apple cider
    2 tablespoons 2% reduced-fat milk
    ½ teaspoon kosher salt
    ¼ teaspoon pumpkin-pie spice
    ⅛ teaspoon pepper
    ½ cup Greek-style plain fat-free yogurt or
       fat-free sour cream (optional)

1. Heat 1 teaspoon oil in a Dutch oven over medium heat. Add squash to pan, stirring to coat. Cover and cook 8 minutes, stirring often. Uncover and cook 4 minutes or until squash begins to brown. Remove squash from pan; keep warm.
2. Add remaining 1 teaspoon oil to pan; add apple and onion. Cover and cook 10 minutes or until onion is tender, stirring often.
3. Return squash to pan. Add broth and cider. Bring to a boil; cover, reduce heat, and simmer 30 minutes or

until squash is tender. Place one-fourth of squash mixture in a blender; process until smooth. Pour pureed mixture into pan. Repeat procedure with remaining three-fourths of squash mixture. Stir in milk and next 3 ingredients. Cook over medium heat 3 minutes or until thoroughly heated, stirring occasionally. Ladle soup into bowls, and top with yogurt, if desired. **YIELD: 6 SERVINGS (SERVING SIZE: 1¼ CUPS).**

PER SERVING: CAL 149 (11% from fat); FAT 1.9g (sat 0.3g); PRO 3.9g; CARB 32.8g; FIB 4.2g; CHOL 0mg; IRON 1.2mg; SOD 455mg; CALC 90mg

GREEN TOMATO SOUP WITH PANCETTA CRISPS

POINTS value: 4

PREP: 23 minutes ■ **COOK:** 46 minutes

Sautéing the onions increases their sweetness, which helps balance the slight tartness of the green tomatoes.

    4 ounces thinly sliced pancetta, coarsely chopped
    2 cups coarsely chopped sweet onion (about 1 large)
    5 green tomatoes, chopped (about 2 pounds)
    2 (14-ounce) cans fat-free, less-sodium chicken broth
    1 (8-ounce) carton light sour cream, divided
    ¼ teaspoon freshly ground black pepper

1. Cook pancetta in a large Dutch oven over medium heat 8 minutes or until crisp. Drain pancetta on a paper towel.
2. Add onion to pan, and sauté 5 minutes. Add tomato and broth; bring to a boil. Cover, reduce heat, and simmer 25 minutes or until tomato is tender.
3. Place one-fourth of tomato mixture in a blender; process until smooth. Pour pureed mixture into a large bowl. Repeat procedure with remaining three-fourths of tomato mixture. Stir in ½ cup sour cream and pepper. Ladle soup into bowls. Top with remaining sour cream and pancetta. **YIELD: 6 SERVINGS (SERVING SIZE: 1¼ CUPS SOUP, 1 TABLESPOON SOUR CREAM, AND 1 TABLESPOON PANCETTA).**

PER SERVING: CAL 185 (54% from fat); FAT 11g (sat 5.6g); PRO 8.2g; CARB 15g; FIB 2.6g; CHOL 28mg; IRON 0.9mg; SOD 729mg; CALC 72mg

Use green tomatoes almost as soon as you buy them. After a day or two, they will begin to turn red and lose their characteristic tartness. If you can't use them immediately, store them in your refrigerator to slow their ripening. Bring them to room temperature before cooking them.

GREEK EGG AND LEMON SOUP

POINTS value: 4

pictured on page 141

PREP: 10 minutes ■ **COOK:** 22 minutes

This traditional Greek soup is also known as *avgolemono* (ahv-goh-LEH-moh-noh), which refers to a group of Mediterranean sauces and soups made with egg yolks, lemon juice, and broth. The result is a smooth, creamy soup, which can best be described as Greek comfort food. Our Test Kitchens gave it their well-deserved highest rating.

  2 teaspoons olive oil
  ¾ cup finely chopped onion
  3 tablespoons all-purpose flour
  8 cups fat-free, less-sodium chicken broth
  1 cup uncooked orzo
  1 tablespoon grated fresh lemon rind
  ½ teaspoon freshly ground black pepper
  2 large eggs
  1 large egg white
  ¼ cup fresh lemon juice
  6 dill sprigs or 3 tablespoons minced fresh dill (optional)

1. Heat oil in a Dutch oven over medium–high heat. Add onion, and sauté 3 minutes. Add flour; cook 1 minute, stirring constantly. Gradually add broth; bring to a boil. Add orzo, rind, and pepper; reduce heat, and simmer 10 minutes.

2. Combine eggs, egg white, and juice, stirring with a whisk until foamy. Gradually add 1 cup hot broth mixture to egg mixture, stirring with a whisk. Return mixture to pan, stirring constantly with whisk. Cook over low heat 2 minutes or until slightly thick. Ladle soup into bowls; top with dill sprigs, if desired. YIELD: 6 SERVINGS (SERVING SIZE: 1½ CUPS).

PER SERVING: CAL 193 (16% from fat); FAT 3.5g (sat 0.6g); PRO 11g; CARB 29.1g; FIB 1.7g; CHOL 60mg; IRON 0.6mg; SOD 794mg; CALC 18mg

WHITE BEAN SOUP WITH CORIANDER ✓

POINTS value: 4

PREP: 16 minutes ■ **COOK:** 4 hours and 14 minutes
■ **OTHER:** 1 hour

Dried beans, which have significantly less sodium than canned beans, are inexpensive and require little attention when prepared in a slow cooker. Plus, one serving provides almost 50% of the daily recommended amount of dietary fiber. Pair this hearty soup with Green Chile Corn Bread on page 31.

  1 pound dried navy beans
  ¾ pound smoked turkey drumstick
  3 (14-ounce) cans fat-free, less-sodium chicken broth
  2 cups water
  1½ cups chopped celery
  1 cup chopped onion
  1 cup chopped carrot
  3 garlic cloves, minced
  1 chicken-flavored bouillon cube
  1 bay leaf
  2 teaspoons ground coriander
  1 teaspoon seasoned salt
  1 teaspoon freshly ground black pepper
Minced fresh cilantro (optional)

1. Sort and wash beans; place in a large Dutch oven. Cover with water 2 inches above beans; bring to a boil. Cook 2 minutes; remove from heat. Cover and let stand 1 hour. Drain beans.

2. Place beans and next 12 ingredients in a 5-quart oval slow cooker. Cover and cook on HIGH 4 hours or LOW 8 hours.

3. Remove bay leaf and turkey drumstick from cooker. Mash soup mixture with a potato masher to desired consistency. Remove skin from turkey drumstick, shred meat with 2 forks, and return to soup. Ladle soup into bowls. Garnish with cilantro, if desired. YIELD: 10 SERVINGS (SERVING SIZE: ABOUT 1¼ CUPS).

PER SERVING: CAL 211 (7% from fat); FAT 1.7g (sat 0.4g); PRO 18g; CARB 31.5g; FIB 11.9g; CHOL 29mg; IRON 3.3mg; SOD 619mg; CALC 95mg

ABOUT CORIANDER

Coriander is the seed from which the cilantro leaf is grown. When crushed, the seeds have a lemony citrus flavor. Coriander is used in Vietnamese, South African, and Middle Eastern cuisines and is a key ingredient in garam masala and Indian curries.

ROASTED GARLIC AND VIDALIA ONION SOUP

POINTS value: 3

PREP: 14 minutes ■ **COOK:** 1 hour and 43 minutes

For a nonalcoholic version, substitute chicken broth or water for the wine.

  1 whole garlic head
Cooking spray
  4 Vidalia or other sweet onions (about 2¾ pounds), peeled and cut into eighths
  6 cups fat-free, less-sodium chicken broth
  ⅓ cup dry white wine
  1 teaspoon dried thyme
  1 bay leaf
  1 tablespoon butter
  ½ teaspoon salt
  ¼ teaspoon freshly ground black pepper
  8 (½-inch-thick) slices diagonally cut French bread baguette
  1 cup shredded Swiss cheese

1. Preheat oven to 375°.
2. Cut off top of garlic head; discard. Spray garlic head generously with cooking spray; wrap in foil.
3. Arrange onion on a jelly-roll pan coated with cooking spray. Spray onion with cooking spray. Place garlic on pan; bake at 375° for 1 hour or until tender and browned, stirring onion after 40 minutes.
4. Unwrap garlic. Squeeze to extract garlic pulp; discard white papery skin. Combine garlic pulp and onion in a Dutch oven. Add broth and next 3 ingredients; bring to a boil. Cover, reduce heat, and simmer 30 minutes. Stir in butter, salt, and pepper. Discard bay leaf.
5. While onion mixture simmers, place baguette slices on a baking sheet coated with cooking spray. Top each slice with 2 tablespoons cheese. Bake at 375° for 5 minutes or until cheese melts. Serve with soup. YIELD: 8 SERVINGS (SERVING SIZE: ABOUT 1 CUP SOUP AND 1 BAGUETTE SLICE).

PER SERVING: CAL 159 (30% from fat); FAT 5.3g (sat 3.3g); PRO 8.6g; CARB 20.9g; FIB 1.8g; CHOL 16mg; IRON 1.1mg; SOD 690mg; CALC 178mg

ROASTED ROOT VEGETABLE SOUP ☑.

POINTS value: 2

PREP: 30 minutes ■ **COOK:** 1 hour and 35 minutes

A dollop of sour cream stirred into each serving of soup blends all the other flavors together.

  4 carrots, peeled
  4 onions, peeled and halved
  4 small red potatoes, halved
  3 beets, peeled and halved
  3 celery stalks, cut into 3-inch pieces
  2 small sweet potatoes, peeled and quartered
Cooking spray
  6 cups organic vegetable broth (such as Swanson Certified Organic), divided
  1 teaspoon dried thyme
  ½ teaspoon salt
  ¼ teaspoon pepper
  10 tablespoons fat-free sour cream

1. Preheat oven to 425°.
2. Arrange first 6 ingredients in a single layer on a 17 x 12½-inch roasting pan coated with cooking spray; coat vegetables generously with cooking spray. Bake at 425° for 1 hour and 10 minutes or until tender and browned.
3. Chop vegetables into 1-inch pieces, and place in a Dutch oven. Add ½ cup broth to pan, scraping pan to loosen browned bits. Add browned bits, remaining 5½ cups broth, thyme, salt, and pepper to vegetables. Bring to a boil; cover, reduce heat, and simmer 15 minutes. Ladle soup into bowls, and top with sour cream. YIELD: 10 SERVINGS (SERVING SIZE: 1 CUP SOUP AND 1 TABLESPOON SOUR CREAM).

PER SERVING: CAL 127 (1% from fat); FAT 0.2g (sat 0.1g); PRO 3.9g; CARB 27.4g; FIB 3.9g; CHOL 3mg; IRON 1mg; SOD 538mg; CALC 68mg

RUSTIC ITALIAN TOMATO AND RED PEPPER SOUP WITH BASIL ✓

POINTS value: 1

PREP: 12 minutes ■ **COOK:** 34 minutes
■ **OTHER:** 10 minutes

Offer Roasted Pepper–Fontina Flatbread, found on page 33, with this chunky, garden-fresh soup.

Cooking spray
1 cup chopped red bell pepper
½ cup chopped onion
1 carrot, peeled and sliced (½ cup)
1 garlic clove, minced
1 (14-ounce) can fat-free, less-sodium chicken broth
⅛ to ¼ teaspoon crushed red pepper
1 pound fresh tomatoes, chopped (about 2 medium)
3 tablespoons chopped fresh basil
2 teaspoons extravirgin olive oil
¼ teaspoon salt

1. Heat a Dutch oven over medium–high heat; coat pan with cooking spray. Add bell pepper, onion, and carrot; coat vegetables with cooking spray. Cook 4 minutes or until onion is translucent, stirring frequently. Add garlic, and cook 15 seconds, stirring constantly. Add broth and crushed red pepper. Bring to a boil; cover, reduce heat, and simmer 15 to 20 minutes or until carrot is very tender.
2. Add tomato to pan. Bring to a boil; cover, reduce heat, and simmer 5 minutes. Remove pan from heat. Stir in basil, oil, and salt; cover and let stand 10 minutes. **YIELD: 4 SERVINGS (SERVING SIZE: 1 CUP).**

PER SERVING: CAL 76 (32% from fat); FAT 2.7g (sat 0.4g); PRO 3.5g; CARB 11.4g; FIB 3.1g; CHOL 0mg; IRON 0.6mg; SOD 451mg; CALC 28mg

CANNED NAVY BEANS

Navy beans are small white beans with a mild flavor and a dense, creamy texture. They are a good source of fiber and folate and are a virtually fat-free source of protein. There is little nutritional difference between canned navy beans and the dried variety you cook yourself.

MEDITERRANEAN CHUNKY SOUP WITH SAUSAGE

POINTS value: 3

PREP: 10 minutes ■ **COOK:** 34 minutes

Multigrain pasta and navy beans contribute 2.5 grams of fiber to this soup.

Cooking spray
6 ounces 50%-less-fat bulk pork sausage (such as Jimmy Dean)
1 cup chopped green bell pepper
1 cup diced zucchini (1 medium)
3 cups water
1 (14.5-ounce) can stewed tomatoes, undrained and chopped
⅔ cup uncooked multigrain rotini (corkscrew pasta; such as Barilla Plus)
1½ teaspoons chili powder
1 teaspoon dried oregano
1 (16-ounce) can navy beans, rinsed and drained
½ teaspoon salt
½ cup (2 ounces) grated fresh Parmesan cheese

1. Heat a Dutch oven over medium–high heat; coat pan with cooking spray. Add sausage; cook until browned, stirring to crumble. Remove sausage from pan; set aside.
2. Coat pan with cooking spray; add bell pepper and zucchini, and coat vegetables with cooking spray. Cook 2 minutes or until zucchini is lightly browned. Add 3 cups water and next 4 ingredients; bring to a boil. Cover, reduce heat, and simmer 20 minutes. Stir in beans, reserved sausage, and salt; cook 5 minutes or until thoroughly heated. Ladle soup into bowls, and sprinkle evenly with cheese. **YIELD: 7 SERVINGS (SERVING SIZE: 1 CUP SOUP AND ABOUT 1 TABLESPOON CHEESE).**

PER SERVING: CAL 175 (34% from fat); FAT 6.6g (sat 2.6g); PRO 11.2g; CARB 19.4g; FIB 3.7g; CHOL 22mg; IRON 2.4mg; SOD 662mg; CALC 116mg

WINTER SQUASH AND LAMB TAGINE

POINTS value: 7

PREP: 24 minutes ■ **COOK:** 1 hour and 45 minutes

A tagine is a slowly cooked North African stew that's named for the unique clay pot in which it's prepared. Similar results can be achieved in a Dutch oven. To save the expense of using the many spices typical in a tagine, we've simplified the recipe with pumpkin-pie spice, which still adds the desired warmth to the dish. See page 157 for how-to information on preparing butternut squash.

- 1 tablespoon olive oil
- 1 pound boneless leg of lamb, trimmed and cut into 1-inch cubes
- 1 butternut squash, peeled, seeded, and cut into 1-inch cubes
- 2 cups chopped onion (about 1 large)
- 2 teaspoons pumpkin-pie spice
- 3 cups fat-free, less-sodium chicken broth, divided
- ¾ cup uncooked couscous
- ⅓ cup raisins
- 3 tablespoons chopped fresh flat-leaf parsley
- ¼ teaspoon salt
- ¼ teaspoon freshly ground black pepper
- 2 tablespoons slivered almonds, toasted

1. Heat oil in a Dutch oven over medium–high heat. Add lamb, and cook 8 to 10 minutes or until browned, turning occasionally. Remove lamb from pan with a slotted spoon, and set aside.
2. Add squash to pan, and cook over medium–high heat 3 minutes, stirring occasionally. Remove squash from pan with a slotted spoon, and set aside.
3. Add onion and pumpkin-pie spice to pan, and cook over medium heat 3 minutes, stirring often. Return lamb and squash to pan. Add 1¾ cups broth. Bring to a boil; cover, reduce heat, and simmer 1 hour. Uncover and cook 25 minutes.
4. While stew simmers, bring remaining 1¼ cups broth to a boil in a saucepan. Stir in couscous; cover and let stand 5 minutes. Stir in raisins and next 3 ingredients.
5. Divide couscous among bowls. Serve stew over couscous, and top with almonds. YIELD: 5 SERVINGS (SERVING SIZE: ABOUT ½ CUP COUSCOUS, 1 CUP LAMB MIXTURE, AND ABOUT 1 TEASPOON ALMONDS).

PER SERVING: CAL 359 (26% from fat); FAT 10.3g (sat 3.1g); PRO 25.8g; CARB 41.5g; FIB 4.9g; CHOL 64mg; IRON 2.8mg; SOD 640mg; CALC 45mg

EASY CHICKEN NOODLE SOUP ✓

POINTS value: 2

PREP: 9 minutes ■ **COOK:** 18 minutes

- 7 cups fat-free, less-sodium chicken broth
- 2 cups shredded cooked chicken breast
- 1 cup sliced celery
- 1 cup matchstick-cut carrots
- 1 cup sliced green onions
- 2 cups cooked whole wheat rotini (corkscrew pasta)
- 1 teaspoon freshly ground black pepper
- ¼ teaspoon salt

1. Place broth in a large Dutch oven; bring to a boil. Add chicken and next 3 ingredients. Cook 3 minutes or until vegetables are crisp-tender. Add pasta, pepper, and salt; cook 3 minutes or until thoroughly heated. YIELD: 10 SERVINGS (SERVING SIZE: 1 CUP).

PER SERVING: CAL 103 (10% from fat); FAT 1.2g (sat 0.3g); PRO 12.5g; CARB 10.5g; FIB 1.7g; CHOL 24mg; IRON 0.8mg; SOD 501mg; CALC 26mg

PAD THAI CHICKEN NOODLE SOUP

POINTS value: 5

pictured on page 144

PREP: 8 minutes ■ **COOK:** 10 minutes
■ **OTHER:** 20 minutes

Peanuts, cilantro, and green onions add crunch, color, and extra flavor to each serving.

- 2 ounces uncooked rice stick noodles (such as Hokan)
- 4 cups fat-free, less-sodium chicken broth
- 1 cup shredded cooked chicken
- ½ cup matchstick-cut carrots
- 1 tablespoon grated peeled fresh ginger
- ¼ cup chopped unsalted peanuts
- ¼ cup chopped fresh cilantro
- ¼ cup sliced green onions

1. Soak rice noodles in warm water to cover according to package directions. Drain.
2. Bring noodles and next 4 ingredients to a boil in a large saucepan; cover, reduce heat, and simmer 5 minutes. Ladle soup into bowls; top with peanuts, cilantro, and green onions. YIELD: 4 SERVINGS (SERVING SIZE: ABOUT 1⅓ CUPS SOUP, 1 TABLESPOON PEANUTS, 1 TABLESPOON CILANTRO, AND 1 TABLESPOON GREEN ONIONS).

PER SERVING: CAL 211 (40% from fat); FAT 9.3g (sat 2g); PRO 15.9g; CARB 17.2g; FIB 1.7g; CHOL 31mg; IRON 1.1mg; SOD 619mg; CALC 21mg

CHICKEN CHILI

POINTS value: 5

PREP: 12 minutes ■ **COOK:** 55 minutes
■ **OTHER:** 10 minutes

To chop canned stewed tomatoes with ease and minimal mess, use kitchen shears to chop them in the can. Make this a Core Plan ☑ recipe by substituting fat-free sour cream for the light version.

Cooking spray
1½ pounds skinless, bone-in chicken thighs, trimmed
1¼ cups chopped red bell pepper (about 1 medium)
1 cup chopped onion
1 garlic clove, minced
1 (14.5-ounce) can stewed tomatoes, undrained and chopped
1 (14-ounce) can fat-free, less-sodium chicken broth
2 tablespoons Louisiana hot pepper sauce (such as Crystal), divided
1 (15-ounce) can navy beans, rinsed and drained
6 tablespoons light sour cream
6 tablespoons chopped fresh cilantro

1. Heat a Dutch oven over medium-high heat; coat pan with cooking spray. Add chicken; cook 4 minutes on each side or until browned. Set aside.
2. Add bell pepper, onion, and garlic to pan. Cook 4 minutes or until tender, stirring frequently. Add reserved chicken, tomatoes, broth, and 1 tablespoon hot pepper sauce. Bring mixture to a boil. Cover, reduce heat, and simmer 40 minutes or until chicken is done.
3. Remove pan from heat. Remove chicken from pan and shred, discarding bones. Stir chicken into broth mixture in pan. Stir in beans and remaining 1 tablespoon hot pepper sauce. Let stand 10 minutes. Top each serving with sour cream and cilantro. **YIELD: 6 SERVINGS (SERVING SIZE: ABOUT 1 CUP CHILI, 1 TABLESPOON SOUR CREAM, AND 1 TABLESPOON CILANTRO).**

PER SERVING: CAL 240 (30% from fat); FAT 8.1g (sat 2.7g); PRO 22.2g; CARB 18.6g; FIB 4.4g; CHOL 62mg; IRON 2.6mg; SOD 651mg; CALC 91mg

WONTON SOUP

POINTS value: 2

PREP: 25 minutes ■ **COOK:** 22 minutes

Look for wonton wrappers in the produce section of your grocery store.

4 ounces ground turkey
2 tablespoons minced garlic, divided
2 tablespoons minced peeled fresh ginger, divided
2 teaspoons dark sesame oil, divided
¼ teaspoon freshly ground black pepper
16 wonton wrappers
1 teaspoon cornstarch
1 cup matchstick-cut carrots
1 cup sliced green onions
1 cup sliced mushrooms
8 cups fat-free, less-sodium chicken broth
1 cup fresh bean sprouts
1 cup diagonally cut snow peas

1. Place turkey, 1 tablespoon garlic, 1 tablespoon ginger, 1 teaspoon sesame oil, and pepper in a food processor; process until smooth. Working with 1 wonton wrapper at a time (cover remaining wrappers with a damp towel to keep them from drying), spoon about ½ tablespoon turkey mixture into center of wrapper. Moisten edges of dough with water; bring 2 opposite corners to center, pinching points to seal. Bring remaining 2 corners to center, pinching points to seal. Pinch 4 edges together to seal. Place dumplings on a large baking sheet sprinkled with cornstarch (cover with a damp towel to keep them from drying). Repeat procedure with remaining wonton wrappers and turkey mixture.
2. Heat remaining 1 teaspoon sesame oil in a Dutch oven over medium-high heat. Add carrot, green onions, and mushrooms; sauté 3 minutes or until tender. Stir in remaining 1 tablespoon garlic and 1 tablespoon ginger; cook 1 minute. Add broth; bring to a boil. Add prepared wontons; reduce heat, and simmer 5 minutes. Stir in bean sprouts and peas; cook 1 minute or until crisp-tender. **YIELD: 8 SERVINGS (SERVING SIZE: 1¼ CUPS).**

PER SERVING: CAL 130 (21% from fat); FAT 3.1g (sat 0.6g); PRO 9.8g; CARB 16.6g; FIB 2g; CHOL 10mg; IRON 1.6mg; SOD 689mg; CALC 46mg

seasonal menus

Roasted Onion and Apple Salad with Apple-Bacon Vinaigrette, *page 172*

WINTER MENU ■ Total *POINTS* value per serving: 13
Beef Tenderloin with Romesco Sauce, page 164
Paprika Potatoes, page 164
Roasted Pear and Walnut Salad with Honey-Cider Vinaigrette, page 165
Almond Angel Food Cake with Fresh Oranges, page 165

SPRING MENU ■ Total *POINTS* value per serving: 13
Curried Yellow Squash Soup, page 166
Penne, Baby Carrot, and Snap Pea Salad, page 166
Grilled Lemon Chicken, page 167
Strawberries and Cream Sundaes, page 167

SUMMER MENU ■ Total *POINTS* value per serving: 14
☑ Tuna Steaks with Roasted Tomato Sauce, page 168
☑ Green Bean Salad with Basil Dressing, page 168
Orzo with Summer Squash, page 169
Nectarine and Berry Crumble, page 169

SUMMER VEGETARIAN MENU ■ Total *POINTS* value per serving: 11
Cranberry-Lime Green Tea Cooler, page 170
Lima Bean Bruschetta, page 170
Summer Vegetable Gratin, page 171
Fresh Peaches with Maple-Raspberry Sauce, page 171

FALL MENU ■ Total *POINTS* value per serving: 14
Rosemary-Maple Pork Tenderloin, page 172
Roasted Onion and Apple Salad with Apple-Bacon Vinaigrette, page 172
☑ Roasted Autumn Vegetables, page 173
Spiced Bread Pudding, page 173

WINTER MENU

Serves 6 ■ Total **POINTS** value per serving: 13

Roasted Pear and Walnut Salad with Honey-Cider Vinaigrette ■ Beef Tenderloin with Romesco Sauce
■ Paprika Potatoes ■ Almond Angel Food Cake with Fresh Oranges

GAME PLAN:

1. **One day in advance:**
   - Prepare **Almond Angel Food Cake.**
   - Section oranges for cake; store in an airtight container in refrigerator.
   - Prepare **Romesco Sauce;** store in an airtight container in refrigerator.

2. **About one hour before the meal:**
   - Roast pears for salad, and prepare **Honey-Cider Vinaigrette;** marinate pears.
   - Prepare and bake beef tenderloin.
   - Place **Romesco Sauce** on counter to warm to room temperature.
   - Prepare **Paprika Potatoes.**

3. **While beef tenderloin stands:**
   - Assemble salad.
   - Slice cake.

BEEF TENDERLOIN WITH ROMESCO SAUCE

POINTS value: 4

PREP: 7 minutes ■ COOK: 27 minutes
■ OTHER: 10 minutes

- **2 teaspoons olive oil**
- **1 (1½-pound) beef tenderloin, trimmed**
- **¾ teaspoon kosher salt**
- **½ teaspoon freshly ground black pepper**
- **1 (12-ounce) bottle roasted red bell peppers, drained**
- **2 tablespoons slivered almonds, toasted**
- **1 tablespoon fresh flat-leaf parsley**
- **1 small garlic clove**
- **1 teaspoon olive oil**
- **1 teaspoon red wine vinegar**
- **⅛ teaspoon salt**
- **⅛ teaspoon crushed red pepper**

1. Preheat oven to 400°.
2. Heat 2 teaspoons oil in a large ovenproof skillet over medium–high heat. Sprinkle beef evenly with kosher salt and black pepper. Add beef to pan, and cook 1 to 2 minutes on all sides or until browned. Place pan in oven. Bake at 400° for 22 minutes or until a thermometer inserted in center of beef registers 145° (medium-rare) or to desired degree of doneness. Place beef on a platter; let stand 10 minutes. Cut into 6 slices.
3. While beef stands, place bell peppers and next 7 ingredients in a food processor; process until sauce is chunky. Serve sauce over beef. YIELD: 6 SERVINGS (SERVING SIZE: 3 OUNCES BEEF AND ABOUT 2 TABLESPOONS SAUCE).

PER SERVING: CAL 182 (53% from fat); FAT 10.8g (sat 3.2g); PRO 18.5g; CARB 1.6g; FIB 0.4g; CHOL 54mg; IRON 2.6mg; SOD 395mg; CALC 13mg

PAPRIKA POTATOES

POINTS value: 3

PREP: 7 minutes ■ COOK: 22 minutes

- **2 pounds red potatoes, cut into 1-inch pieces**
- **⅓ cup 1% low-fat milk**
- **1 tablespoon butter**
- **1¼ teaspoons hot or Hungarian sweet paprika**
- **1 teaspoon salt**

1. Place potato in a Dutch oven; cover with water. Bring to a boil; reduce heat, and simmer 10 minutes or until tender. Drain. Return potato to pan. Add milk and remaining ingredients. Mash potato mixture with a potato masher until desired consistency, and serve immediately. YIELD: 6 SERVINGS (SERVING SIZE: ¾ CUP).

PER SERVING: CAL 157 (13% from fat); FAT 2.2g (sat 1.3g); PRO 3.4g; CARB 31.8g; FIB 3.1g; CHOL 6mg; IRON 1.8mg; SOD 418mg; CALC 30mg

ROASTED PEAR AND WALNUT SALAD WITH HONEY-CIDER VINAIGRETTE

POINTS value: 3

PREP: 13 minutes ■ COOK: 30 minutes ■ OTHER: 10 minutes

        3 Bartlett pears, cored
        1 teaspoon olive oil
      ⅛ teaspoon salt
      ⅛ teaspoon freshly ground black pepper
    Cooking spray
    Honey-Cider Vinaigrette
        1 (5-ounce) package mixed baby salad greens
        2 tablespoons chopped walnuts, toasted

1. Preheat oven to 400°.
2. Cut each pear into 8 wedges. Combine pears and next 3 ingredients in a bowl; toss gently to coat. Arrange pears, cut sides down, on a baking sheet coated with cooking spray. Bake at 400° for 30 minutes or until lightly browned, turning once.
3. Drizzle baked pears with 1 tablespoon Honey-Cider Vinaigrette, and toss gently to coat. Cool to room temperature.
4. Toss salad greens with remaining vinaigrette. Divide salad greens among 6 plates. Top evenly with pears and walnuts. YIELD: 6 SERVINGS (SERVING SIZE: 1 CUP SALAD GREENS, 4 PEAR SLICES, 1 TEASPOON WALNUTS, AND ABOUT 1 TABLESPOON VINAIGRETTE).

PER SERVING: CAL 130 (48% from fat); FAT 6.9g (sat 0.8g); PRO 1.4g; CARB 17.6g; FIB 3.3g; CHOL 0mg; IRON 0.6mg; SOD 253mg; CALC 24mg

Honey-Cider Vinaigrette

POINTS value: 2

        2 tablespoons olive oil
        2 tablespoons white wine vinegar
        2 tablespoons apple cider
        1 tablespoon honey
      ½ teaspoon salt
      ½ teaspoon ground cumin
      ⅛ teaspoon freshly ground black pepper

1. Combine all ingredients in a small bowl; stir with a whisk. YIELD: ⅓ CUP.

PER TABLESPOON: CAL 61 (75% from fat); FAT 5.1g (sat 0.7g); PRO 0.1g; CARB 4.2g; FIB 0.1g; CHOL 0mg; IRON 0.1mg; SOD 222mg; CALC 2mg

ALMOND ANGEL FOOD CAKE WITH FRESH ORANGES

POINTS value: 3

PREP: 18 minutes ■ COOK: 25 minutes
■ OTHER: 40 minutes

This cake doesn't rise as much as a traditional angel food cake because the ground almonds weigh it down slightly. You'll need to buy 4 oranges to yield 3 cups of segments.

      ¾ cup slivered almonds
      ¼ cup cornstarch
        1 cup sifted cake flour
      ⅛ teaspoon salt
      12 large egg whites
      ½ teaspoon cream of tartar
      ¼ teaspoon almond extract
      ¾ cup sugar
        3 cups orange sections

1. Preheat oven to 350°.
2. Place almonds and cornstarch in a food processor; process until almonds are finely ground. Transfer to a bowl; add flour and salt, stirring with a whisk to combine. Set aside.
3. Place egg whites and cream of tartar in a large bowl; beat with a mixer at medium speed until foamy. Beat in almond extract. Gradually add sugar, 1 tablespoon at a time, beating at high speed until stiff peaks form.
4. Add one-fourth of flour mixture to egg white mixture; gently fold in. Repeat procedure with remaining flour mixture, one-fourth of mixture at a time. Pour batter into an ungreased 10-inch tube pan.
5. Bake at 350° for 25 minutes or until cake springs back when lightly touched. Invert pan, and cool cake completely in pan. Loosen cake from sides of pan with a thin knife or a narrow metal spatula. Invert cake onto plate. Serve cake with orange sections. YIELD: 12 SERVINGS (SERVING SIZE: 1 SLICE CAKE AND ¼ CUP ORANGE SECTIONS).

PER SERVING: CAL 178 (18% from fat); FAT 3.6g (sat 0.3g); PRO 6.4g; CARB 30.8g; FIB 2.1g; CHOL 0mg; IRON 1.2mg; SOD 80mg; CALC 39mg

SPRING MENU

Serves 6 ■ Total **POINTS** value per serving: 13

Curried Yellow Squash Soup ■ Grilled Lemon Chicken ■ Penne, Baby Carrot, and Snap Pea Salad
■ Strawberries and Cream Sundaes

GAME PLAN:

1. **One day in advance:**
   - Prepare **Curried Yellow Squash Soup**; store in an airtight container in refrigerator.

2. **Two hours before the meal:**
   - Prepare Step 1 of **Grilled Lemon Chicken.**

3. **One hour before the meal:**
   - Prepare **Penne, Baby Carrot, and Snap Pea Salad.**
   - Prepare **Lemon Sauce.**
   - Prepare grill.

4. **Prepare Step 3 of Grilled Lemon Chicken.**

5. **Prepare sundaes just before serving.**

CURRIED YELLOW SQUASH SOUP

POINTS value: 1

PREP: 12 minutes ■ COOK: 36 minutes
■ OTHER: 2 hours and 20 minutes

This cool, creamy soup with a hint of curry is the perfect start to this fresh spring menu. Make the soup a day ahead and chill to allow the flavors to meld.

- 1 teaspoon olive oil
- 1 onion, chopped (about ¾ cup)
- 1 garlic clove, minced
- 2 teaspoons curry powder
- 2½ cups fat-free, less-sodium chicken broth
- 4 yellow squash (about 1¼ pounds), chopped
- ½ cup light sour cream
- 1 tablespoon fresh lemon juice
- ½ teaspoon salt
- 2 tablespoons chopped fresh cilantro

1. Heat oil in a Dutch oven over medium heat. Add onion; sauté 5 minutes. Add garlic and curry powder, and sauté 30 seconds. Add broth and squash. Bring to a boil; reduce heat, and simmer, covered, 20 minutes.
2. Place one-third of squash mixture in a blender; process until smooth. Pour pureed squash mixture into a large bowl. Repeat procedure with remaining two-thirds

of squash mixture. Cool soup to room temperature. Stir in sour cream, lemon juice, and salt. Cover and refrigerate at least 2 hours or until chilled. Garnish with chopped cilantro. YIELD: 6 SERVINGS (SERVING SIZE: ABOUT ¾ CUP).

PER SERVING: CAL 70 (45% from fat); FAT 3.5g (sat 1.7g); PRO 3.6g; CARB 7.3g; FIB 1.6g; CHOL 10mg; IRON 0.6mg; SOD 450mg; CALC 55mg

PENNE, BABY CARROT, AND SNAP PEA SALAD

POINTS value: 4

PREP: 12 minutes ■ COOK: 13 minutes

Crisp vegetables and tangy feta team up to create a salad full of color and flavor.

- 2 cups uncooked penne pasta
- 2 cups baby carrots, quartered lengthwise
- 2 cups sugar snap peas, trimmed
- 3 tablespoons white balsamic vinegar
- 1 tablespoon olive oil
- ¾ teaspoon salt
- ⅛ teaspoon freshly ground black pepper
- 3 tablespoons crumbled feta cheese
- 3 tablespoons chopped fresh dill

1. Cook pasta in boiling water 8 minutes, omitting salt and fat. Add carrot; cook 2 minutes. Add sugar snap peas; cook 1 minute. Drain, and rinse with cold water until vegetables are cool. Drain well.

2. While pasta cooks, combine vinegar and next 3 ingredients in a large bowl, stirring with a whisk. Add pasta mixture, feta, and dill; toss well. YIELD: 6 SERVINGS (SERVING SIZE: ABOUT 1 CUP).

PER SERVING: CAL 204 (17% from fat); FAT 3.9g (sat 1g); PRO 6.5g; CARB 35.2g; FIB 2.2g; CHOL 4mg; IRON 1.2mg; SOD 375mg, CALC 53mg

GRILLED LEMON CHICKEN

POINTS value: 5

PREP: 17 minutes ■ COOK: 14 minutes ■ OTHER: 2 hours

You'll need 6 lemons for this recipe, and all parts of the lemons—rind, juice, and sections—will be used. The unique lemon sauce helped this simple grilled chicken recipe earn our Test Kitchens' highest rating.

    1 tablespoon grated fresh lemon rind
    ¼ cup fresh lemon juice
    1 tablespoon olive oil
    2 garlic cloves, minced
    6 (6-ounce) skinless, boneless chicken breast halves
    ½ teaspoon salt
    ¼ teaspoon freshly ground black pepper
    Cooking spray
    1 lemon, cut into 6 thin slices
    Lemon Sauce

1. Combine first 4 ingredients in a large zip-top plastic bag; add chicken. Seal, and shake to coat chicken. Marinate in refrigerator 2 hours.

2. Prepare grill.

3. Remove chicken from bag; discard marinade. Sprinkle chicken with salt and pepper. Place chicken on grill rack coated with cooking spray; cook 6 minutes on each side or until chicken is done. Place lemon slices on grill; grill 1 to 2 minutes on each side or until lightly browned. Serve chicken with Lemon Sauce, and garnish with grilled lemon slices. YIELD: 6 SERVINGS (SERVING SIZE: 1 CHICKEN BREAST HALF, ABOUT 1½ TABLESPOONS SAUCE, AND 1 SLICE LEMON).

PER SERVING: CAL 250 (24% from fat); FAT 6.7g (sat 1.2g); PRO 39.8g; CARB 6.7g; FIB 1.2g; CHOL 99mg; IRON 1.6mg; SOD 358mg; CALC 33mg

Lemon Sauce

POINTS value: 1

    2 large lemons
    1 tablespoon sugar
    1 tablespoon water
    ⅛ teaspoon salt
    ⅛ teaspoon freshly ground black pepper
    1 tablespoon olive oil
    1 tablespoon chopped fresh flat-leaf parsley

1. Cut a thin slice from top and bottom of each lemon, exposing flesh. Stand each lemon upright, and, using a sharp knife, cut peel from lemon, removing all white pith and membrane. Holding lemon over a bowl, section lemon, allowing sections to fall into bowl. Squeeze membranes to extract juice into bowl. Break sections into small pieces.

2. Add sugar and next 3 ingredients to lemon pieces; slowly add oil, stirring with a whisk. Stir in parsley. YIELD: ½ CUP.

PER TABLESPOON: CAL 25 (61% from fat); FAT 1.7g (sat 0.2g); PRO 0.2g; CARB 3g; FIB 0.4g; CHOL 0mg; IRON 0.1mg; SOD 37mg; CALC 5mg

STRAWBERRIES AND CREAM SUNDAES

POINTS value: 3

PREP: 15 minutes

Top each sundae with 2 reduced-fat vanilla wafers to provide some extra crunch, with a *POINTS* value of 4 per serving. Try experimenting with other berries and flavors of sorbet to find your favorite combination.

    3 cups sliced strawberries, divided
    3 tablespoons sugar
    1½ cups vanilla light ice cream (such as Edy's)
    1½ cups strawberry sorbet

1. Combine 1½ cups strawberries and sugar in a blender; process until smooth.

2. Place ¼ cup ice cream and ¼ cup sorbet in each of 6 bowls. Top each with ¼ cup strawberries and 2 tablespoons strawberry sauce. YIELD: 6 SERVINGS (SERVING SIZE: 1 SUNDAE).

PER SERVING: CAL 173 (10% from fat); FAT 2g (sat 1g); PRO 2.1g; CARB 37.8g; FIB 2.2g; CHOL 0mg; IRON 0.3mg; SOD 23mg; CALC 43mg

SUMMER MENU

Serves 6 ■ Total **POINTS** value per serving: 14

Green Bean Salad with Basil Dressing ■ Tuna Steaks with Roasted Tomato Sauce
■ Orzo with Summer Squash ■ Nectarine and Berry Crumble

GAME PLAN:

1. **One day in advance:**
   ■ Prepare **Green Bean Salad with Basil Dressing;**
   store in an airtight container in refrigerator.

2. **One and a half hours before the meal:**
   ■ Prepare **Roasted Tomato Sauce.**
   ■ Prepare **Nectarine and Berry Crumble.**

3. **While crumble bakes:**
   ■ Prepare **Orzo with Summer Squash.**
   ■ Prepare tuna steaks.

TUNA STEAKS WITH ROASTED TOMATO SAUCE ☑.

POINTS value: 5

PREP: 10 minutes ■ COOK: 40 minutes

Create a tasty vegetarian side dish by serving this tomato sauce over pasta. A ¼-cup serving of the sauce has a **POINTS** value of 1.

- 6 plum tomatoes, halved lengthwise (about 1½ pounds)
- 4 teaspoons olive oil, divided
- ½ teaspoon salt, divided
- ½ teaspoon freshly ground black pepper, divided
- Cooking spray
- 4 garlic cloves, minced
- 2 tablespoons chopped fresh basil
- ¼ cup chopped pitted kalamata olives
- 1 tablespoon fresh lemon juice
- 6 (6-ounce) tuna steaks

1. Preheat oven to 400°.
2. Combine tomatoes, 2 teaspoons oil, ¼ teaspoon salt, and ¼ teaspoon pepper; toss to coat. Place tomato halves, cut sides up, on a jelly-roll pan coated with cooking spray. Top each tomato half evenly with garlic. Bake at 400° for 30 minutes or until tomatoes are soft and browned on the bottom; cool slightly.
3. Place tomatoes and basil in a food processor; pulse 3 times or until coarsely chopped. Combine tomato mixture, olives, and lemon juice in a bowl; stir well. Set aside.

4. Heat 1 teaspoon oil in a large nonstick skillet over medium-high heat; coat pan with cooking spray. Sprinkle steaks with remaining ¼ teaspoon salt and remaining ¼ teaspoon pepper. Add 3 steaks to pan; cook 2 to 3 minutes on each side or until desired degree of doneness. Remove from pan, and keep warm. Repeat procedure with remaining 1 teaspoon oil and 3 steaks. Serve steaks with sauce. YIELD: 6 SERVINGS (SERVING SIZE: 1 STEAK AND ⅓ CUP SAUCE).

PER SERVING: CAL 234 (25% from fat); FAT 6.4g (sat 1.2g); PRO 38.2g; CARB 4g; FIB 0.9g; CHOL 80mg; IRON 2.4mg; SOD 359mg; CALC 63mg

GREEN BEAN SALAD WITH BASIL DRESSING ☑.

POINTS value: 1

PREP: 13 minutes ■ COOK: 14 minutes

Crisp green beans are tossed with a fresh basil vinaigrette for a simple side.

- 1½ pounds green beans, trimmed
- 2 tablespoons white wine vinegar
- 1 tablespoon olive oil
- 1 garlic clove, minced
- ½ teaspoon salt
- ½ teaspoon Dijon mustard
- ⅛ teaspoon freshly ground black pepper
- ¼ cup thinly sliced red onion
- 3 tablespoons chopped fresh basil

1. Cook green beans in boiling water 5 minutes or until crisp-tender. Drain. Rinse with cold water, and drain.
2. Combine vinegar and next 5 ingredients in a large bowl, stirring with a whisk. Add onion, basil, and green beans, and toss gently to coat. YIELD: 6 SERVINGS (SERVING SIZE: ABOUT ¾ CUP).

PER SERVING: CAL 54 (40% from fat); FAT 2.4g (sat 0.3g); PRO 2g; CARB 7.8g; FIB 3.6g; CHOL 0mg; IRON 1.2mg; SOD 206mg; CALC 42mg

ORZO WITH SUMMER SQUASH

POINTS value: 4

PREP: 14 minutes ■ COOK: 13 minutes

Serve this pasta salad at room temperature or chilled.

2 cups fat-free, less-sodium chicken broth
2 cups water
1 cup uncooked orzo (rice-shaped pasta)
2 yellow squash, diced
1 large zucchini, diced
½ cup (2 ounces) grated fresh Parmesan cheese
1 tablespoon extravirgin olive oil
2 teaspoons white wine vinegar
¼ teaspoon salt
⅛ teaspoon freshly ground black pepper
2 tablespoons pine nuts, toasted

1. Combine broth and water in a large saucepan; bring to a boil. Add orzo, and cook 5 minutes. Stir in squash and zucchini; cook 3 minutes. Drain well.
2. Return orzo mixture to pan; add cheese and next 4 ingredients, stirring well. Sprinkle with pine nuts. YIELD: 6 SERVINGS (SERVING SIZE: ⅔ CUP).

PER SERVING: CAL 193 (32% from fat); FAT 6.9g (sat 1.7g); PRO 8.8g; CARB 24.4g; FIB 1.9g; CHOL 6mg; IRON 0.6mg; SOD 391mg; CALC 87mg

NECTARINE AND BERRY CRUMBLE

POINTS value: 4

PREP: 18 minutes ■ COOK: 35 minutes
■ OTHER: 10 minutes

This combination of succulent fruits and a crunchy-sweet topping received our Test Kitchens' highest rating. You'll need to buy 2 to 3 lemons to yield 1 tablespoon of grated fresh lemon rind.

4 nectarines (about 2¼ pounds), sliced
1 cup blackberries
1 cup blueberries
2 tablespoons all-purpose flour
1 tablespoon grated fresh lemon rind
Cooking spray
½ cup packed brown sugar
½ cup regular oats
½ teaspoon ground cinnamon
2 tablespoons chilled butter, cut into small pieces
¼ cup sliced almonds

1. Preheat oven to 350°.
2. Combine first 5 ingredients in a large bowl, and toss gently to combine. Place nectarine mixture in an 8-inch square baking dish coated with cooking spray. Set aside.
3. To prepare topping, combine brown sugar, oats, and cinnamon, stirring well. Cut in butter with a pastry blender or 2 knives until mixture resembles coarse meal. Stir in almonds. Sprinkle brown sugar mixture evenly over nectarine mixture. Bake at 350° for 35 minutes or until filling is bubbly. Let stand 10 minutes before serving. YIELD: 6 SERVINGS (SERVING SIZE: ABOUT 1 CUP).

PER SERVING: CAL 227 (27% from fat); FAT 6.8g (sat 2.7g); PRO 3.6g; CARB 41.4g; FIB 4.8g; CHOL 10mg; IRON 1.5mg; SOD 35mg; CALC 48mg

SUMMER VEGETARIAN MENU

Serves 6 ■ Total **POINTS** value per serving: 11

Cranberry-Lime Green Tea Cooler ■ Lima Bean Bruschetta ■ Summer Vegetable Gratin
■ Fresh Peaches with Maple-Raspberry Sauce

GAME PLAN:

1. **One day in advance:**
   - Prepare **Cranberry-Lime Green Tea Cooler;** cover and chill.

2. **Two hours before the meal:**
   - Prepare **Summer Vegetable Gratin.**

3. **While gratin bakes:**
   - Place baguette slices in oven to toast.
   - Prepare Steps 3 and 4 of **Lima Bean Bruschetta.**
   - Prepare **Maple-Raspberry Sauce.**

4. **Assemble Fresh Peaches with Maple-Raspberry Sauce just before serving.**

CRANBERRY-LIME GREEN TEA COOLER

POINTS value: 3

PREP: 4 minutes ■ COOK: 5 minutes
■ OTHER: 17 minutes

This green tea cooler, which is loaded with antioxidants, is refreshing any time of year.

    4 cups water, divided
    ¾ cup sugar
    4 green tea bags
    2 cups cranberry juice cocktail, chilled
    ¼ cup fresh lime juice (about 1 lime)
    Lime slices (optional)

1. Bring 1 cup water and sugar to a boil in a small saucepan, stirring until sugar dissolves. Remove pan from heat; add tea bags, and steep 2 minutes. Remove tea bags with a slotted spoon (do not squeeze). Cool tea to room temperature.
2. Combine tea, remaining 3 cups water, cranberry juice cocktail, and lime juice in a pitcher; cover and chill. Serve over ice; garnish with lime slices, if desired. YIELD: 6 SERVINGS (SERVING SIZE: 1 CUP).

PER SERVING: CAL 145 (1% from fat); FAT 0.1g (sat 0g); PRO 0g; CARB 37.3g; FIB 0g; CHOL 0mg; IRON 0.1mg; SOD 2mg; CALC 4mg

LIMA BEAN BRUSCHETTA

POINTS value: 2

PREP: 11 minutes ■ COOK: 7 minutes

Lemon, mint, and limas blend to create a creamy spread that's also delicious on sandwiches or as a dip for pita chips or raw vegetables. A serving of two tablespoons has a **POINTS** value of 1. Store it in the refrigerator up to 3 days.

    12 (¼-inch-thick) slices diagonally cut French bread baguette
    Cooking spray
     1 (10-ounce) package frozen baby lima beans
     3 tablespoons chopped fresh mint
     3 tablespoons fresh lemon juice (about 1 lemon)
     3 tablespoons water
     1 tablespoon olive oil
     1 garlic clove
     ½ teaspoon salt
     ⅛ teaspoon freshly ground black pepper
     1 tablespoon thinly sliced green onions

1. Preheat oven to 400°.
2. Place baguette slices on a baking sheet; coat slices with cooking spray. Bake at 400° for 5 minutes or until toasted; set aside.

3. While baguette slices bake, cook lima beans in boiling water 2 minutes or until tender. Drain. Rinse with cold water; drain.

4. Place lima beans, mint, and next 6 ingredients in a food processor; process until smooth. Spread 1 tablespoon lima bean mixture on each bread slice, and sprinkle with green onions. YIELD: 6 SERVINGS (SERVING SIZE: 2 BRUSCHETTA).

PER SERVING: CAL 87 (11% from fat); FAT 1.1g (sat 0.2g); PRO 3.2g; CARB 16.9g; FIB 1.6g; CHOL 0mg; IRON 1.1mg, SOD 218mg; CALC 9mg

SUMMER VEGETABLE GRATIN

POINTS value: 4

PREP: 22 minutes ■ COOK: 1 hour and 20 minutes ■ OTHER: 15 minutes

This hearty casserole celebrates summer's bounty by using garden vegetables topped with crusty breadcrumbs and cheese.

- 1 (1½-pound) eggplant, peeled and cut into ½-inch slices
- Cooking spray
- 6 plum tomatoes, sliced
- 3 medium zucchini (1½ pounds), cut into ¼-inch slices
- 1 yellow bell pepper, cut into thin strips
- 1 red bell pepper, cut into thin strips
- 1 small onion, halved and sliced
- 4 garlic cloves, minced
- 1 tablespoon chopped fresh thyme
- ¾ teaspoon salt
- ¼ teaspoon freshly ground black pepper
- 1 tablespoon olive oil
- ⅔ cup dry breadcrumbs
- ⅔ cup shredded fontina cheese
- ⅓ cup grated fresh Parmesan cheese

1. Preheat oven to 400°.

2. Place eggplant slices on a large baking sheet coated with cooking spray. Lightly coat eggplant with cooking spray. Bake at 400° for 20 to 25 minutes or until lightly browned, turning once. Cool eggplant slightly.

3. Reduce oven temperature to 350°.

4. Combine eggplant, tomato, and next 8 ingredients in a large bowl. Drizzle vegetable mixture with oil, and toss to coat. Spoon mixture into a 13 x 9–inch baking dish coated with cooking spray. Bake, uncovered, at 350° for 45 minutes.

5. While vegetable mixture bakes, combine breadcrumbs, fontina cheese, and Parmesan cheese in a

medium bowl. Sprinkle breadcrumb mixture evenly over vegetable mixture; bake 15 minutes or until top is browned. Let stand 10 minutes before serving. YIELD: 6 SERVINGS (SERVING SIZE: ABOUT 1½ CUPS).

PER SERVING: CAL 207 (38% from fat); FAT 8.8g (sat 3.6g); PRO 11.4g; CARB 23.8g; FIB 6.5g; CHOL 18mg; IRON 2.2mg; SOD 558mg; CALC 179mg

FRESH PEACHES WITH MAPLE-RASPBERRY SAUCE

POINTS value: 2

PREP: 11 minutes

If your peaches are firm, let them stand on the kitchen counter for a few days or until they're fragrant and soft to the touch.

- 1 cup raspberries
- ¼ cup maple syrup
- 1½ cups vanilla light ice cream (such as Edy's)
- 6 small peaches (about 2 pounds), peeled and sliced

1. Combine raspberries and syrup in a medium bowl; gently mash raspberries with a spatula, leaving some berries whole.

2. Place ¼ cup ice cream in each of 6 stemmed glasses or bowls. Top evenly with peach slices and raspberry mixture. Serve immediately. YIELD: 6 SERVINGS (SERVING SIZE: ¼ CUP ICE CREAM, 1 SLICED PEACH, AND 2 TABLESPOONS SAUCE).

PER SERVING: CAL 126 (15% from fat); FAT 2.1g (sat 1g); PRO 2.5g; CARB 26.4g; FIB 2.5g; CHOL 0mg; IRON 0.5mg; SOD 24mg; CALC 49mg

FALL MENU

Serves 6 ■ Total **POINTS** value per serving: 14

Roasted Onion and Apple Salad with Apple-Bacon Vinaigrette ■ Rosemary-Maple Pork Tenderloin
■ Roasted Autumn Vegetables ■ Spiced Bread Pudding

GAME PLAN:

1. **One day in advance:**
   - Prepare **Apple-Bacon Vinaigrette** (except bacon); store in an airtight container in refrigerator.
   - Prepare **Spiced Bread Pudding;** cover and chill.

2. **About one and a half hours before the meal:**
   - Prepare Steps 1 and 2 of **Roasted Onion and Apple Salad.**
   - Prepare **Roasted Autumn Vegetables.**

3. **While vegetables bake:**
   - Prepare **Rosemary-Maple Pork Tenderloin,** and place in oven to bake with vegetables.

4. **Warm bread pudding. Add bacon to dressing, and assemble individual salads just before serving.**

ROSEMARY-MAPLE PORK TENDERLOIN

POINTS value: 5

PREP: 6 minutes ■ **COOK:** 23 minutes ■ **OTHER:** 10 minutes

   2 (¾-pound) pork tenderloins, trimmed
   ½ teaspoon salt
   ½ teaspoon freshly ground black pepper
   2 tablespoons chopped fresh rosemary
   2 teaspoons olive oil
   ⅓ cup maple syrup
   2 tablespoons fat-free, less-sodium chicken broth
   1 tablespoon light brown sugar
   1 tablespoon Dijon mustard

1. Preheat oven to 425°.

2. Sprinkle pork with salt and pepper. Sprinkle with rosemary, pressing lightly to adhere to pork. Place pork in a roasting pan; drizzle with oil. Bake at 425° for 20 to 25 minutes or until a thermometer inserted in center of pork registers 155°. Remove pork from pan; cover and let stand 10 minutes.

3. While pork bakes, combine maple syrup and next 3 ingredients, stirring with a whisk.

4. To prepare sauce, place roasting pan on stovetop after removing pork. Add maple syrup mixture to roasting pan, scraping pan to loosen browned bits.

Cook over medium heat 3 minutes or until mixture thickens. Cut pork into ½-inch-thick slices; serve with maple sauce. YIELD: **6 SERVINGS (SERVING SIZE: 3 OUNCES PORK AND ABOUT 1½-TABLESPOONS SAUCE).**

PER SERVING: CAL 206 (24% from fat); FAT 5.5g (sat 1.6g); PRO 23.9g; CARB 14.2g; FIB 0.1g; CHOL 74mg; IRON 1.7mg; SOD 328mg; CALC 22mg

ROASTED ONION AND APPLE SALAD WITH APPLE-BACON VINAIGRETTE

POINTS value: 2

pictured on page 142

PREP: 11 minutes ■ **COOK:** 34 minutes

   1 large sweet onion, cut into 12 thin wedges
   4 teaspoons olive oil, divided
   ½ teaspoon salt, divided
   ½ teaspoon freshly ground black pepper, divided
Cooking spray
   ¼ cup apple butter (such as Dickinson's)
   2 tablespoons cider vinegar
   1 tablespoon water
   2 slices bacon, cooked and crumbled
   9 cups fresh baby spinach
   2 large Gala apples, cored and sliced

1. Preheat oven to 400°.
2. Combine onion, 1 teaspoon oil, ¼ teaspoon salt, and ¼ teaspoon pepper in a bowl; toss to coat. Place onion mixture on a jelly-roll pan coated with cooking spray. Bake at 400° for 34 minutes or until lightly browned and tender, turning once. Cool slightly.
3. While onion cools, combine apple butter, vinegar, water, remaining ¼ teaspoon salt, and remaining ¼ teaspoon pepper in a medium bowl. Slowly add remaining 1 tablespoon oil, stirring with a whisk. Stir in bacon just before serving.
4. Divide spinach among 6 plates; top evenly with onion mixture and apple slices. Drizzle dressing evenly over salads. YIELD: 6 SERVINGS (SERVING SIZE: 1⅔ CUPS).

PER SERVING: CAL 130 (28% from fat); FAT 4.1g (sat 0.7g); PRO 2.4g; CARB 23.1g; FIB 4.4g; CHOL 2mg; IRON 1.4mg; SOD 308mg; CALC 43mg

ROASTED AUTUMN VEGETABLES ☑

POINTS value: 1

PREP: 16 minutes ■ COOK: 45 minutes

Make sure you give the vegetables enough space to cook. If they're too crowded in the pan, they'll steam, not roast.

    6 small carrots (about ¾ pound), peeled and cut into ½-inch cubes
    1 large red potato (about ¾ pound), cut into ½-inch cubes
    2 turnips (about 1 pound), peeled and cut into ½-inch cubes
    3 cups halved Brussels sprouts
    ¾ teaspoon garlic powder
    ½ teaspoon salt
    ¼ teaspoon freshly ground black pepper
    2 teaspoons olive oil
 Cooking spray

1. Preheat oven to 425°.
2. Combine first 4 ingredients in a large bowl. Combine garlic powder, salt, and pepper in a small bowl. Sprinkle garlic powder mixture over vegetables, and toss. Drizzle oil over vegetables, and toss until thoroughly coated.
3. Spread vegetables in a single layer on a large rimmed baking sheet coated with cooking spray. Bake at 425° for 25 minutes. Stir vegetables, turning roasted sides over. Bake an additional 20 minutes or until vegetables are browned. YIELD: 10 SERVINGS (SERVING SIZE: ½ CUP).

PER SERVING: CAL 103 (17% from fat); FAT 1.9g (sat 0.3g); PRO 3.4g; CARB 20.3g; FIB 4.8g; CHOL 0mg; IRON 1.3mg; SOD 276mg; CALC 55mg

SPICED BREAD PUDDING

POINTS value: 6

PREP: 12 minutes ■ COOK: 43 minutes
■ OTHER: 15 minutes

Enjoy the tantalizing spicy aroma as this pudding bakes.

    1¼ cups 1% low-fat milk
    ¾ cup packed light brown sugar
    2 large eggs
    1 teaspoon vanilla extract
    ¾ teaspoon pumpkin-pie spice
    ⅛ teaspoon salt
    6 cups (1-inch) cubed French bread
    ¼ cup raisins
 Cooking spray
    1 tablespoon butter, melted

1. Preheat oven to 350°.
2. Combine first 6 ingredients in a large bowl, stirring with a whisk. Add bread and raisins, stirring to coat. Let stand 15 minutes or until almost all liquid is absorbed, stirring occasionally.
3. Spoon bread mixture into a 1½-quart baking dish coated with cooking spray. Place dish in a 13 x 9–inch baking pan; add hot water to pan to a depth of 1 inch. Bake at 350° for 43 minutes or until top of bread pudding is golden. Remove baking dish from baking pan. Brush top of bread pudding with butter. Serve warm.
YIELD: 6 SERVINGS (SERVING SIZE: ⅙ OF BREAD PUDDING).

PER SERVING: CAL 285 (15% from fat); FAT 4.8g (sat 2.2g); PRO 8g; CARB 53.6g; FIB 1.3g; CHOL 78mg; IRON 2.3mg; SOD 345mg; CALC 114mg

One day's menu provides at least two servings of dairy and at least five servings of fruits and/or vegetables.

	MONDAY	**TUESDAY**	**WEDNESDAY**	**THURSDAY**
BREAKFAST	**Weight Watchers blueberry muffin**, 1 **fat-free milk**, 1 cup ☑ **banana**, 1 small ☑	**hard-cooked egg**, 1 large ☑ **high-fiber English muffin**, 1 **peach slices**, 1 cup ☑ **all-fruit spread**, 1 tablespoon	**hot cooked farina (such as Cream of Wheat)**, 1 cup cooked ☑ **blueberries**, 1 cup ☑ **light cranberry juice**, 1 cup	**low-fat multigrain waffles**, 2 frozen **reduced-calorie pancake syrup**, 2 tablespoons **fat-free milk**, 1 cup ☑
LUNCH	**Chicken Waldorf Salad** (Top 2 cups mixed greens with ½ cup shredded skinless rotisserie chicken breast; ¼ cup each of halved grapes, chopped tomato, and chopped celery; 2 tablespoons each of crumbled blue cheese and light balsamic dressing; and 1 tablespoon chopped walnuts. Toss gently - **POINTS value: 6**.) **whole wheat crackers**, 6	**ham and cheese hot sandwich**, 1 reduced-fat frozen pocket **cucumber slices**, 1 cup ☑ **nectarine**, 1 ☑ **cherry-vanilla fat-free yogurt**, 1 (6-ounce) carton	**Turkey Pepperoni Pizza** (Gently spread 2 tablespoons tomato-basil pasta sauce over 1 side of a pita round, leaving a ½-inch border around edge. Top with 8 turkey pepperoni slices and ⅓ cup shredded reduced-fat mozzarella cheese; broil until cheese melts - **POINTS value: 6**.) **baby carrots**, 10 ☑ **fat-free milk**, 1 cup ☑	**corn chowder**, ¾ cup canned **mixed greens**, 2 cups ☑ **light balsamic dressing**, 2 tablespoons **raspberries**, 1 cup ☑
DINNER	**tuna steak**, 6 ounces cooked ☑ **wild rice**, ½ cup ☑ **steamed snow peas**, 1 cup ☑	**Chicken Italiano**, page 106, 1 serving **Fresh Herb Insalata**, page 113, 1 serving	**macaroni and cheese**, 1 frozen entrée **steamed broccoli**, 1 cup ☑	**pork tenderloin**, 4 ounces cooked ☑ **plain mashed potatoes**, ½ cup ☑ **Braised Brussels Sprouts with Cranberries and Bacon**, page 148, 1 serving
SNACK	**lemon chiffon fat-free yogurt**, 1 (6-ounce) carton **94% fat-free popcorn**, 5 cups ☑	**raspberries**, 1 cup ☑ **graham cracker crisps**, 1 (100-calorie) pack **fat-free milk**, 1 cup ☑	**Apple Butter Pound Cake**, page 37, 1 serving **fat-free milk**, 1 cup ☑	**Creamy Peanut-Buttery Java Dip**, page 19, 1 serving **apple slices**, 1 cup ☑ **vanilla fat-free yogurt**, 1 (6-ounce) carton
POINTS VALUE	**POINTS** value for the day: 25	**POINTS** value for the day: 28	**POINTS** value for the day: 25	**POINTS** value for the day: 24

FRIDAY	SATURDAY	SUNDAY	
Weight Watchers blueberry muffin, 1 peach slices, 1 cup ☑ fat-free milk, 1 cup ☑	Maple-Banana Hot Cereal (Stir ½ cup banana slices, 1 tablespoon reduced-calorie maple pancake syrup, and a dash of salt into 1 cup hot cooked farina [such as Cream of Wheat] - *POINTS* value: 4.) fat-free milk, 1 cup ☑	Breakfast Egg Sandwich (Split and toast 1 high-fiber English muffin. Place a poached large egg on bottom half of muffin; top with 1 [¾-ounce] American cheese slice and top half of muffin - *POINTS* value: 5.) blueberries, 1 cup ☑ light cranberry juice, 1 cup	**BREAKFAST**
Tuna–White Bean Salad (Toss together 2 ounces drained chunk light tuna, ½ cup rinsed and drained cannellini beans, ¼ cup chopped tomato, 2 tablespoons light olive oil vinaigrette, 1 tablespoon finely chopped fresh basil, and a dash each of salt and pepper. Gently spoon over 1 cup mixed greens - *POINTS* value: 3.) warm pita bread, 1 round, cut into quarters strawberry fat-free yogurt, 1 (6-ounce) carton	chicken soft taco, 1 fast food with lettuce and tomato apple, 1 medium ☑ fat-free milk, 1 cup ☑	Cranberry-Walnut Sweet Potato (Split 1 large baked sweet potato down center lengthwise; gently push ends toward center to soften flesh of potato. Stuff potato with 2 tablespoons each of vanilla fat-free yogurt and dried cranberries and 1 tablespoon each of chopped walnuts and brown sugar - *POINTS* value: 6.) fat-free milk, 1 cup ☑	**LUNCH**
Mushroom and Swiss Panini, page 128, 1 serving Sweet Lemon-Jicama Slaw, page 114, 1 serving baked potato chips, 11	Miso-Glazed Salmon, page 68, 1 serving brown rice, ½ cup ☑ Sautéed Bok Choy with Ginger and Garlic, page 148, 1 serving ☑	grilled chicken breast tenders, 3 ounces cooked ☑ black-eyed peas, ½ cup ☑ steamed green beans, 1 cup ☑ Tomatoes with Feta (Top 3 [1.5-inch] tomato slices with 2 tablespoons feta cheese; drizzle with 2 tablespoons light balsamic dressing - *POINTS* value: 2.)	**DINNER**
mixed fruit salad, 1 cup ☑ hummus, ¼ cup baby carrots and cucumber slices, 1 cup ☑	mixed berry light smoothie, 1 (7-ounce) container orange, 1 large ☑	Sticky Toffee Pudding, page 38, 1 serving fat-free milk, 1 cup ☑	**SNACK**
POINTS value for the day: 24	*POINTS* value for the day: 26	*POINTS* value for the day: 27	**POINTS VALUE**

7-Day Menu Planner

WEEK 1

One day's menu provides at least two servings of dairy and at least five servings of fruits and/or vegetables.

	MONDAY	TUESDAY	WEDNESDAY	THURSDAY
BREAKFAST	whole-grain puffed cereal, 1 cup ☑ strawberries, 1 cup sliced ☑ fat-free milk, 1 cup ☑ light orange juice, 1 cup	grits, 1 cup cooked ☑ light butter, 2 teaspoons honeydew melon, 1 cup cubed ☑	fruit and nut granola bar, 1 fat-free cottage cheese, ½ cup ☑ peach slices, 1 cup ☑	whole-grain puffed cereal, 1 cup ☑ raspberries, 1 cup ☑ fat-free milk, 1 cup ☑
LUNCH	Mexican Chicken Salad (Place 11 baked tortilla chips on a plate. Top 2 cups mixed salad greens with ½ cup shredded skinless rotisserie chicken breast and ¼ cup each of rinsed and drained canned corn, rinsed and drained canned black beans, and chopped tomato. Combine ¼ cup salsa with 2 tablespoons light sour cream, and drizzle over salad - *POINTS* value: 6.)	hamburger, 1 fast food apple slices with low-fat caramel dip, 1 fast food fat-free milk, 1 cup ☑	Chef Salad (Top 2 cups mixed greens with 2 ounces julienne-cut lean deli honey ham, 1 ounce julienne-cut reduced-fat mozzarella cheese, ½ cup each of halved grape tomatoes and cucumber slices, and 1 diced hard-cooked large egg. Serve with 2 tablespoons fat-free Italian dressing - *POINTS* value: 6.) saltine crackers, 6 fat-free milk, 1 cup ☑	Grilled Cheese-Basil Sandwich (Top 1 reduced-calorie whole wheat bread slice with 1 [1-ounce] reduced-fat mozzarella cheese slice. Sprinkle 1 tablespoon finely chopped fresh basil over cheese; layer with an additional cheese slice and bread slice. Cook sandwich in a hot nonstick skillet in 2 teaspoons melted light butter until both sides are golden brown and cheese melts. Serve with 2 tablespoons warm tomato-basil pasta sauce - *POINTS* value: 6.) honeydew melon, 1 cup cubed ☑ baby carrots, 10 ☑
DINNER	Creamy Shrimp and Cheese Grits, page 75, 1 serving steamed asparagus, 12 spears ☑	thin-crust cheese pizza, 1 large slice cherries, 1 cup ☑ mixed green salad, 2 cups ☑ light balsamic dressing, 2 tablespoons	Sesame Chicken Stir-Fry, page 102, 1 serving Strawberry-Orange Toss (Combine ½ cup strawberry slices with ½ cup drained canned unsweetened mandarin oranges. Whisk together 2 tablespoons light orange juice, 1 tablespoon honey, and 2 teaspoons finely chopped fresh mint. Pour mixture over fruit; toss gently to combine - *POINTS* value: 2.)	Rosemary-Garlic Pork Tenderloin, page 95, 1 serving ☑ Orzo with Summer Squash, page 169, 1 serving steamed green beans, 1 cup ☑
SNACK	Cranberry-Walnut Bread, page 34, 1 serving fat-free milk, 1 cup ☑	Key Lime Pie Dessert (Spoon half of a 6-ounce carton of key lime pie fat-free yogurt into a parfait glass; top with 1 crumbled sheet of low-fat graham crackers and 1 tablespoon thawed reduced-calorie frozen whipped topping. Repeat layers once - *POINTS* value: 4.)	blackberry fat-free yogurt, 1 (6-ounce) carton grapes, 1 cup ☑	apple, 1 medium ☑ peanut butter, 2 tablespoons fat-free milk, 1 cup ☑
POINTS VALUE	*POINTS* value for the day: 24	*POINTS* value for the day: 26	*POINTS* value for the day: 28	*POINTS* value for the day: 25

FRIDAY	SATURDAY	SUNDAY	
Strawberry-Banana Smoothie (Combine 1 small banana, 1 [6-ounce] carton strawberry-banana fat-free yogurt, and 1 cup strawberry slices in a blender, and process until smooth - **POINTS value: 3.**)	**Chocolate Waffles with Dark Cherry Sauce,** page 30, 1 serving **fat-free milk,** 1 cup ☑	**Bacon-Tomato Grits** (Stir 1 cooked and crumbled turkey bacon slice, ¼ cup chopped tomato, and 2 tablespoons reduced-fat shredded Cheddar cheese into 1 cup hot cooked grits - **POINTS value: 4.**) **raspberries,** 1 cup ☑ **blueberry fat-free yogurt,** 1 (6-ounce) carton	BREAKFAST
fat-free cottage cheese, ¾ cup ☑ **mixed fruit,** 1 cup ☑ **whole wheat crackers,** 6	**Honey Ham Sandwich** (Lightly toast 2 reduced-calorie whole wheat bread slices. Spread 1 tablespoon low-fat honey mustard dressing over 1 side of bread; top with 2 ounces lean deli honey ham, 1 green lettuce leaf, 1 tomato slice, and remaining bread slice - **POINTS value: 5.**) **banana,** 1 small ☑ **celery sticks,** 1 cup ☑ **fat-free milk,** 1 cup ☑	**Catfish Sandwiches with Tartar Sauce,** page 122, 1 serving **baked potato chips,** 11 **baby carrots,** 10 ☑ **fat-free milk,** 1 cup ☑	LUNCH
grilled or baked salmon, 6 ounces cooked ☑ **Pasta with Fresh Tomatoes, Herbs, and Lemon,** page 153, 1 serving **sautéed zucchini squash,** 1 cup ☑	**Mojito Chicken Thighs,** page 106, 1 serving ☑ **Fresh Orange and Spring Greens Salad,** page 112, 1 serving **whole wheat French bread,** 1 ounce	**grilled or broiled flank steak,** 4 ounces trimmed and cooked ☑ **baked sweet potato,** 1 large **Asian Broccoli Stir-Fry** (Heat 1 teaspoon olive oil in a small nonstick skillet. Add ½ teaspoon peanut oil; heat just until hot. Add 2 cups shredded broccoli slaw; sauté until crisp-tender. Spray slaw with 10 sprays (or add 2 teaspoons) low-fat sesame ginger vinaigrette; toss gently to combine - **POINTS value: 2.**)	DINNER
Quick S'mores (Break 1 sheet of low-fat graham crackers into 2 halves. Top each half with 1 miniature milk-chocolate bar and 1 large marshmallow. Broil 1 minute or until marshmallows begin to brown and chocolate softens - **POINTS value: 5.**) **fat-free milk,** 1 cup ☑	**mozzarella string cheese,** 1 **pear,** 1 medium ☑	**mixed berry light smoothie,** 1 (7-ounce) container **cherries,** 1 cup ☑	SNACK
POINTS value for the day: 25	**POINTS** value for the day: 27	**POINTS** value for the day: 27	POINTS VALUE

7-Day Menu Planner

WEEK 2

One day's menu provides at least two servings of dairy and at least five servings of fruits and/or vegetables.

	MONDAY	TUESDAY	WEDNESDAY	THURSDAY
BREAKFAST	**wheat bran flake cereal with raisins**, 1 cup **fat-free milk**, 1 cup ☑ **apple juice**, ½ cup	**oatmeal**, 1 cup cooked ☑ **blueberries**, 1 cup ☑ **peach fat-free yogurt**, 1 (6-ounce) carton	**Southwest Breakfast Wrap** (Whisk together 1 large egg, 2 large egg whites, and a dash of salt; scramble egg mixture in a hot nonstick skillet. Spoon eggs down center of a warm 8-inch whole wheat tortilla; top with 2 tablespoons each of preshredded reduced-fat 4-cheese Mexican blend cheese and salsa. Roll up burrito-style - **POINTS value: 5.**) **light orange juice**, 1 cup	**Pumpkin–Chocolate Chip Muffins, page 28**, 1 serving **vanilla fat-free yogurt**, 1 (6-ounce) carton **light orange juice**, 1 cup
LUNCH	**Tuna Salad Pita** (Combine 2 ounces chunk light tuna; 2 table-spoons each of chopped celery and light mayonnaise; 1 tablespoon finely chopped red onion; and a dash each of salt, pepper, and lemon juice. Mix well. Line half of a split pita round with 1 green lettuce leaf and 1 tomato slice; gently spoon tuna mixture into pita half - **POINTS value: 5.**) **watermelon**, 1 cup cubed ☑ **lemon chiffon fat-free yogurt**, 1 (6-ounce) carton	**Feta and Fruit Spinach Salad** (Top 2 cups torn fresh spinach leaves with ¼ cup blueberries, 2 tablespoons each of dried cherries and feta cheese, and 1 tablespoon chopped walnuts. Drizzle with 2 tablespoons light olive oil vinaigrette; toss well - **POINTS value: 5.**) **warm pita bread**, 1 round, cut into quarters	**teriyaki chicken and vegetable bowl**, 1 frozen entrée **fat-free milk**, 1 cup ☑ **nectarine**, 1 ☑	**Caesar Romaine with Black Bread Croutons, page 113**, 2 servings **tomato soup**, 1 cup canned made with fat-free milk ☑ **saltine crackers**, 6
DINNER	**Baked Chicken and Risotto Casserole, page 105**, 1 serving **steamed broccoli**, 1 cup ☑	**steamed shrimp**, 6 ounces cooked and shelled ☑ **Creamy Cocktail Sauce, page 19**, 2 servings **corn**, 1 small ear ☑ **steamed green beans**, 1 cup ☑ **light butter**, 2 teaspoons	**whole wheat cheese ravioli**, 1 cup cooked **tomato-basil pasta sauce**, ½ cup **Parmesan-Garlic Spinach** (Sauté ½ teaspoon garlic in 1 teaspoon olive oil. Add 2 cups torn baby spinach leaves; stir gently until leaves wilt. Sprinkle with 2 tea-spoons grated fresh Parmesan cheese - **POINTS value: 2.**)	**Grilled Grouper with Mango Salsa, page 66**, 1 serving **Rosemary–Olive Oil Potatoes** (Cut 2 [4-ounce] red potatoes into [1.5-inch] cubes. Toss with 1 teaspoon olive oil, ¼ teaspoon finely chopped fresh rosemary, and ⅛ teaspoon salt. Roast potatoes at 450° for 40 minutes, stirring occasionally - **POINTS value: 3.**) ☑ **steamed asparagus**, 12 spears ☑
SNACK	**light creamy cheese wedges**, 2 **pretzels**, 15 small twists	**Chocolate-Strawberry Parfait** (Spoon half of a chocolate fat-free pudding cup into a parfait glass. Top with ½ cup strawberry slices and 1 crumbled reduced-fat chocolate sandwich cookie; repeat layers - **POINTS value: 5.**) **fat-free milk**, 1 cup ☑	**orange-mango fat-free yogurt**, 1 (6-ounce) carton **gingersnaps**, 4 cookies	**reduced-fat chocolate sandwich cookies**, 3 **fat-free milk**, 1 cup ☑
POINTS VALUE	**POINTS value for the day: 25**	**POINTS value for the day: 25**	**POINTS value for the day: 26**	**POINTS value for the day: 24**

	FRIDAY	SATURDAY	SUNDAY	
BREAKFAST	oatmeal, 1 cup cooked ☑ scrambled eggs, 1 large egg and 3 large egg whites ☑ light orange juice, 1 cup	wheat bran flake cereal with raisins, 1 cup strawberries, 1 cup sliced ☑ fat-free milk, 1 cup ☑	Cherry-Walnut Oatmeal (Stir 2 tablespoons dried cherries and 1 tablespoon chopped walnuts into 1 cup cooked plain oatmeal - *POINTS* value: 4.) fat-free milk, 1 cup ☑	
LUNCH	grilled chicken sandwich, 1 fast food without mayonnaise side salad, 1 fast food light Italian dressing, 1 packet fat-free milk, 1 cup ☑	Roasted Pepper–Spinach Wrap (Spread 2 tablespoons whipped garlic-and-herb cream cheese over an 8-inch whole wheat tortilla. Top with 1 cup torn baby spinach leaves and ⅓ cup chopped roasted red bell peppers. Gently roll up tortilla - *POINTS* value: 4.) baby carrots, 10 ☑ key lime pie fat-free yogurt, 1 (6-ounce) carton	chili with beans, 1 cup mixed green salad, 2 cups ☑ fat-free Ranch dressing, 2 tablespoons saltine crackers, 6 nectarine, 1 ☑	
DINNER	Tofu, Corn, and Black Bean Enchiladas, page 86, 1 serving watermelon, 1 cup cubed ☑	lean pork loin, 4 ounces trimmed and cooked ☑ Brown Rice and Onion Pilaf, page 154, 1 serving Lemony Broccoli, page 147, 1 serving	Turkey and Greens Noodle Bowl, page 110, 1 serving grapes, 1 cup ☑ raspberry fat-free yogurt, 1 (6-ounce) carton	
SNACK	Blueberry-Banana Smoothie (Combine 1 small banana, 1 cup frozen blueberries, and 1 [6-ounce] carton blueberry fat-free yogurt in a blender; process until smooth - *POINTS* value: 3.)	Iced Mocha Latte, page 25, 1 serving pretzels, 15 small twists	light creamy cheese wedges, 2 whole wheat crackers, 6	
POINTS VALUE	*POINTS* value for the day: 26	*POINTS* value for the day: 24	*POINTS* value for the day: 26	

7-Day Menu Planner

WEEK 3

One day's menu provides at least two servings of dairy and at least five servings of fruits and/or vegetables.

	MONDAY	TUESDAY	WEDNESDAY	THURSDAY
BREAKFAST	**Breakfast Berry Parfait** (Spoon half of a 6-ounce carton of raspberry fat-free yogurt into a parfait glass or bowl; top with ½ cup each of strawberry slices and high-fiber flake cereal. Repeat layers - **POINTS** value: 5.)	**Weight Watchers bagel,** 1 split and toasted **light cream cheese,** 2 tablespoons **cantaloupe,** 1 cup cubed ☑	**high-fiber flake cereal,** 1 cup **grapefruit,** half of 1 medium ☑ **fat-free milk,** 1 cup ☑	**poached egg,** 1 large ☑ **reduced-calorie whole wheat bread,** 2 slices, toasted **all-fruit spread,** 1 tablespoon **strawberry-kiwi fat-free yogurt,** 1 (6-ounce) carton
LUNCH	**Turkey BLT** (Lightly toast 2 slices reduced-calorie whole wheat bread. Spread 2 teaspoons light mayonnaise evenly over 1 slice; top with 2 ounces lean deli turkey, 1 green lettuce leaf, 2 tomato slices, and 1 turkey bacon slice, halved. Top with remaining toasted bread slice - **POINTS** value: 5.) **cucumber slices,** 1 cup ☑ **fat-free Ranch dressing,** 2 tablespoons ☑ **fat-free milk,** 1 cup ☑	**Artichoke Quesadillas,** page 78, 1 serving **pineapple,** 1 cup cubed ☑ **cherry-vanilla fat-free yogurt,** 1 (6-ounce) carton	**Chicken and Tortellini Salad** (Toss together ½ cup cooked and chilled cheese tortellini, ½ cup each of cooked and shredded skinless chicken breast and chopped tomato, 2 tablespoons each of light balsamic dressing and finely chopped basil, and a dash each of salt and pepper. Serve over 1 cup mixed greens; sprinkle with 2 teaspoons grated fresh Parmesan cheese - **POINTS** value: 7.) **orange,** 1 medium ☑	**Greek Spinach Salad,** page 113, 1 serving **warm pita bread,** 1 round, cut into quarters **hummus,** ¼ cup **pear,** 1 medium ☑
DINNER	**Seared Scallops with Lemon-Butter Sauce,** page 73, 1 serving **whole wheat angel hair pasta,** 1 cup ☑ **steamed asparagus,** 12 spears ☑	**Blue Cheeseburger** (Mix 1 table-spoon crumbled blue cheese into 4 ounces very lean ground beef; shape into patty. Grill or broil until done. Split and toast 1 light whole wheat bun. Spread 1 tablespoon fat-free blue cheese dressing over cut side of bottom half of bun; top with 1 green lettuce leaf, 1 tomato slice, patty, and top half of bun - **POINTS** value: 6.) **baked potato chips,** 11 **Crunchy Coleslaw with Spring Peas,** page 114, 1 serving	**veggie pizza,** 1 frozen entrée **cantaloupe,** 1 cup cubed ☑ **fat-free milk,** 1 cup ☑	**Chipotle Meat Loaf,** page 88, 1 serving **plain mashed potatoes,** ½ cup ☑ **steamed carrots, cauliflower, and broccoli,** 1 cup ☑
SNACK	**apple slices,** 1 cup ☑ **peanut butter,** 2 tablespoons	**Raspberry Blondies with White Chocolate and Pecans,** page 48, 1 serving **fat-free milk,** 1 cup ☑	**fat-free chocolate and vanilla swirl pudding,** 1 cup **Cheddar cheese thin crisps,** 1 (100-calorie) pack (such as Cheese Nips)	**mozzarella string cheese,** 1 **blueberries,** 1 cup ☑ **fat-free milk,** 1 cup ☑
POINTS VALUE	**POINTS** value for the day: 26	**POINTS** value for the day: 27	**POINTS** value for the day: 27	**POINTS** value for the day: 27

	FRIDAY	SATURDAY	SUNDAY
BREAKFAST	**PB and Banana Bagel** (Split and toast 1 Weight Watchers bagel. Evenly spread 2 tablespoons peanut butter over cut sides of bagel. Slice 1 small banana, and top peanut butter with banana slices. Serve bagel open-faced - **POINTS value: 5.**) fat-free milk, 1 cup ☑	**Southwestern Eggs** (Whisk together 1 large egg, 2 large egg whites, 2 tablespoons each chopped ham and tomato, 1 tablespoon chopped green onions, and a dash each of salt and pepper. Scramble mixture in a hot nonstick skillet until done. Remove from pan; sprinkle with 2 tablespoons reduced-fat Cheddar cheese - **POINTS value: 4.**) orange sections, 1 cup ☑ fat-free milk, 1 cup ☑	**high-fiber flake cereal**, 1 cup **strawberries**, 1 cup sliced ☑ **fat-free milk**, 1 cup ☑
LUNCH	**roast beef submarine sandwich**, 1 (6-inch) on wheat bread without mayonnaise and with cheese, lettuce, and tomato **apple**, 1 medium ☑ **fat-free milk**, 1 cup ☑	**Italian wedding soup**, 1 cup canned **saltine crackers**, 6 **pineapple**, 1 cup cubed ☑ **blackberry fat-free yogurt**, 1 (6-ounce) carton	**Turkey Bagel Melt** (Split and lightly toast 1 Weight Watchers bagel. Spread 1 teaspoon light mayonnaise over each cut side of bagel. Top one bagel half with 2 ounces lean deli turkey and 1 ounce reduced-fat Swiss cheese. Broil until melted; top with 1 tomato slice, 1 green lettuce leaf, and remaining toasted bagel half - **POINTS value: 7.**) **baked potato chips**, 11 **baby carrots**, 10 ☑
DINNER	**Grilled Chicken with Avocado Salsa**, page 103, 1 serving ☑ **black beans and rice**, ½ cup prepared mix **iceberg lettuce wedge**, one-fourth head ☑ **Bacon Ranch Dressing** (Stir together 2 tablespoons fat-free Ranch dressing, 1 tablespoon salsa, and 1 tablespoon crumbled bacon - **POINTS value: 2.**)	**grilled or baked halibut**, 6 ounces cooked ☑ **Sun-Dried Tomato and Goat Cheese Salad**, page 114, 1 serving **French bread roll**, 1	**Moroccan Lamb with Tomato Chutney**, page 92, 1 serving **Parmesan couscous**, 1 cup **steamed green beans**, 1 cup ☑
SNACK	**plums**, 2 small ☑	**Frozen Blueberry-Lime Margaritas**, page 26, 1 serving **baked tortilla chips**, 30 bite-sized **salsa**, ¼ cup ☑	**peach fat-free yogurt**, 1 (6-ounce) carton **Cheddar cheese thin crisps**, 1 (100-calorie) pack (such as Cheese Nips)
POINTS VALUE	**POINTS** value for the day: 27	**POINTS** value for the day: 28	**POINTS** value for the day: 27

7-Day Menu Planner

WEEK 4

GENERAL RECIPE INDEX

ABOUT OUR RECIPES

Each recipe has a complete list of nutrients—including calories (CAL), fat, saturated fat (sat), protein (PRO), carbohydrates (CARB), dietary fiber (FIB), cholesterol (CHOL), iron, sodium (SOD), and calcium (CALC)—as well as a serving size and the number of servings. This information makes it easy for you to use the recipes in any weight-loss program that you may choose to follow. Measurements are abbreviated g (grams) and mg (milligrams). Nutritional values used in our calculations either come from The Food Processor, Version 7.5 (ESHA Research) or are provided by food manufacturers. Numbers are based on these assumptions:

■ Unless otherwise indicated, meat, poultry, and fish refer to skinned, boned, and cooked servings.

■ When we give a range for an ingredient (3 to 3½ cups flour, for instance), we calculate using the lesser amount.

■ Some alcohol calories evaporate during heating; the analysis reflects this.

■ Only the amount of marinade absorbed by the food is used in calculation.

■ Garnishes and optional ingredients are not included in an analysis.

Safety Note: Cooking spray should never be used near direct heat. Always remove a pan from heat before spraying it with cooking spray.

A Note on Diabetic Exchanges: You may notice that the nutrient analysis for each recipe does not include Diabetic Exchanges. Most dietitians and diabetes educators are now teaching people with diabetes to count total carbohydrates at each meal and snack, rather than counting exchanges.

Almost all of our recipes can be incorporated into a diabetic diet by using the carbohydrate amount in the nutrient analysis and incorporating that into the carbohydrate amount recommended by your physician.

POINTS® Value and Core Plan® Index

Toffee Sauce, 38
Tomatoes with Feta, 175
Tuscan Spread, 18
Wonton Soup, 162

3 *POINTS* value

Almond Angel Food Cake with Fresh
  Oranges, 165
Blueberry-Banana Smoothie, 179
Blueberry–Brown Sugar Muffins, 28
Brown Rice and Onion Pilaf, 154
Coconut-Pineapple Sherbet, 43
Cranberry-Lime Green Tea
  Cooler, 170
Cranberry-Walnut Bread, 34
☑ Edamame and New Potatoes with
  Rosemary, 146
Gingered Carrot Soup, 156
Iced Mocha Latte, 25
☑ Lentil and Garden Vegetable
  Salad, 117
Maple-Glazed Acorn Squash, 153
Maple-Roasted Carrots and
  Parsnips, 150
Mediterranean Chunky Soup with
  Sausage, 160
Mini Party Burgers with Cheese, 21
Paprika Potatoes, 164
Quick Cranberry Crescent Rolls, 32
Raspberry-Orange Sauce with
  Ice Cream, 43
Roasted Garlic and Vidalia Onion
  Soup, 159
Roasted Pear and Walnut Salad with
  Honey-Cider Vinaigrette, 165
☑ Rosemary-Garlic Pork Tenderloin, 95
☑ Rosemary–Olive Oil Potatoes, 178
Scalloped Potato and Fennel
  Gratin, 152
Smoked Salmon Bruschetta with
  Sun-Dried Tomato Relish, 21
Strawberries and Cream Sundaes, 167
Strawberry-Banana Smoothie, 177
Sunshine Scones, 29
Tuna–White Bean Salad, 175
Watermelon and Feta Salad, 112

4 *POINTS* value

Adobo-Rum Grilled Shrimp, 74
Asparagus and Tomato Frittata, 86
Bacon-Tomato Grits, 177

Banana Pancakes with Peanut Butter–
  Honey Syrup, 30
Bananas Peach Foster with Pecans, 41
Beef Tenderloin with Romesco
  Sauce, 164
Braised Brussels Sprouts with
  Cranberries and Bacon, 148
Buttermilk Banana Cake with Rum-
  Soaked Strawberries, 36
Cherry-Walnut Oatmeal, 179
Chicken Sausage and Apple
  Skillet, 108
Chocolate-Cherry Baked Alaskas, 44
Chocolate Waffles with Dark Cherry
  Sauce, 30
Coffee-Marinated Grilled Pork
  Chops, 94
Crispy Calamari with Citrus Aïoli, 76
Eight-Spice Chicken Salad, 119
☑ Garden Vegetable Shrimp Salad, 118
Gingerbread Pumpkin Cream Trifle, 41
Greek Egg and Lemon Soup, 158
Greek Spinach Salad, 113
Green Chile Corn Bread, 31
Green Chile Rice, 154
Green Tomato Soup with Pancetta
  Crisps, 157
Grilled Grouper with Mango
  Salsa, 66
☑ Grilled Turkey Cutlets with Basil-Mint-
  Tomato Relish, 110
Key Lime Pie Dessert, 176
Korean Beef, 89
Leek and Potato Soup, 156
Mahimahi with Pineapple-Green
  Onion Salsa, 67
Maple-Banana Hot Cereal, 175
Moussaka, 80
Nectarine and Berry Crumble, 169
Orzo with Summer Squash, 169
Peach Melba Panna Cotta, 40
Penne, Baby Carrot, and Snap Pea
  Salad, 166
Pomegranate Martini, 26
Prune-Stuffed Pork Tenderloin, 95
Pumpkin Bundt Cake with Cider
  Sauce, 38
Pumpkin–Chocolate Chip Muffins, 28
Raspberry Blondies with White
  Chocolate and Pecans, 48
Roasted Pepper–Spinach Wrap, 179

Seared Pork Tenderloin with Dark
  Cherry Relish, 96
Southwestern Eggs, 181
Spicy Thai Fish, 66
Steak Diane, 91
Sticky Toffee Pudding, 38
Summer Vegetable Gratin, 171
☑ Taco Pepper Rice, 154
Tropical Tea Bread, 32
☑ Tuna, Bean, and Tomato Salad, 118
Upside-Down Pineapple Spice
  Cake, 37
Vanilla and Peach Shortcakes, 39
☑ White Bean Soup with Coriander, 158

5 *POINTS* value

Artichoke Quesadillas, 78
Baked Potatoes with Mushroom
  Stroganoff, 81
Blueberry–Cream Cheese
  Cupcakes, 36
Blueberry-Pineapple Buckle, 45
Breakfast Berry Parfait, 180
Breakfast Egg Sandwich, 175
Chicken and Mushroom Enchilada
  Casserole, 98
Chicken Chili, 162
Chocolate Malt Crème Brûlée, 40
Chocolate-Strawberry Parfait, 178
Chorizo-Chicken Kebabs, 99
Crab Salad Sandwiches with Arugula,
  Bacon, and Tomato, 122
Cranapple Cobbler, 46
Cumin'd Black Beans and Rice, 78
Feta and Fruit Spinach Salad, 178
Filet Mignon with Sherried
  Shiitakes, 90
Grilled Lemon Chicken, 167
Honey Ham Sandwich, 177
Italian Cobb Salad, 120
Moroccan Lamb with Tomato
  Chutney, 92
Oven-Barbecued Chicken, 103
Pad Thai Chicken Noodle Soup, 161
PB and Banana Bagel, 181
Port and Spice–Braised Beef Roast, 91
Pumpkin Risotto, 83
Quick S'mores, 177
Rosemary-Maple Pork Tenderloin, 172
Salmon Mini Loaves with Homemade
  Tartar Sauce, 70

10 SIMPLE CORE PLAN® SIDE DISHES

Vegetable	Servings	Preparation	Cooking Instructions
Asparagus	3 to 4 per pound	Snap off tough ends. Remove scales, if desired.	To steam: Cook, covered, on a rack above boiling water 2 to 3 minutes. To boil: Cook, covered, in a small amount of boiling water 2 to 3 minutes or until crisp-tender.
Broccoli	3 to 4 per pound	Remove outer leaves and tough ends of lower stalks. Wash; cut into spears.	To steam: Cook, covered, on a rack above boiling water 5 to 7 minutes or until crisp-tender.
Carrots	4 per pound	Scrape; remove ends, and rinse. Leave tiny carrots whole; slice large carrots.	To steam: Cook, covered, on a rack above boiling water 8 to 10 minutes or until crisp-tender. To boil: Cook, covered, in a small amount of boiling water 8 to 10 minutes or until crisp-tender.
Cauliflower	4 per medium head	Remove outer leaves and stalk. Wash. Break into florets.	To steam: Cook, covered, on a rack above boiling water 5 to 7 minutes or until crisp-tender.
Corn	4 per 4 large ears	Remove husks and silks. Leave corn on the cob, or cut off kernels.	To boil: Cook, covered, in boiling water to cover 8 to 10 minutes (on cob) or in a small amount of boiling water 4 to 6 minutes (kernels).
Green beans	4 per pound	Wash; trim ends, and remove strings. Cut into 1½-inch pieces.	To steam: Cook, covered, on a rack above boiling water 5 to 7 minutes. To boil: Cook, covered, in a small amount of boiling water 5 to 7 minutes or until crisp-tender.
Potatoes	3 to 4 per pound	Scrub; peel, if desired. Leave whole, slice, or cut into chunks.	To boil: Cook, covered, in boiling water to cover 30 to 40 minutes (whole) or 15 to 20 minutes (slices or chunks). To bake: Bake at 400° for 1 hour or until done.
Snow peas	4 per pound	Wash; trim ends, and remove tough strings.	To steam: Cook, covered, on a rack above boiling water 2 to 3 minutes. Or sauté in cooking spray or 1 teaspoon oil over medium-high heat 3 to 4 minutes or until crisp-tender.
Squash, summer	3 to 4 per pound	Wash; trim ends, and slice or chop.	To steam: Cook, covered, on a rack above boiling water 6 to 8 minutes. To boil: Cook, covered, in a small amount of boiling water 6 to 8 minutes or until crisp-tender.
Squash, winter *(including acorn, butternut, and buttercup)*	2 per pound	Rinse; cut in half, and remove all seeds. Leave in halves to bake, or peel and cube to boil.	To boil: Cook cubes, covered, in boiling water 20 to 25 minutes. To bake: Place halves, cut sides down, in a shallow baking dish; add ½ inch water. Bake, uncovered, at 375° for 30 minutes. Turn and season, or fill; bake an additional 20 to 30 minutes or until tender.